SCHOOL LIBRARY MEDIA SERIES
Edited by Diane de Cordova Biesel

1. *Chalk Talk Stories,* written and illustrated by Arden Druce, 1993.
2. *Toddler Storytime Programs,* by Diane Briggs, 1993.
3. *Alphabet: A Handbook of ABC Books and Book Extensions for the Elementary Classroom, second edition,* by Patricia L. Roberts, 1994.

ALPHABET
A Handbook of ABC Books and Book Extensions for the Elementary Classroom

Second Edition

by
PATRICIA L. ROBERTS

School Library Media Series, No. 3

The Scarecrow Press, Inc.
Metuchen, N.J., & London
1994

Alphabet: A Handbook of ABC Books and Activities for the Elementary Classroom published by Scarecrow Press, 1984.

British Library Cataloguing-in-Publication data available

Library of Congress Cataloging-in-Publication Data

Roberts, Patricia, 1936–
   Alphabet : a handbook of ABC books and book extensions for the
elementary classroom / by Patricia L. Roberts. — 2nd ed.
      p.   cm.—(School library media series ; no.3)
   Includes bibliographical references (p.   ) and index.
   ISBN 0-8108-2823-5 (acid-free paper)
   1. English language—Alphabet—Textbooks—Abstracts. 2. Creative
activities and seat work—Handbooks, manuals, etc.—Abstracts. I. Title.
LB1525.65.R64   1994
372.6—dc20   93-42444

CONTENTS

Contents

EDITOR'S FOREWORD

The School Library Media Series is directed to the school library media specialist, particularly the building level librarian. The multifaceted role of the librarian as educator, collection developer, curriculum developer, and information specialist is examined. The series includes concise, practical books on topical and current subjects related to programs and services.

In Part One of this book, Dr. Roberts has grouped alphabet books by themes useful either to the classroom teacher or to the librarian (animals as humans and letter transformations). Creative extensions suggest areas for further study by curious young minds. The sequence of letters is the focus for Part Two.

This useful handbook belongs in the professional collection of every elementary school.

Diane de Cordova Biesel,
Series Editor

ACKNOWLEDGMENTS

My acknowledgments are many:
- to Robert Whitehead, Professor of Education, California State University, Sacramento, who supported this review of alphabet books in a unique, humorous way;
- to Roz Van Auker, curriculum librarian, California State University, Sacramento;
- to Kathryn King of the InterLibrary Loan Department, California State University, Sacramento;
- to James Michael, my helpful son; and
- to James E. Roberts, my understanding husband, who supported the writing of this handbook.

P. L. R.

Dedication

To James E. and James M.,—
the two most important, valued, and loved people in my life.

The alphabet in a topic collection consists of ABC books that have words and illustrations related to a selected theme or topic. Some of the books follow a simple plot line or tell a story in alphabetical sequence. Other books are a series of episodes.

ABOUT ALPHABET BOOKS

"From alleycat and antenna to zick-zxack and Zelma, the ubiquitous alphabet book forms part of every nusrey school and kindergarten environment. Several of the alphabet books available are also appropriate for older children. . . . Early childhood educators use alphabet books for several purposes. Most alphabet books can help teach the letter sequence, form, and style, and sound-symbol correspondence. Some can also teach concepts. Alphabet books also serve the important purpose of helping children achieve visual and verbal literacy."

—John Warren Stewig
Children and Literature

"Several alphabet books are designed to provide information to older students rather than to teach letter/sound relationships to younger ones. . . . When adults share alphabet books with older children . . . pages rich with detail and numerous objects may help children develop their observational and discussion skills."

—Donna E. Norton
Through the Eyes of a Child

"Try the unusual, challenging alphabet . . . books. Leonard Baskin designed Hosie's Alphabet, aided by his children Hosea, Tobias, and Lisa, with dramatic varieties of typography and illustration for such items as 'the carrion crow' and the 'rhinoceros express.'"

—Sam Leaton Sebesta and William J. Iverson
Literature for Thursday's Child

Part One
Alphabet Books in a
Topic/Theme Collection

Numbers appearing within parentheses following book titles refer to entry numbers in the Annotated Bibliography.

In two examples from past alphabets, an apple pie introduces the letter *A* in a reprint edition of *The Adventures of A, Apple Pie* (92) by George Burgess and in Kate Greenaway's *A Apple Pie* (100). In Wanda Gág's *The ABC Bunny* (7), a book published almost one hundred years after the alphabets of Burgess and Greenaway, an "apple, big and red" introduces the letter. In contemporary alphabets, the letter *A* shows readers an image quite different from apples and the pies in which they're hidden. As readers browse through the books about animals, they will find the letter *A* is introduced by a colorful armadillo, an angwantibo, a small African lemur who crosses Boston Common, and a caribou's antlers. The letter *A* also stands for a small animal such as an alley cat or an anteater cub as well as a large creature—the alligator—or larger still—the dinosaur ankylosaur.

Introduced by animals acting as humans, the letter *A* gives readers verse such as Edward Lear's about ants that "never stood still," rhymes about an ape in a cape and other animals, and prose about a small elephant, Alexander, who eats everything from A to Z for a midnight snack. Presented in various ways, a letter can be a push-and-pull type and hide a brown ape or be a distorted image that

3

hides an ant and anteater, which are revealed with the help of a silver cylinder. A letter can be found in a picture wheel, on strips of flip pages, and in scenes viewed through die-cut openings. In addition to the topic of animals, the letter *A* can introduce readers in the elementary classroom to other topics of interest. In Part One, selected alphabet books are grouped into collections of topics that represent themes:

- Animals as Animals;
- Animals as Humans;
- City Life;
- Country Life;
- History;
- Letter Transformations;
- Puzzles and Games;
- Sign Language; and
- Specific Places.

In Part Two, the alphabet books in a milieu collection are found. In the milieu collection, the key objects for the letters are not related to a particular topic or theme. In both Parts One and Two, more than eighty alphabet books considered among the best for children[1] are reviewed and extended with selected activities. In Part Three, over two hundred and fifty alphabet books in the annotated bibliographies arranged by themes are entered by the author's last name and include bibliographic information. Footnotes and suggested readings are at the end of the book. This work is intended for librarians, teachers, and classroom aides, who are new to the elementary classroom and are considering extending some of the alphabet books they read to children with selected activities. The purpose of the book is to assist readers in building a collection of alphabet books that is varied in topics, illustrators' techniques, and art style; to foster interest in using ABC books creatively; and to offer alternative ways of putting the books to their widest use—ways an educator can sort through and select from. In some cases where the details for the book extensions are specific—examples that relate to the importance of taking nothing for granted when introducing an activity to children (for some, it may be their first time to participate in that type of activity in an American classroom) and related to a teaching error of assuming that today's children in today's pluralistic classrooms will automatically understand a teacher's general directions—the specificity is not meant to be condescending. As a cautionary note, the activities are not recipes for "extending" the included alphabet books "to death." Rather, it is hoped that the bibliographies will spark a reader's interest in reading and discussing alphabet books with children for aesthetic enjoyment of the use of language and the illustrators' techniques, and when appropriate, the activities will generate an interest in following a particular book with a creative activity developed by the reader.

*ANIMALS AS ANIMALS THEME

Alphabets provide a variety of animals as characters. In the alphabet books related to the theme of animals as animals, children will find that in an alphabetical sequence, the animals are shown realistically and the illustrations or drawings support the key word choices about their traits, habitat, and behaviors.

THE A B C BUNNY (7)

By Wanda Gág. Hand lettered by Howard Gág. Illustrated by the author. New York: Putnam, 1933. Copyright renewed in 1961 by Robert Hansen.

Gág's book offers words and music for the story of a searching bunny who hops through the adventure and meets a fat frog, a jaunty jay, and a lazy lizard in attractive black-and-white illustrations. Short sentence stems and rhymes introduce large red capitals and reflect the quick hop of a young bunny as it first dashes away from a crashing apple, runs away from hail that falls during a gale, eyes a sunning lizard, and finally takes a nap in the woods.

Extension: Sing the alphabet

Purpose: To identify the alphabet set to music

Materials: Copy of *The ABC Bunny* (7), opaque projector displaying song, musical instruments, tape recorder, blank tape for recording

Suggested Grade: K-1

Show children the words of *The ABC Bunny* song on the opaque projector and point out key words in the sequence. Display the words again on a chart, chalkboard, or on transparency on overhead projector. Review the words of the song with children and using a pitch pipe or other musical instrument, play some of the beginning notes. Play the music on the piano or sing the song for the children and then ask them to sing along with you as you point to the words. If an extended ABC sing-along time is desired, other alphabet books that include music and have songs to sing may be introduced:

The True-to-Life Alphabet Book Including Numbers (258) by Johan Polak (familiar ABC Song)
All in the Woodland Early: An ABC Book (199) by Jane Yolen (accumulating song with surprise ending)
Professor Breads' Alphabet (146) by Tom Besche (accompanying record)
My ABC Book (256) Illustrated by Alys Nugent (when opened, a microchip plays the music of "The Alphabet Song")
The ABC Song (245) by Demi and illustrated by Leonard Shortall (music box book and a milieu of objects to recognize)

For the children's listening enjoyment, record the singing of the children on tape and invite them to listen to their voices and join in the singing again. Save the tape and place it at a listening center along with the alphabet books to meet students' individual interest and replay it on request.

Extension: Singing an abecedarius

Purpose: To identify animal names in alphabetical order and sing them to the music of "The Alphabet Song"

Materials: Copy of *A Peaceable Kingdom: The Shaker Abecedarius* (120), tape recorder, blank tape for recording, duplicated list of animal names (or overhead transparency or list on board)

Suggested Grade: 4–6

Another alphabet book, *A Peaceable Kingdom: The Shaker Abecedarius* (120), illustrated by Alice and Martin Provensen, offers animal names in alphabetical order and the words may be sung to the tune of "The Alphabet Song." Review the names of the animals in alphabetical order with a duplicated list, an overhead transparency, or with a list of the names on the board. Rehearse the tune of "The Alphabet Song." Invite volunteers to lead the singing and then record the singing of the students on tape. Invite them to listen to their voices when the tape is replayed and join in the singing again. Place the tape and a copy of the book in a listening center so interested students can read the words on the pages when the tape is replayed.

ANIMAL ALPHABET (10)

By Bert Kitchen. Illustrated by the author. New York: Dial, 1984.

On white backgrounds, carefully detailed animals introduce large capitals and the animals are shown in, on, or nearby the letters. After predicting the names of the animals, the initial letters in the animals' names may be matched with the large capitals found in black type. As an example, the letter X is introduced by x-ray fish that swim in blue water enclosed by the sides of X. To verify the names of the animals predicted on the previous pages, children may turn to the last page to find a list of animals from armadillo to zebra.

Extension: Animal identification

Purpose: To identify the animals and give each its name and provide some descriptive words; to review animal names and alphabet letters in a musical format

Materials: Copy of *Animal Alphabet* (10)

Suggested Grade: K-1

Invite the boys and girls to locate where each animal is on the page and to give each a name. Some such as dodo, jerboa, quetzal, umbrella bird may be unfamiliar to some young children. Ask the girls and boys to think of words that describe some of the animals. For a self-check, the animals' names are on a final page.

After reviewing the song "Skip to My Lou" with the children, introduce the following words for the tune. The number of animals seen on the pages and their names are included in the verses:

> A for armadillo, one will do,
> A for armadillo, one will do,
> A for armadillo, one will do,
> One will do . . . for A . . . a . . .
>
> B for bats, two will do,
> B for bats, two will do,
> B for bats, two will do,
> Two will do . . . for B . . . b . . .
>
> C for chameleon, one will do,
> C for chameleon, one will do,
> C for chameleon, one will do,
> One will do . . . for C . . . c . . .
>
> M for mole and magpie, two will do,
> M for mole and magpie, two will do,
> M for mole and magpie, two will do,
> Two will do . . . for M . . . m . . .
>
> X for x-ray fish, five will do,
> X for x-ray fish, five will do,
> X for x-ray fish, five will do,
> Five will do . . . for X . . . x . . .
>
> Z for zebra, one will do,
> Z for zebra, one will do,
> Z for zebra, one will do,
> One will do . . . for Z . . . z . . .

Older students can write their own "Animal Alphabet" verses for the various animals in Kitchen's illustrations. A group of students interested in animals can be organized in which the girls and boys compare the various collections of animal illustrations and how different artists have interpreted the animals in alphabet books. Variations in the text may also be studied.

AS I WAS CROSSING BOSTON COMMON (6)

By Norma Farber. Illustrated by Arnold Lobel. New York: Dutton, 1975.

Some alphabet books are designed to introduce children to unfamiliar animals, and Farber's book does just that. Twenty-six animals, in turn, meet a turtle who crosses the Common. Descriptions for animals are on the concluding pages in a list beginning with an angwantibo, a small West African lemur, and ending with an East Indian civet cat—a Zibet. Pronunciation guide.

Extension: Unusual animal names

Purpose: To become aware of names of some unfamiliar animals and the beginning letters of the names; to write selected letters in manuscript or in cursive; to predict where the animals might be going.

Materials: Copy of *As I Was Crossing Boston Common* (6)

Suggested Grade: 2–3

With children, discuss some of the unusual animals they have seen (and where they saw them). Read Farber's story about the turtle meeting animals as it crossed the Common and ask children to predict where the animals might be going. Clarify words i. e., *tow*, with additional phrases, i. e., *tow* means *dragged,* and if needed, invite children to act out related motions. Reread the words and invite the girls and boys to chime in on the familiar phrase, "As I was crossing Boston Common—not very fast, not very slow—." Ask them to review the illustrations and the sequence of the letters as you turn the pages and discuss them with the children. Encourage them to listen as you present this supplementary verse. The second time, invite children to chime in:

> Animals, animals,
> All you can see,
> Let's learn their names

From A to Z.
Twenty-six animals,
All in a row,
The angwantibo says,
'Alphabet show!'

When "Alphabet show!" is said, you hold up a writing paper (or individual chalkboard) to show the children the letter *A* for angwantibo. Repeat this with the children and invite them to hold up their writing papers or individual chalkboards to show each other the letter each has written—*A* for angwantibo. In the second verse, the second animal, the Boobook says, "Alphabet show!" and the children write *B* to hold up and to show others. If desired, match some of the children's letters with the letter you write on the board. Continue the activity with the letters you and the children select. Invite volunteers to discuss the animals and what they look like in the illustrations and then ask the children to chime in on a final verse to end the book extension:

Animals, animals,
All you can see,
We learned their names
From A to Z.
Twenty-six animals,
All in a row,
The Zibet says,
'This ends alphabet show!'

As an option for older students, ask them to select some of their favorite animals from the alphabet book and find the geographical locations of some of the animals on a world map or a globe. For an extension into creative writing, ask the students to discuss the unusual animals they know about, list the animals' names on board in alphabetical order, and suggest that they write original sentences or write endings for a sentence pattern: "As I was crossing _____ (name of a place in students' town), not very fast, not very slow; I met someone with a _____(name of animal) in tow." As a link to art, suggest to the students that they illustrate some of their favorite sentences. For those who will benefit from a read-along situation, place a tape cassette of the story and its read-along reader (Listening Library) at a listening center so they can listen to the narrator and follow along.[2]

THE BABY ANIMAL ABC (4)

By Robert Broomfield. Illustrated by the author. New York: Penguin, 1968.

Broomfield introduces girls and boys to cubs, calves, foals, and other young animals. Animal babies called cubs are shown with their mothers, i.e., the anteater, fox, jaguar, koala, lion, tiger, and wolf. The young of bison, cow, elephant, rhinoceros, and yak are identified as calves. Foals of the donkey, pony, and zebra are represented by the letters d, p, and z and some animal young are given names unique to their species—the goat kid, the impala fawn, seal pup, a lamb, owlets, and quail chicks. Some babies are known simply as the young—of hedgehogs, newts, and xerus. Drawings show some of the playful behavior of the babies, e.g., an anteater cub rides on its mother's back, an elephant calf grasps its mother's tail, and fox cubs play with a snail.

Extension: Baby with a b

Purpose: To listen to descriptions of baby animals, to become aware of names given to baby animals, and to gain information about young animals

Materials: Copy of *The Baby Animal ABC* (4)

Suggested Grade: Pre-K

With children, discuss some of the baby animals they have seen (and where they saw them). Read *The Baby Animal ABC* and ask children to predict (guess, tell a hunch) the name for each baby animal. Reread and invite students to chime in on names of baby animals familiar to them. Do a third reading of each page and feature each baby animal with this supplementary chant:

> Baby, baby with a B
> I see a baby animal.
> What do you see?
> (leader points to student and student
> names baby animal) I see _____

Encourage children to use terms such as cubs, calves, foals with:

teacher: Baby, baby with a B.
             Which baby animal do YOU see?

children: Baby, baby with a B
             I see a baby animal.
             What do I see?
             The _____ (anteater cub) is what I see.
             (students name animal and the term for its young)

Ask children to review the illustrations and the names of the baby animals as the pages are turned again for another review and discussed. Encourage the girls and boys to dictate names of baby animals and cluster the names under terms for animal young in a word web similar to the one that follows:

Baby Animals

cubs	calves	foals	unique names	known as young
anteater	bison	donkey	goat kid	hedgehogs
fox	cow	pony	impala fawn	newts
jaguar	elephant	zebra	owlets	xerus
koala	rhinoceros		quail chicks	
lion	yak		seal pup	
tiger			urial lamb	

If desired, use the web above as a writing resource in the classroom. Some of the children may be ready to write/dictate sentences or produce drawings that illustrate something they have learned about baby animals.

A CARIBOU ALPHABET (16)

By Mary Beth Owens. Illustrated by the author. New York: Dog Ear Press, 1988.

Owens's book introduces children to the world of the caribou, North America's reindeer. From *A* for antlers to *Z* for zero weather, the couplets describe the characteristics, habitat, and ways of caribou. Unfamiliar words for some children may be *ungulate, kalmia, lichen, predator,* and *xalibu* (a Micmac word for "pawer of snow"). "A Caribou Compendium" by Mark McCollough at the end of the book gives information about the key words.

Extension: Caribou characteristics

Purpose: To become aware of facts about the caribou

Materials: Copy of *A Caribou Alphabet* (16)

Suggested Grade: 3–4

With students, discuss some of the characteristics, ways, and habitat of "America's reindeer." Read some of the rhyming couplets about caribou and ask the students to predict the last rhyming word in the last line of each couplet. Clarify words that may be unfamiliar ones, i. e., *kalmia,* (favorite plant of caribou that grows in a bog); *lichen* (small spongy plant of the tundra); and *ungulate* (mammal whose toes have horned covering called hooves). Reread and invite students to chime in on words they remember. Ask the students to review the illustrations and letters as pages are turned and discussed. After the discussion, the students may work in pairs, illustrate the couplets, produce oversize alphabet books to share with younger children, and "research" additional information about a selected animal.

Work in Pairs. Once the students see the pattern of the book's organization, engage them in working in pairs to select an animal, to do research to discover the animal's characteristics and habitat, and to write couplets of information about the animal.

Illustrate Couplets. When the couplets are finished, invite the students to illustrate them with large illustrations (perhaps 18'' x 24''). With the use of watercolor or tempera, the students paint backgrounds and then use art paper and crayons and scissors to draw, color, and cut out shapes of animals and other objects for the scenes. They punch holes in the margins of their illustrations and tie with yarn ties to make an oversize alphabet book to donate to a kindergarten class.

Produce Oversize Alphabet Books. Invite the students to introduce the big alphabet book to younger students in a primary classroom. If desired, leave the book(s) in the primary classroom for a week and then return to collect the books and leave others for the younger students to read.

Look for Information. Additional alphabet books are useful for research and the students can find information about some of the animals they are studying. Suggest titles of alphabet books such as:

Animal	*Alphabet Book*
African animals	*African Treehouse* (234)
Australian animals	*ABC of Australian Animals* (233)
prehistoric animals	*The ABC Dinosaur Book* (9)
	100 Dinosaurs A to Z (24)
unusual animals	*Incredible Animals from A to Z* (19)
animal companions	*The Kittens' ABC* (15)
zoo animals	*Alphabet Zoo* (11)

The animals the students see in the illustrations can be categorized in a word web such as the one that follows:

Animals

Prehistoric Animals	*Today's Animals*
_____	_____
_____	_____
_____	_____

THE KITTENS' ABC (15)

By Clare Turlay Newberry. Illustrated by the author. New York: Harper, 1965.

With watercolor and wet paper, Newberry created appealing, lifelike kittens with touches of yellow in the large black-and-white illustrations. Large capitals, also in yellow, are introduced by verses about kittens, how they look, and how they act. The kittens are inside when weather is bad and outside when it is nice. Inside, they drink milk, play, and claw the furniture. Outside, they purr, grrr, quarrel, and climb trees. Invite the children to look for specific examples, e.g., the alley cats, the tomcat, and the cross-eyed Siamese with eyes of blue.

Extension: Add meow to verses

Purpose: To become aware of ways to orally interpret verses and to add a meow effect to selected verses about kittens

Materials: Copy of *The Kittens' ABC* (15) and musical instruments

Suggested Grade: K-1

Ask children to tell some of the things they know about kittens. With the word *kittens* as the center of a word map on the board, write the children's dictations around the center and cluster the children's ideas to show relationships. Read aloud Newberry's verses and then introduce musical notes (perhaps D, C, and E in C major) with a piano, pitch pipe or musical bells. Invite the boys and girls to match the tones you play with their voices and to sing up and down the musical notes with the meow of a kitten. Then, ask the children to help you add a "meow effect" to the verses by singing the notes with "meow" at the end of some of the verses read aloud. Invite the children to engage in oral interpretation and decide on other appropriate kitten or cat meows and growls to accompany a rereading of selected verses. For instance, certain situations in verses may suggest oral interpretations similar to the following ones:

situations in verses	suggested effect
kitten drinking warm milk	contented purr
kitten washing its face and ears	satisfied meow
kitten scared	hissing and grr-rr
kitten sleeping	purr-purr
kitten calling for its mother	mew
kitten pretending to quarrel and fight	a pretend spit and growl
kitten afraid to climb down a tree	frightened mew

After reading another alphabet book about cats, invite the girls and boys to engage in more oral interpretation and suggest meows, growls, and other sounds to accompany a rereading. For an example, their suggestions could accompany Nancy Jewell's descriptive words about the family cat in *ABC Cat* (8). Older students could volunteer to lead this activity for younger children in a preschool setting, kindergarten, or first grade.

* ANIMALS AS HUMANS THEME

In the alphabet books related to the theme of animals acting like humans, girls and boys will discover such characters as an ape in a cape, a small elephant who eats a midnight snack, Aster Aardvark who begins alphabetical adventures in an airplane, and Appley Dabbley, one of Beatrix Potter's animal characters.

A IS FOR ANGRY: AN ANIMAL AND ADJECTIVE ALPHABET (28)

By Sandra Boynton. Illustrated by the author. New York: Workman, 1983.

Boynton's alphabet book introduces children to animals acting like humans, their names, and selected adjectives. After a zany zebra hangs upside down from a large *Z*, a second ending shows that *Z* also stands for zoo and the animals sleeping with Zzzzs. A picture review at the end shows all the animals and letters.

Extension: What do you see?

Purpose: To identify selected animal names, beginning letters, adjectives associated with animals acting with human behaviors, and to write selected letters in manuscript or in cursive

Materials: Copy of *A Is for Angry* (28)

Suggested Grade: K-1

After reading the book, encourage the children to use different words to describe the animals they saw on the pages. Introduce this review of adjectives with a verse to say together:

I see an anteater
looking at me.
When I read the page
How will anteater be? (*A* is for angry)

I see a zebra
looking at me.
When I read the page
How will zebra be? (*Z* is for zany)

And for a second ending:

I see a zoo
looking at me.
I read the page
How will it be? (*Z* is for zzzzzz—
and sleeping animals).

For each animal, provide some descriptive information during rereadings. Unfamiliar animals for some may be the iguana, jaguar, koala, newt, opossum, unau, and yak.

For a second chant-aloud, focus on the sequence and the subsequent letters. After showing the letter *A* and its related animals, anteater and ant, provide opportunities for the children to respond to examples:

I see a letter *B* looking at me.
When I call *your* name, _____, (leader calls name)
What do *you* see? (student says, "bashful bear and bunny")

I see a letter I looking at me.
When I call *your* name, _____,
What do *you* see? (ill iguana)

ALEXANDER'S MIDNIGHT SNACK:
A LITTLE ELEPHANT'S ABC (55)

By Catherine Stock. Illustrated by the author. New York: Ticknor, 1988.

Stock's alphabet book introduces children to names of foods in an amusing way. Alexander, the little elephant, wakes up and wants a glass of water, but once in the kitchen, he finds that the apple pie looks good. He proceeds to eat (or do) something for every letter, beginning with apple pie and buns, and ending with a yawn and sleep (ZZZZZZZZ). The key words are shown with red capitals in black text, and the letter *X* is for an X-ray of what Alexander's stomach looks like. For a second ending, Mother sees the mess in the kitchen the next morning.

Extension: Chant for Alexander

Purpose: To participate in telling an alphabet story by emphasizing a chant about the little elephant, Alexander

Materials: Copy of *Alexander's Midnight Snack* (55)

Suggested Grade: Pre-K

With children, discuss some of the foods Alexander found for his late-night snack (and where). Ask the children to predict some of the foods they think are "suitable" for a midnight snack and begin the story about the little elephant. As you read, clarify the words related to any unfamiliar foods. Reread Alexander's story and invite the girls and boys to chime in on any words they remember. Ask the children to review the illustrations and the letters with you as pages are turned and discussed. Encourage the children to listen and chime in on the following refrain as you present the words to summarize:

Who ate _____ (name of food representing *A*)?
It was Alex-and-er,
The Mid-night Snack-er.
Who ate _____(name of food representing *B*)?
It was Alex-and-er,
The Mid-night Snack-er.
Who ate _____(name of food representing *C*)?
It was Alex-and-er,
The Mid-night Snack-er.

After each page is reread and the children are aware of each food that Alexander eats, substitute the name of that food into the lines.

Apple pie	Buns with raisins
Cinnamon cookies	Dish of doughnuts
Eggs, hard-boiled	Fishcakes
Gingersnaps	Honey
Ice cream	Jam (raspberry)
Ketchup	Lemon
Milkshake	Nuts
Orange	Pickle
Quarter of a pound of Swiss cheese	Roast beef

To develop a word map, invite the children to contribute other food names and write the names on the board. Ask the children for their suggestions about placing the words in related clusters, i.e., all the names of desserts in one cluster, dairy products in another, and so on. Ask the children to give some reasons for their suggestions.

ALLIGATOR ARRIVED WITH APPLES: A POTLUCK ALPHABET FEAST (38)

By Crescent Dragonwagon. Illustrated by Jose Aruego & Ariane Dewey. New York: Macmillan, 1987.

Dragonwagon's rhymes introduce children to a Thanksgiving potluck party with the foods and guests in alphabetical order. Two pink pigs wait for the guests at a table set with name tags for animals from alligator to Zebra. There is no name tag *X.* The letter *X* is for excellent yams and yogurt brought by a blue Yak. The turkey is not part of the feast, but a guest instead, and brings tomatoes, trifle, and turnips. The animals take Thanksgiving naps at the end of the book and the endpapers show the labeled foods from the alligator's apples to the zebra's zucchini. Full-color illustrations.

Extension: alphabet rhythms

Purpose: To participate in chanting rhythmic language about a Thanksgiving potluck attended by animals from *A* to *Z*

Materials: Copy of *Alligator Arrived with Apples* (38)

Suggested Grade: K-1

With children, discuss some of the foods they like to eat around Thanksgiving time, and write the words on the board as the children dictate them. Cluster the words in groups to show relationships.

Dragonwagon's rhymes about foods are effective ones and can lead to a visual display of the way the guests and foods accumulated. In a row of empty "boxes" drawn side by side on the chalkboard (or on individual paper sheets), place arrows between the boxes to show the direction that follows the book's rhymes. The first box represents the first guest and the foods that were brought, and so on. In the first box, the words *alligator, apples,* and *allspice* are written (or sketches are drawn). The next box represents the second guest and foods, and so on.

Give the children the empty word boxes with the first one completed and help the children finish filling in the remainder of the boxes with appropriate guests and foods. Encourage the girls and boys to write original sentences beneath the boxes or to draw some small illustrations to show the foods or the guests. Some of the words from the story may be listed as resources for writing since some of them may be unfamiliar ones to some children:

letter	*guest*	*foods for potluck*
A	alligator on motorcycle	apples, allspice
B	bear on unicycle	banana bread, biscuits, butter
C	cat on hang glider	cranberry compote, cherry cobbler
D	dragon and deer on bicycle built for two	diced dates
E	elephant on tricycle	elderberry elixir
F	flamingo on roller skates	fresh figs

After rereading Dragonwagon's verses aloud, discuss the different transportation used by the animals to deliver the food, i.e., motorcycle, unicycle, hang glider, and others. If a food-tasting extension activity is desired, invite the children to take a small sample of some of the foods as they are mentioned in the book.

ALPHABEARS: AN ABC BOOK (42)

By Kathleen Hague. Illustrated by Michael Hague. New York: Holt, 1984.

In full-color illustrations, teddy bears with human behaviors introduce the colorful block letters and the rhymes in large print. For example, *A* is for Amanda who carries apples in a wheelbarrow, *Y* is for York, a young bear who sits in a high chair at the table, and *Z* is for Zak, who thinks zippers are better than buttons. The letter *X* is for a mark in the sand so an unnamed bear can return to the same spot on the beach.

Extension: Alphabet rhythms

Purpose: To listen to the behaviors of teddy bears in rhyme

Materials: Copy of *Alphabears: An ABC Book* (42)

Suggested Grade: K-1

With children, introduce the letters of the alphabet with the teddy bear rhymes about their humanlike behavior and invite the girls and boys to discuss the bears' behavior when it reminds them of a behavior they've seen in younger siblings. Hague's rhymes are effective in showing the different qualities of the bears. For example, Byron Bear wants a kiss from mother at bedtime, Elsie Bear explores the jungle, and Freddie Bear makes a frightful muddy mess.

If desired, introduce this book of rhymes with a word web of the names of Hague's teddy bears. Demonstrate to the children a way to substitute the name(s) of their teddy bear characters for Hague's bear names in the book's rhymes. If the rhymes are used to initiate creative dictation/writing, invite the children to think of some of their own original teddy bear characters and use them as characters for sentences.

As the children pantomime the behavior of the bears, the names and qualities of the teddy bears may be discussed with the children and recorded on charts for future writing resources:

letter	teddy bear	qualities and behaviors
A	Amanda	good, carries apples in wheelbarrow
B	Byron	snuggles in bed
C	Charles	stuffy, old, wears bow tie
D	Devon	looks like his pop, big nose, floppy ears
E	Elsie	explores the jungle
F	Freddie	makes a muddy mess
G	Gilbert	gruff, growls
H	Henry	likes hot cakes, honey, butter
I	Ivan	itches and likes to be scratched
J	John	likes jam and jelly

THE AMAZING ANIMAL ALPHABET BOOK (32)

By Roger Chouinard & Mariko Chouinard. Illustrated by Roger Chouinard. New York: Doubleday, 1988.

In full-color illustrations, the animal characters introduce letter pairs and alliterative phrases. For example, *A* is for an anteater waiting for August, *M* is for a mole making a molehill out of a mountain, and *Z* is for a zebra with zippers on his zoot suit. The letter *X* is for an x-ray fish playing on the xylophone at "Xmas." Engage some of the children in looking for the hidden letter in every illustration, e.g., the letter *Y* is hidden in the flag on the yak's yacht.

Extension: Alliterative phrases

Purpose: To listen to alliterative phrases about animal characters from anteater to zebra

Materials: Copy of *The Amazing Animal Alphabet Book* (32)

Suggested Grade: K-1

Introduce this book of alliterative phrases about animal characters with a chart to show the animals' names, looks, and behaviors. Invite the children to discuss the animals' behaviors and descriptions and point out ways the alliterative phrases support the humorous full-color illustrations. For examples, "Bear bathes in a bathtub, Cat catches a cab," and "Dog and Duck dance divinely together." If the alliterative phrases are used to begin creative dictation/writing, invite the children to think of some original animal characters and use them as the characters in additional alliterative sentences. Further, alliterative words about the animal characters can be listed as a writing resource and the children can suggest the additional words they want to add:

letter	alliterative words
A	anteater, August
B	bear, bath, bathtub
C	cat, catch, cab
D	dog, duck, dance
E	elephant, emu, eat

F	frog, feeling, forlorn
G	gorilla, girdle
H	hippo, hiding, hill
I	iguana, ice cream
J	jackrabbit, jumping, Jacuzzi
K	kangaroos, kiss, kayaks
L	lions, lamb, lifeboat

APE IN A CAPE: AN ALPHABET OF ODD ANIMALS (40)

By Fritz Eichenberg. Illustrated by the author. New York: Harcourt Brace Jovanovich, 1952.

Still other alphabet books, such as Eichenberg's, offer a rich background for rhyme. Eichenberg creates an unusual assortment of animals in the illustrations along with a short rhyming caption for each one. For example, the children see a tall lizard standing beside a wizard who is dressed in a bright red gown. The wizard waves a wand to sprinkle sparkling stars in a bright blue sky.

Extension: Put rhyming words to music

Purpose: To create alphabet verses with rhyming words and to dictate words for the song, "Here We go 'Round the Mulberry Bush."

Materials: Copy of *Ape in a Cape* (40)

Suggested Grade: K-1

With the children, review Eichenberg's alphabet book to see and hear his brief alphabet captions again. Engage the children in adding some rhyming words to a song they know to create an original alphabet song and to promote the recognition of words that sound alike. To see how this was done in another class, the boys and girls may be interested in hearing some of the words another first-grade class selected and sang to the tune, "Here We Go 'Round the Mulberry Bush." Encourage the children to say the words along with you as you introduce these original verses:

Verse for key word for letter *F*: fox

And here's the fox wearing some sox,
wearing some sox,
wearing some sox.
And here's the fox wearing some sox,
Fox and sox are rhyming.

Verse for key word for letter *G*: goat

And here's the goat buttoning a coat,
buttoning a coat,
buttoning a coat,
And here's the goat buttoning a coat,
Goat and coat are rhyming.

Verse for key word for letter *C*: carp

And here's a carp playing a harp,
playing a harp,
playing a harp,
And here's a carp playing a harp,
Carp and harp are rhyming.

Continue through selected letters and encourage the children to talk about the animals and their actions. For instance, some children may want to talk about the large, white goat wearing a long scarf around his neck and who is in a rowboat looking toward shore; or about the lighthouse and wonder aloud what could have happened before the scene in the illustration (where the goat has been and what motivated the animal to get in a rowboat) and what might happen next (the events that happen when the goat reaches the lighthouse). Some children will notice that the color blue is the pre-dominant one in the illustrations and that red highlights the ape's cape, hare's jacket, a wizard's long cloak, unicorn's mane, and a kingly lion's royal coat.

Older students may turn to the book as an art resource—not to copy the work that the artist has done, but to look and see the ways the artist used color in the illustrations. If a student likes the way the artist achieved a particular effect, a student may want to try achieving a similar effect in a scene. Some of the features to point out to a student can include: the way a student responds to the colors; an observation of the artist's lines of hard work; an observation of which lines are single ones and which are close together; the directions the lines take; and the texture achieved by the use of lines; the way the artist uses the entire page; and the way an artist arranges the objects in the space.

ASTER AARDVARK'S ALPHABET ADVENTURES (44)

By Steven Kellogg. Illustrated by the author. New York: Morrow, 1987.

Having an aversion to the alphabet, Aster Aardvark receives an airplane from her Aunt Agnes, who hopes it will help increase Aster's academic achievement. On her adventures, Aster meets several animal characters beginning with Bertha Bear and her Brooklyn buddies and ending with sleeping zebras. The letter *X* is for Xerxes Ox, who became exhausted from exertion after exercise. The catchy alliterative sentences may be chanted aloud and fingers and feet tapped to keep the beat.

Extension: Alliteration overhead bingo

Purpose: To identify the alliterative letter in a selected sentence or phrase

Materials: Copy of *Aster Aardvark's Alphabet Adventures* (44)

Suggested Grade: 2–3

After reading the book to the students, discuss the alliterative letters in some of the sentences. For instance, read a sentence aloud and invite the students to listen for the sound that repeats itself and to identify the letter that represents the sound. Ask the students to listen for the sound of *H* in the sentence about hibernating Harris Hare, for the sound of *K* in the sentence about Kenilworth, the kind kangaroo, and for the sound of *L* in the sentence about Lana, a lazy lioness from Louisiana. Invite the children to tap their fingers or toes to the chant.

Introduce Alliteration Overhead Bingo and distribute a teacher-produced Alliteration Bingo Card to each student. Receiving the card, each student writes in the word FREE in a space and fills in the other spaces with alphabet letters.

When students have filled in the spaces, display the first of several transparencies with a circle divided into pie shapes. In each pie shape is an alliterative phrase (with the name of the animal character deleted) from Kellogg's book. Place a spinner in the center of the circle on the transparency and ask a student to spin the spinner. When the spinner stops, the arrow will stop on one of the phrases. Ask the students to read the alliterative phrase together as a choral reading and see if they can recall the name of the animal character that relates to the phrase. When a student recalls the animal character's name, he/she identifies the beginning letter on the bingo card and finds the matching letter written on the card. They cross out the letter with a crayon or pencil, and with inventive or conventional spelling, write in the animal character's name.

For the bingo game, examples of alliterative phrases and names of animal characters are:

alliterative phrase	*letter*	*animal character's name*
_____ and her Brooklyn buddies were being bothered by a bratty baboon	B	Bertha Bear
_____ cleverly coordinated a chorus of caterwauling cats, cawing crows, and croaking condors.	C	Cyril Capon
Desperate for dinner after a day of digging up dinosaurs		

in the desert, _____ dined on delicious delicacies.	D	Dr. Delphius Dog
_____ encountered eight ermines who ecstatically extolled the elegance of her eyeglasses.	E	Estelle Egret

BABAR'S ABC (35)

By Laurent de Brunhoff. Illustrated by the author. New York: Random House, 1983.

In Celesteville, Babar and the other animals introduce the alphabet beginning with Arthur, the little elephant with an accordion, and ending with Zephir, the little monkey. Each object represents a key word shown in bold that is used in an alliterative sentence. The sentences are beneath either the large illustrations or smaller inserts and both capitals and lowercase letters are presented.

Extension: I was looking at a book

Purpose: To review the alphabet with an alphabet rhyme

Materials: Copy of *Babar's ABC* (35)

Suggested Grade: K-1

Review the alphabet on the pages with the children. With children, introduce the rhyme "I was looking at a book" and invite children to say the words with you as they snap their fingers or tap their toes. Hold up *Babar's ABC* and say the words for the rhyme:

I Was Looking At a Book

I was looking
at a book,
the oth-er day,
When I met Ba-bar
going my way.

I said,
Dear Ba-Bar
What did you see?
And this is what
he said to me:

I said,
Dear Ba-Bar
What have you seen?
He said,
"I've seen the letters
in an elephant's dream."

"I saw the a, b, c, d,
and the e, f, g, h;
the i, j, k, l,
and the m, n, o, p;
I saw the q, r, s, t,
and the u and the v;
I saw the w and x
and the y and the z."

FAINT FROGS FEELING FEVERISH AND OTHER TERRIFICALLY TANTALIZING TONGUE TWISTERS (52)

By Lilian Obligado. Illustrated by the author. New York: Viking, 1983.

A student who takes time to look carefully at this book discovers such humorous pictures as a green frog "feeling feverish" and resting in a wicker chair with an ice pack on his head, a thermometer in his mouth, and a paper fan in his hand; an energetic flamingo who fans the frog "faint with fever"; and pandas who patrol for pickpockets (panthers) and are armed with purple pistols. Juggling jackrabbits, zipping zebras, whistling wombats, and adding aardvarks are found in alliterative sentences that offer choices to students for tongue twister sessions.

Extension: Say the secret word . . .

Purpose: To locate identified words in alphabet books

Materials: Copy of *Faint Frogs Feeling Feverish* (52)

Suggested Grade: 4–6

With older students, mention that the secret alphabet word(s) for the day is _____ (a word or phrase from an alphabet book in the room or school library). Display the word(s) on the bulletin board or in another conspicuous place. Invite students to look for the word(s) while in school during the day. When a student locates the book in which the word(s) are found, the student whispers to the teacher, "I know the secret word." And in turn, the teacher asks for the secret word(s) (title of the alphabet book in which the words were located). Unusual words for the teacher to consider as "secret words" are:

- *Primordial* describes protozoa, the simple one-cell animals who live in water and are so small they are seen only with a microscope; *bumptious* describes a brown blue-eyed baboon; and *eight-tentacled* describes a floating green octopus from *Hosie's Alphabet* (3) by Leonard Baskin;
- "*Terrible lizards,*" in *The ABC Dinosaur Book* (9) by Jill Kingdon, refers to the dinosaurs, a term that includes many prehistoric creatures from the ankylosaur, a sharp-spiked dinosaur with a clubbed tail, to the zanclodon, a meat gulper with small "hands" who walked on strong back legs.
- A *bandicoot* is an animal who eats a chocolate cupcake, and a *dormouse* is one who dances in *A Comic and Curious Collection of Animals, Birds, and Other Creatures* (33) by Bobbie Craig.
- *Brolgas* is from *ABC of Australian Animals* (231) by Robert E. Smith; and
- *Ossifers* is one of Edward Lear's coined words in *A Learical Lexicon* (107) collected by Myra Cohn Livingston.
- *Zoo suit* is in *The Amazing Animal Alphabet Book* (32) by Roger and Mariko Chouinard.
- *Aquawalker* is found in Jim Davis's *Garfield A to Z Zoo* (34).
- *Zany* is in Stan Mack's *The King's Cat Is Coming* (47).

Schedule a brief browsing time each day, and invite the student who was first to find the secret word to be the one to select the next secret word so the searching can continue. Further, the first student who identifies the alphabet book correctly is awarded an ABC token recognition such as a Secret Word certificate or is given a valued responsibility or role in the room for that period, day, or week.

THE GUINEA PIG ABC (39)

By Kate Duke. Illustrated by the author. New York: Dutton,
1983.

Duke's full-color illustrations show the actions of guinea pigs, which
introduce large colorful letters and key words in capitals. The
guinea pigs get dirty, get clean, are loud, are timid, and hang upside
down. The letter *X* is for finding an extra shoe.

Extension: Guinea pigs act out

Purpose: To identify selected actions of guinea pigs and beginning
letters of key words

Materials: Copy of *The Guinea Pig ABC* (39)

Suggested Grade: Pre-K

With the children, discuss guinea pigs they have seen (and where).
Read the key words about the guinea pigs and their actions and ask
the children to predict what the guinea pigs might be doing for each
key word before showing the related action in the illustration. For
instance, after showing the illustration for the letter *A* where the
sleeping guinea pig is rudely "awakened" by another guinea pig
beating a drum, announce, "*B* is for bouncy. What are some of the
things the guinea pig might be doing to show the meaning of the
word *bouncy?*" Wait for the children's predictions, then show the illustration of the guinea pig bouncing on a pogo stick. Clarify some
of the unfamiliar words, i.e., *vain,* and discuss why the guinea pig is
looking into a mirror. Reread the book and invite the boys and girls
to chime in on the key words that are beneath the illustrations.
Invite them to select another animal and prepare an ABC to show
that animal's characteristics. Together, brainstorm some of the different characteristics the animals might have, and as words are dictated by the children, put the words in alphabetical order on a wall
chart. Ask children to record them in alphabetical order, too, on papers at their desks:

ABC Order	Dictated words	ABC Order	Dictated Words
A is for		N is for	
B is for		O is for	
C is for		P is for	
D is for		Q is for	
E is for		R is for	
F is for		S is for	
G is for		T is for	
H is for		U is for	
I is for		V is for	
J is for		W is for	
K is for		X is for	
L is for		Y is for	
M is for		Z is for	

If desired, invite the children to look for illustrations that show something about the words and to paste the pictures on the chart near the related words.

Older students may contribute alternatives for the adjectives in the book. When the text for a page is read, e.g., "A is for angry," a student may respond with, "I'm tired of guinea pigs being angry. I wish that guinea pigs were_____ (student selects word that begins with the appropriate letter)." Other students take turns responding with adjectives for other letters.

LETTERS TO TALK ABOUT (46)

By Leo Lionni. Illustrated by the author. New York: Pantheon, 1985.

On white backgrounds, gray mice act like humans and play near, around, and on top of capital block letters in collage illustrations. The actions of the mice have no relationship to the letters of the alphabet on the pages. One mouse juggles on top of the letter *F*, another does a headstand on top of *H*, and still another balances the letter *I* on its nose. The sturdy small cardboard pages have no objects or key words.

Extension: Sing the alphabet

Purpose: To identify the letters and review the sequence in song

Materials: Copy of *Letters to Talk About* (46)

Suggested Grade: Pre-K

With the children, discuss the actions of the mice around the letters. Show the illustrations of the mice playing among letters and name the letters. Review the letters a second time and invite the girls and boys to sing some different words to the familiar song, "Three Blind Mice." Ask them to sing along with these words:

> *Mice, Mice, Mice*
> (tune of "Three Blind Mice")
>
> Mice, mice, mice
> See how they play
> See how they play
> They know the letters from A to Z.
> They know the letters from A to Z
> Mice, mice, mice.
>
> *Dashing Through the Letters*
> (tune of "Jingle Bells")

Dashing through the letters	*Chorus*
With their voices bright and gay,	Oh—
The mice say ABCs today—	ABCs—
Sounding all the way.	ABCs—
The mice alphabet is clear	Saying letters bright.

with letters big and bright.
What fun it is to sound and say
The ABCs just right.

What fun it is to sound
and say
The ABCs just right.

PETER RABBIT'S ABC (53)

By Beatrix Potter. Reproductions of original illustrations by the
author. London, England: Warne, 1987.

The endpapers, designed by Colin Twinn, show several of Potter's
characters from the original illustrations—from Appley Dappley
and Benjamin Bunny to Yock-Yock, the pig, and Zzz, bzz, the bees.
Capitals and lowercase letters are in the corners of the pages in color
inserts, the key object and key phrase are on left-hand pages and the
reproductions in full color are on the right-hand pages. Quotes
from the stories are beneath the reproductions.

Extension: Who's in Potter's picture?

Purpose: To identify an object or animal from Beatrix Potter's stories

Materials: Copy of *Peter Rabbit's ABC* (53)

Suggested Grade: K

Discuss what the children know about Peter Rabbit and the other
characters developed by Potter and place their dictated words on a
word map. With the children, discuss some of the experiences with
rabbits they have seen, had as a pet, or touched at a nearby petting
zoo. Read the excerpts from *Peter Rabbit's ABC.* After reading to the
children, help them construct a "web of characters" with the names
of Potter's animal characters around a central circle showing the author's name, Beatrix Potter. Encourage students to add several descriptive words for each character, e.g., "Cecily Parsley is furry,
brown, and dressed in blue." Characters from the ABC to place on
a character web are:

Cecily Parsley (rabbit) from *Cecily Parsley's Nursery Rhymes*
Ribby (cat) and Dr. Maggotty (bird) from *The Tale of the Pie
    and The Patty-Pan*
Mittens, Moppet, and Tom (kittens) from *The Tale of Tom
    Kitten*
Tom Thumb and Hunca Munca (mice) from *The Tale of Two
    Bad Mice*
Miss Moppet (mouse) from *The Story of Miss Moppet*
Jemima (duck) from *The Tale of Jemima Puddle-Duck*
Alexander and Bland (pigs) *The Tale of Pigling Bland*
Timmy Willie (mouse) from *The Tale of Johnny Town-Mouse*

While showing the illustrations again with an opaque projector, point to the key object(s): *A* is for the apples gathered by Cecily Parsley, and *Z* is for Zzz of the bee in *The Tale of Mrs. Tittlemouse*. The letter *X* is found in fox's name. For each object, ask the question, "What's in Potter's picture, her picture, HO? and invite children to chant the response with, "It's apples, apples, SO!"

Showing the illustrations again one at a time, ask the children to identify Potter's characters:

    leader: Here's B and butter carried by a cat:
                Who's in Potter's picture,
                her picture, HO?

    children: It's Ribby,
                Ribby, SO!

After showing Peter in Mr. McGregor's garden:

    leader: Here's G and a garden entered by a rabbit:
                Who's in Potter's picture,
                her picture, HO?

    children: It's Peter,
                Peter, SO!

If interested further in Peter Rabbit and the other animal characters as a topic, the children can select sentences from other Potter books and use them as captions for their own original illustrations.

To trace the beginning of the modern picture storybook, older students may research information about the stories of Beatrix

Potter. In each, the pictures are an integral part of the story, so much so that a child can tell the story from the illustrations. Further, the students can discuss the use of watercolors to show the effects of the English countryside, the meadows, the small animals dressed in country clothes, and the interiors of their homes. For instance, in a letter to *The Horn Book*, May 1929, Potter tells how she happened to write *The Tale of Peter Rabbit*. The students may be interested in knowing that Potter said that her method of writing was to "scribble, and cut out, and write it again and again."

POOH'S ALPHABET BOOK (51)

By A. A. Milne. Illustrated by E. H. Shepard. New York: Dutton, 1965.

Milne's character, Pooh, takes a child on an alphabetical tour to meet his animal friends and to see some of their problems. For example, small Piglet tries hard to be brave; taking a bath bothers little Piglet when Kanga gets soap in his mouth; and baby Roo is not bothered at all, but delighted when Tigger takes Roo's medicine by mistake. Both Pooh and Wise Owl are bothered by some spelling problems, and brave Pooh meets a tree-roosting Jagular, dreams of a big Heffalump in his sleep, and tells how he likes Rabbit's short, one-syllable words.

Extension: Pooh's classroom corner

Purpose: To introduce the alphabet and key words with quotations from Milne's Pooh stories

Materials: Copy of *Pooh's Alphabet Book* (51), cardboard, spray paint, green art paper, glue, scissors, green paper grass

Suggested Grade: K

With the children, discuss the idea of giving a classroom corner to Pooh and his friends. Ask them to prepare a bulletin board display to decorate the corner. Using cardboard, encourage them to draw/trace the shape of a large tree trunk and three large circles. Ask students to experiment with moving the circles around, overlapping them, to form a stylized treetop. Paint the tree trunk brown and the treetop green. Invite children to add original shapes of leaves of different sizes and shapes cut from art paper. Using paper grass (the kind used to fill holiday baskets) ask children to decorate the tree's base and the horizontal ground line on the bulletin board.

Invite the girls and boys to bring any favorite stuffed Pooh character or special books to the corner and to display the items on a table in the classroom. Later in the week, encourage the children to bring stuffed bears to class and read aloud some of the books the children bring from home. Prepare a book display and, if desired, include these bears: the bears with personalities in *Alphabears* (42) by Michael Hague; the bear in *Mr. Lion's I Spy ABC* (236) by Pam Adams; the bear bathing in a bathtub in *The Amazing Animal Alphabet Book* (32) by Roger and Mariko Chouinard; and the yellow outlined bear in *B Is for Bear: An ABC* (238) by Dick Bruna.

Read the make-believe adventure—a lunchtime game—of a small boy and a teddy bear who have soup for lunch in *Alphabet Soup* (144) by Kate Banks and illustrated by Peter Sis. Listening to the story, children learn the power of letters to make words, and as the boy daydreams, he spells out what he needs with the letters in his soup:

-When a pepper mill becomes an ogre at the table, the boy spells S-W-O-R-D, and a sword appears in his hand to scare away the ogre.

-When the boy and bear reach a lake, the boy spells B-O-A-T, and a boat appears to take them across.

-When they reach shore and face a mountain of fruit, the boy spells R-O-P-E, and a rope appears to help them climb.

-When they get hungry at the end of their adventure, both bear and the boy drink all the soup.

Invite the parents to come to school for a Teddy Bear Get-Together to watch the children as they listen to their favorite bear stories and to escort their child and bear home. An outline of a teddy bear can be the shape for the invitations. At the get-together, project some of the illustrations selected from *Pooh's Alphabet Book* (51) after reading the stories that the children request. When the children see the illustrations enlarged with an opaque projector, ask

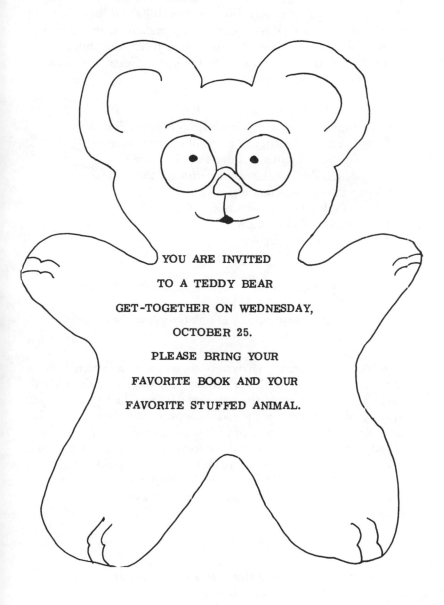

YOU ARE INVITED
TO A TEDDY BEAR
GET-TOGETHER ON WEDNESDAY,
OCTOBER 25.
PLEASE BRING YOUR
FAVORITE BOOK AND YOUR
FAVORITE STUFFED ANIMAL.

them to capture some of Pooh's poses that are seen on the pages. Discuss Pooh in a variety of poses—writing, sitting, stuck in Rabbit's door, helping Eeyore find his tail, walking with Piglet, and taking a sky ride hanging to a balloon. Further, the children can mime the actions of Piglet, Eeyore, Owl, and Tigger. For instance, some may choose to act out the following:

- Piglet hides in a hole in a large tree
- Rabbit tries to unwedge Pooh from Rabbit's door.
- Piglet runs and carries a large balloon to Eeyore.
- Christopher Robin attaches a tail to Eeyore.
- Piglet and Pooh walk together through the woods.
- Pooh talks to a Heffalump.
- Pooh finds a Jagular on a tree branch.
- Kanga gives Piglet a bath.
- Kanga watches Baby Roo.

WHERE IS EVERYBODY? AN ANIMAL ALPHABET (49)

By Eve Merriam. Illustrated by Diane De Groat. New York: Simon & Schuster, 1989.

In full color, the animal characters show up in unexpected places and introduce the letters. With humanlike behaviors, the animals range from an alligator in the attic and a bear in the bakery to a yak in the yard and a zebra at the zoo. In most of the illustrations, a little mole is behind a camera and takes pictures of the animals. He is found in such places as a laundry basket, a passing car, and behind a fence. Words that may be unfamiliar to some children are *ibex, narwhal,* and *vicuna.* The letter *X* is for xenosaurid at the X-ray machine. Some alliteration is in the sentences placed beneath the illustrations.

Extension: Where is everybody?

Purpose: To introduce the alphabet and key words with the question, "Where is everybody?"

Materials: Copy of *Where Is Everybody?* (49)

Suggested Grade: 2

With children, discuss the idea of unexpected places to see animals dressed like humans. Read aloud the alliterative sentences and discuss the humor in the illustrations:

- Alligator is dressed as an angel;
- Bear in bakery is making bagels;
- Cat is playing Camelot Commando on a computer;
- Dog is playing doctor at daycare center;
- Rabbit is riding on a roller coaster;
- Unicorn is diving under water; and
- Monkeys are in the food market.

Make rows of empty "boxes" (rectangle, squares) for a sequence map, and use them to recognize the animal characters and their locations in the story. The first box represents the first animal character for *A* and the animal's location. The next box represents the next animal character for *B* and its location, and so on. Write the names of the first two animals in the alphabet book and their locations in the first two boxes.

If needed, review the letter sequence with the students by rereading the book aloud and give students the empty boxes for a word map with the first two boxes completed. The words *alligator* and *attic* are in the first box. The words *bear* and *bakery* are in the second box. Help students finish completing the remainder of the boxes with the appropriate characters and locations from the story or with alliterative characters and locations that the children want to select. If desired, the students can write sentences beneath the boxes or draw pictures to show their ideas of the alligator in the attic, the bear in the bakery, and so on.

* CITY LIFE THEME

The alphabet books in this section give children a glimpse of city life. Vicariously, girls and boys can see what other children do during the day and evening, learn something about life in a housing project in an inner city, and observe an artwork painted on the side of a tall building. They can get a close look at fire fighters in their working environment, the equipment they use, and ways they operate as a team to fight fires. In contrast to these realistic presentations, they can see a whimsical account of a city tour when Grandpa takes Louie and Mary Ann on an alphabetical trip and starts off with a ride on the Alligator Airlines.

A-B-Cing: AN ACTION ALPHABET (60)

By Janet Beller. Illustrated by the author. New York: Crown, 1984.

Actions are illustrated by children in scenes, and 26 words that end in "ing" tell what's going on. In lowercase letters, each word is at the foot of the page below a black-and-white photograph of the action. Girls and boys climb, read, and zip up clothing. There are no single letters to guide the sequence of the alphabet, so a young child will have to recognize the first letter in each action word or know the sequence of letters in the alphabet.

Extension: Kids in motion

Purpose: To recognize an action word for each letter of the alphabet

Suggested Grade: K-1

Materials: Copy of *A-B-Cing: An Action Alphabet* (60)

Discuss with children what they do during the day and evening and write what they suggest on the board. After singing "The Alphabet Song," demonstrate how to write their suggestions in the order of the song's letters. Review their suggestions from A to Z and invite volunteers to act out the ideas facing partners as an audience. Examples of motions are blowing bubbles, climbing, licking lollipops, examining a xylophone, yawning, and zipping a jacket.

Extension: Kids on film

Purpose: To recognize an action word for each letter of the alphabet

Materials: Copy of *A-B-Cing: An Action Alphabet* (60)

Suggested Grade: 1–2

If available, use a Polaroid™ camera to take photographs of the children as they show motions from *A* to *Z*. Identify the motion with a key word, label the photographs, and place them in alphabetical order on the pages of a big book. Read the book aloud and let children see themselves in the illustrations. Reread the text and ask children to chime in. For a third reading, read the words aloud in a choral setting. If children identify more actions, add the words and the photographs in the appropriate place in the alphabetical arrangement. Place the book in a classroom book corner for children interested in the material.

BEN'S DAY (61)

By Terry Berger. Illustrated by Alice Kandell. New York: Lothrop, Lee, & Shepard, 1981.

Berger's alphabet book is about doing things in a child's world. Each of Ben's activities begins with a letter of the alphabet from *A*, awakening, to *Z*, quiet snoring with zzzzzzzz. Clear, full-color photographs provide a photo essay for children. Illustrations for such actions as joking and questioning may be unclear to viewers at first and will need elaboration.

Extension: Activities through the alphabet

Purpose: To recognize a child's activities in alphabetical order

Materials: Copy of *Ben's Day* (61)

Suggested Grade: K

With children, discuss some of the activities they do throughout the day. As children mention activities, develop a word web with headings of work or play (or morning, afternoon, and night), and write key words for activities under the headings. If needed, draw stick-figure sketches to clarify actions. After singing the alphabet song along with the letters on the endpapers, read the alphabet book to the children and discuss the photographs. With each action, let children relate what is happening in the photograph to their daily lives—awakening, brushing, combing. Where appropriate, encourage children to mime the actions—putting on socks, eating cereal, feeding the cat.

Option: Elicit actions of children for another letter sequence by marking off sections for each letter on long mural paper. Distribute discarded magazines and invite children to find illustrations of children and their actions, to cut out the illustrations, and discuss them with others. Engage children in naming the action and pasting the illustration in the appropriate letter section of the mural.

CITY SEEN FROM A TO Z (64)

By Rachel Isadora. Illustrated by the author. New York: Greenwillow, 1983.

Striking city scenes prepared in textured black-and-white illustrations include a lion design on a T-shirt, an umbrella over a vendor's cart, and a graffiti zoo on a city sidewalk. At first glance, Isadora's illustrations may remind an older viewer of a modern black-and-white pointillistic approach. Block letters in tan are introduced by key words. Subjects are fresh ones, i.e., Art for the letter *A*, which shows a large mural of children's faces on a brick building; entrance for *E*, an opening to the subway; and *P* for pigeon, a familiar bird in a city.

Extension: ABC city silhouettes

Purpose: To prepare silhouettes of city sights and to present them in alphabetical order

Materials: Copy of *City Seen from A to Z* (64), black paper, scissors, transparent drinking straws, overhead projector

Suggested Grade: 1–2

With children who will benefit from an observational extension activity, discuss some of shapes of the objects seen in the city environment. Show some of the objects in silhouette shapes made from black paper. Invite the children to draw and cut out silhouette shapes of some objects they have seen or could see in a city.

Using black paper and scissors, invite children to cut out silhouettes in shapes of city objects. Once shapes are drawn and cut, tape or staple each one to a transparent drinking straw. Engage each student in holding the shape on the overhead stage by its drinking straw handle and telling others about the silhouette.

As each silhouette is discussed, write its key word on the chalkboard in alphabetical order. When all of the shapes are identified, lead the class in recognizing which silhouette's name is now first in the alphabetical sequence, which name is second, and so on through the alphabet.

For a review, invite the child with the *A* silhouette to walk to the overhead, put the silhouette on it, and project the shape again. Talk about what the shape represents and where children might see it in the city. Invite the child with the *B* silhouette to do the same, and so on through the alphabet. If there are any letters without silhouette shapes, invite children to suggest ideas for objects seen in the city and ask them to cut the needed shapes. Engage children in adding lightweight tissue-paper shapes to go with their silhouette shapes in some manner. Demonstrate ways that tissue paper could form shapes of clouds, billowing smoke, or wings of birds or butterflies.

After attaching a tissue-paper cutout to a transparent drinking straw, a child can tap these shapes on the overhead or move the transparent handle any way he or she wants to get the movement that is needed. Add another overhead projector to this activity and

show children a way to create still more action by focusing both pro-
jectors on the same classroom screen.

Older students may want to begin special notebooks and record
their reflections about selected alphabet books. Their records should
include the title, author, artist, the topic or theme, notes about the
features that interested them, the part they enjoyed the most, and
other thoughts. In pairs or small groups, the students may share
their thoughts about the books. For instance, each small group
meeting could begin with a time-limited sharing (perhaps two min-
utes) by a member of the group. Encourage the group members to
prepare their thoughts beforehand and to chose a book the member
has enjoyed. If desired, the sharings can focus on a theme, e.g., city
life, country life, animals acting as humans, and so on. The
thoughts recorded in the notebooks may be used as a resource when
a member is ready to create an original alphabet of his or her city,
town, or state.

FIRE FIGHTERS A TO Z (65)

By Jean Johnson. Illustrated by the author. New York: Walker, 1985.

Johnson's alphabet book looks at fire fighters in their working environment, the equipment, and ways they operate as a team. Black-
and-white photographs introduce the informational paragraphs,
guiding capital letters, and capitalized key words from alarm to
zone. The letter *X* is for Xavier, a Dalmatian who might have been
a fire station mascot some time ago. A concluding section, "More
About Fire Fighters," provides further discussion material about fire
and ways to fight it. Children living in Charlotte, North Carolina,
will appreciate the dedication to the fire fighters of their city.

Extension: Interact with information

Purpose: To foster awareness of importance of fire fighters in the
community and review information in alphabetical order

Materials: Copy of *Fire Fighters A to Z* (65)

Suggested Grade: K-1

With primary-grade children, discuss the fire fighters seen in the photographs, where they work, the equipment they use, and ways they work together as a team. Select another community helper and discuss their work, equipment, and need for teamwork. As key words come into the discussion, write them on the board in alphabetical order or arrange in a word web according to related categories.

With older children (grades 3 and up), read selections from the book, discuss key word choices, and review the author's notes at the end of the book. Discuss the information arrangement in alphabetical order and the way the arrangement is used to organize information in a report about a selected topic, i.e., other community servicemen and women. Invite the students to select a community-service person, locate information, and record what is found in an alphabetical arrangement similar to Johnson's format. Each letter of the alphabet may introduce a topic related to the topic selected. Invite students to draw illustrations to go along with key word choices. With partners, encourage the students to read selections from their original books, discuss key word choices, and tell about the notes at the end of the book that they included as authors.

Option: Display of *Alphabet Books for Thematic Reading about Community Workers.* Display, read, and discuss additional books that feature men and women who serve the communities. Other titles in this series (65) by Johnson are: *Librarians A to Z* with related entries from art to zigzag book (a folding book); *Police Officers A to Z* with topics from accident to zone map; *Postal Workers A to Z* with information from addresses to zip codes; *Sanitation Workers A to Z* with topics from animals to zero garbage; and *Teachers A to Z* with entries from alphabet to zipper.

GRANDPA'S GREAT CITY TOUR: AN ALPHABET BOOK (69)

By James Stevenson. Illustrated by the author. New York: Greenwillow, 1983.

Flying with an alligator pilot on Alligator Airlines, Grandpa takes Louie and Mary Ann on an alphabetical tour of the city through to

X, Y, and *Z* with a zebra playing a xylophone in the gondola of a balloon decorated with *X* s and advertising Yummy yogurt. Each double-page spread shows a part of the city—the harbor, the park with a carousel, shops, and the museum. The concluding page shows a review with twenty-six colorful balloons each featuring one of the capitals flying above the city.

Extension: Great city tour

Purpose: To identify places related to child's city or town for each letter

Materials: Copy of *Grandpa's Great City Tour: An Alphabet Book* (69)

Suggested Grade: 1–2

With children, discuss some of the places in their city/town they have seen (and where). Review the story about Grandpa taking the children on a city tour and ask children to suggest key words for their city. As words are suggested, write them in alphabetical order on the board. Suggest research for any letters that are difficult, i.e., *Q* and *X.* For each letter, ask children, working independently or in pairs, to create large illustrations (preferably 18″ x 24″) that incorporate as many of the key words as possible.

When illustrations are finished, invite children to show their drawings and to talk about them with others. Invite children to cut out large block letters, both capitals and lowercase, and paste them in corners of the drawings. Ask one or two children to make a title page and illustrate a cover. With a paper punch, punch holes in left margins of illustrations and tie pages together with yarn ties.

As the pages are turned, invite the children to look at their own alphabet book, Tour of a City, and see all of the things that can happen where they live.

Option: Display of *Alphabet Books for Thematic Reading about City Life Ah! Belle Cite!* (67) by Poulin; *Big City ABC* (66) by Moak; *City Seen From A to Z* (64) by Isadora; *Idalia's Project ABC/Proyecto ABC: An Urban Alphabet Book in English and Spanish* (68) by Rosario; and *Lucy and Tom's ABC's* (63) by Hughes.

LUCY AND TOM'S A. B. C. (63)

By Shirley Hughes. Illustrated by the author. New York: Viking, 1986.

Lucy and her younger brother, Tom, engage in daily activities that introduce the alphabet letters as they meet people and visit places in their town. The letter *A* is for apples, and *Z* is for zoo. The letter *X* is for xylophone. Author includes questions for children to answer, i.e., Can you see where the children live? Can you guess what it is? and Which voice do you like best of all? Full-color illustrations and capitals and lowercase letters in bold on pages.

Extension: A Day with ABCs

Purpose: To identify daily activities and develop awareness of alphabetical order

Materials: Copy of *Lucy and Tom's A. B. C.* (63)

Suggested Grade: Pre-K

With children, discuss all the people and places they went during one day of a past weekend. Show children ways to group dictated words in alphabetical order or place words in an alphabetical word web on the board. Reread the story about Lucy and her younger brother as they read books together, listen to stories at bedtime, and play with Mops, their cat. Unusual word choices are ill for the letter *I*, voices for *V*, and yachts for *Y*. Reread selected pages and invite students to chime in on the familiar opening phrase for each letter, *A* is for . . . ; *B* is for . . . and the other letters.

* COUNTRY LIFE THEME

In this section related to life in the country, a reader finds an alphabet of trees, an alphabet of fruits and vegetables, and an alphabet of rural life. There are activities of children through the day, including a child's trip to a country fair.

A B CEDAR: AN ALPHABET OF TREES (79)

By George Ella Lyon. Illustrated by Tom Parker. New York: Watts, 1989.

Lyon's alphabet book introduces children to leaves from a variety of trees. The letter sequence is in bold block capitals across the tops of pages, and the names of leaves of trees from Aspen for *A* to Zebrawood for *Z* are introduced in order. Featured letters are shown in red. *X* is for Xolisma. Book ends with short phrases about usefulness of trees. On white backgrounds, illustrations show hands of children from different ethnic groups holding leaves, catching nuts, and pulling leaves aside to look through branches. Final page mentions a tree's contribution to make the book.

Extension: Collecting leaves

Purpose: To identify names of trees, beginning letters, and to write selected letters in manuscript or in cursive

Materials: Copy of *A B Cedar: An Alphabet of Trees* (79)

Suggested Grade: K-1

With children, discuss taking an alphabet walk to look at trees and gather leaves. Together with children, plan what should be done on the walk, i.e., taking sketchbooks to record drawings of different trees seen or to record usefulness of trees. Take several copies of the alphabet book with you as a guide to trees and let children refer to the black silhouette shapes on each paper for beginning identification.

Before leaving the room, review safety rules for a safe walk. Walk a distance near or around the school or neighborhood. Back in the classroom, place the collected leaves, one at a time, on the overhead projector stage, and discuss features. Establish groups for leaves by features and write group headings on chart paper and affix each leaf in its place on the paper. Introduce a mystery leaf and let children discuss, predict where it should go, and establish a new category for it.

Option: Mark off mural paper into twenty-six sections, one section for each letter. Invite children to dictate names of trees for each letter and write in the names. Students in pairs do research to find the shapes of leaves in reference books and draw appropriate leaf shapes in each section. When new tree names are found, students may add the names to their section or to another section. Ask students to sign their names after finishing their research and drawing work.

Option: Display titles of other alphabet books about plants and nature and discuss the features found in them. One title to consider for a classroom collection is *A Wildflower Alphabet* (73) by Elizabeth Cameron, where every flower from anemone, *A,* to zigzag clover, *Z,* is illustrated and annotated with a hand-lettered passage about the flower's name, habitat, and uses. For older students who are ready for a further extension activity in composing ways to prepare reports about plants, Cameron's composition is a useful model. Students see several features: her letter to her grandchildren stating the purpose of the book, the alphabetical order with guiding letters at the tops of pages, the manuscript print, marginalia, accompanying full-page illustrations with captions, and author's note at the end.

AARON AWOKE: AN ALPHABET STORY (72)

By Marilee Robin Burton. Illustrated by the author. New York: Harper & Row, 1982.

Some alphabet books are designed around a topic from which the story progresses, and Burton's book is one of these. During one day at the farm, Aaron wakes up, takes a bubble bath, and has an alphabetical day of work and play with his friends. For each letter, a reader looks for objects in the illustrations that begin with the letter. Hidden objects are found again on the end pages in a right-to-left ABC sequence that follows the margins. Alliteration.

Extension: Alliteration add-ons

Purpose: To help tell an alphabetical story by adding sounds

Materials: Copy of *Aaron Awoke* (72)

Suggested Grade: K-1

With a small group of children, read *Aaron Awoke* to the children. Devote some time to looking carefully at the illustrations. Since they are small, show the illustrations with an opaque projector. Invite the children to listen to the alliterative story a second time. Suggest the children choose some sound effects and actions and agree on what sounds and actions will be mentioned where. Read the story again and wait at certain places for the children to add their sound effects. Following is a collection of effects suggested by some first graders:

Where in the story	*Possible sound effects*
boy wakes up	Yawn, say "Good Morning"(Put up arms and stretch.)
boy takes bubble bath	Say "Gurgle, gurgle" for draining water (Pretend to scrub with soap.)
boy combs his hair	Say "Comb, comb." (Make combing actions.)
boy ties his shoes	"I can do it." (Pretend to tie shoes.)

boy walks to barn	Stamp feet. (Pretend to walk.)
boy feeds chickens	Say "Here, Chick-chick." (Pretend to throw feed to chickens.)
boy gathers eggs	Say "Here's one." (Pretend to put eggs in basket.)
boy hitches horse to wagon	Say "Giddyap." (Pretend to put collar around horse's neck.)
boy talks to friends	Say "Can you come to my house for dinner?" (Pretend to talk to a friend next to you.)
boy runs home	Pretend to run home and run in place.
boy makes fire with logs	Say "Snap, crackle, pop." (for burning logs) (Pretend to throw more logs on the fire.)
boy stirs beans	Say "Round and round. The beans are stirred." (Pretend to stir pot of beans.)
boy puts mushrooms on table	Say "Let's measure this." (Pretend to put mushrooms on table.)
boy nibbles on mushrooms	Say "Nibble, nibble." (Pretend to eat mushrooms.)
boy opens door for friends	Say "Come in." (Pretend to open door and welcome friends.)
boy gets puzzles and paints	Say "Let's play with puzzles. Let's paint." (Pretend to play with puzzles or paint pictures.)
boy quiets the dog	Say "Sh sh sh" to the dog. (Put your finger to your lips.)

boy rests on the rug	Say "I'm resting." (Pretend to lay back on the rug or on your stomach with your elbows under your chin.)
boy gets supper for friends	Say, "Let me get a chair." (Pretend to pull out a chair for a friend to be seated.)
boy unfolds cots for beds	Say "This is your bed." (Pretend to unfold a cot to pull it out to make a bed.)
boy and friends sit on beds	Whisper "Sweet Dreams." (Pretend to fluff up pillows and straighten blankets.) Whisper "Good Night." (Pretend to yawn, stretch, and get ready for bed.)
boy sleeps soundly in his own bed	Snore loudly with Zs (Pretend to be fast asleep

Begin the story *Aaron Awoke*, letting children make sound effects and noises. Other sounds are made for the other scenes. Continue the story, giving all an opportunity to help tell this by making their sounds and actions lively ones.

APPLEBET: AN ABC (85)

By Clyde Watson. Illustrated by Wendy Watson. New York: Farrar, Straus & Giroux, 1982.

Bet and her mother attend a country fair and see entertaining acts and find good foods to eat. At the end of the day, they drive their cart home down a zigzag road. An astute student may discover that a bright red apple appears somewhere in each illustration and create a visual game to locate it on each page.

Extension: What's in an illustration?

Purpose: To view an artist's work

Materials: Copy of *Applebet: An ABC* (85)

Suggested Grade: K-1

With children, discuss ways the artist shows what goes on at a country fair—juggling, kite flying, magic acts, puppet shows, good things to eat, food judging, and prizes. Clarify words, i.e., *uproar,* that is, the commotion caused by a thief. Reread and invite students to look closely at the illustrations when they are shown on the opaque projector to locate a bright red apple in each picture. Ask children to review the illustrations again to look for any discrepancies they find between the print and the pictures. For example, a student may mention that there is no egg basket for the speckled eggs of the egg woman who drives a cart into town. Another student may point out that the bright red apple is seen in each illustration but not mentioned in the text.

Option: Where's the apple?

Purpose: To observe carefully

Materials: Copy of *Applebet: An ABC* (85)

Suggested Grade: 2 up

Sitting with a single child, invite the child to locate the bright red apple on each page with the introductory rhyme of "Where's the apple?/ It's in front of my eyes./It's in _____. (state location)/ What a surprise!" Invite the child to turn the page, look for the apple, repeat the rhyme, and state the apple's location. A child may notice some of the locations: The apple is picked from the tree, carried to the cart, and then is found on a fence post beside the road as Bet and her mother drive to the fair. When Bet and her mother wave to a farmer, the apple is seen in his back pocket. In other scenes, the apple is found on a flagstone walk, a second-story windowsill, and in a juggling act at the fair. The apple hides in a magician's hat with a white rabbit and is a snack for someone at Arthur's Nifty Haircut Tent. It is seen in the fork of a tree, in a knapsack, and dangling from a tent-top. A child will find it in a lady's string shopping bag, on a judging table, and in the air when it is thrown at a thief. As a variation, student partners can take turns participating in the activity.

Option: Working in the manner of the artist

Purpose: To experiment with an artist's technique

Materials: Copy of *Applebet: An ABC* (85)

Suggested Grade: 2 up

Discuss with children the idea of placing an object that is important to a story on every illustration in an original book. Invite children to tell their ideas about what objects they could place in illustrations of books they could create in the classroom and encourage them to think of unusual settings and unusual objects. For example, the children may discuss placing an illustration of a "hidden" baby dinosaur on each page of an ABC book that has these phrases:

A Different Dinosaur Family

A All dinosaurs in this family act up.   N Never need to nap
   They. . .
B blow bubbles   O order oranges
C claw in caves   P pull pterodactyls
D dart deftly   Q quarrel with quartz
E eat eagerly   R run rapidly
F fan themselves frantically   S slumber silently
G glare at gardens   T taste trees
H help   U understand
I irritate insects   V vault with vines
J jump   W wait
K keep   X eXpect danger
L look and listen   Y yell with yowls
M munch   Z zigzag

Discuss different media and uses for illustrations and suggest the children try out some of the media at an activity table in the corner of the classroom. Some children many want to use black ink or charcoal for drawings. Others may select colored chalk, crayons, markers, or splatter paints—using a discarded toothbrush or other small brush to splatter paint through wire screen over silhouettes to form splattered outlines of objects. Still others may want to make vegetable prints, gather items for a collage, and cut pictures and designs from cards, wrapping paper, magazines, and newspapers.

EATING THE ALPHABET:
FRUITS AND VEGETABLES FROM A TO Z (75)

By Lois Ehlert. Illustrated by the author. New York: Harcourt Brace Jovanovich, 1989.

Fruits and vegetables are clearly labeled and shown in large bright watercolor collages. Some are familiar edibles—apples, potatoes, tomatoes—and others unfamiliar e.g., radicchio, jalapeño peppers, and xigua, a Chinese name for watermelon. A glossary of the edibles with informative notes ends the book.

Extension: Recognizing fresh foods popular all over the world

Purpose: To recognize selected fruits and vegetables presented in alphabetical order

Materials: Copy of *Eating the Alphabet* (75)

Suggested Grade: Pre-2

Invite children to "Come, take a look" at the fruits and vegetables in the book. If appropriate, prepare tiny slivers of some of the edibles and invite the girls and boys to sample some of the unfamiliar foods. During a second reading, prepare cards for a pocket chart of the names of the fruits and vegetables, and as each is shown on a page, invite a child to help categorize the edible as a fruit or a vegetable by placing the name card under the heading "Fruits" or "Vegetables." Invite other volunteers to draw pictures of the edibles with crayons and markers on the cards.

Encourage students to say some of the key words aloud with you as you point out the usefulness of the glossary at the end of the book. Discuss what can be learned from the glossary and mention some of the informative facts:

1. We can read the name of the edible e.g., jicama.
2. We can locate the letters that spell the name e.g., j-i-c-a-m-a.
3. We can find a small illustration of the edible.
4. We can find a way to pronounce the name of the edible, e.g., HEE-cah-mah.
5. We receive information about the edible: The jicama is a native of Mexico, a country that borders the United States. It is a root that grows underground. It is shaped like a turnip, is white inside, and has a sweet and crunchy taste.

Invite the children to participate in preparing their own alphabet book about edibles and begin by inviting them to suggest a favorite fruit or vegetable for each letter of the alphabet. Encourage them to illustrate the edible and place it in a class book for others to see. Schedule time to ask the children to discuss what they selected and drew. If desired, locate the geographic areas for each edible. This discussion may introduce the whole class to some foods that may be unfamiliar:

kiwi fruit: from China and New Zealand; related to the chinese gooseberry;
kohlrabi: from Europe originally; related to the cabbage;
kumquat: from eastern Asia; related to a miniature orange;
radicchio: from Europe originally; related to lettuce and sometimes called chicory;
star fruit: from Portugal and Asia; with sweet or sour slices that look like stars;
ugli fruit: from the far East and Jamaica; and related to the tangerine and grapefruit.

FARM ALPHABET BOOK (81)

By Jane Miller. Illustrated by the author. London: J. M. Dent & Sons, Ltd., 1981/New York: Prentice-Hall, 1984.

Miller's clear, colorful photographs greet children when they open the book. Bright shiny apples are still on the tree, a stern-looking bull is in the farmyard, and ten tan hen's eggs wait to be collected. A brown-and-white foal, a white goat and a brown hen all take a viewer into the farm's surroundings. A child sees an incubator, jam, and a white kitten who lolls on a rock in the warm sun. A young lamb looks toward the viewer while a nibbling mouse ignores the viewer. Information tells a reader that a sow is the name of the mother pig, a boar is the father, and a piglet is a young pig. Unfamiliar words for some children may be quill and incubator. The letter *X* is for the markings on the sides of a sheep and a lamb to show that the animals belong to the farmer.

Extension: On the farm-o

Purpose: To participate in telling information from an alphabet book

Materials: Copy of *Farm Alphabet Book* (81)

Suggested Grade: Pre-K

With children, after each page of Miller's alphabet book is read, ask the children to help tell the information by saying, on the farm-o, for each one of the farm objects or animals. Introduce the children to the following short saying—one that can be chanted by the children about the key word after each page is read:

Teacher and Children:

Key word: apples
On the farm-O,
Apples-O,
Apples-O,
Apples are
on the farm-O.

Invite children to select their own key words for the illustrations. After seeing and talking about the illustration for the key word, *foal,* the children may decide to say horses:

Key word: foal

On the farm-O,
Horses-O,

Horses-O,
Horses are
on the farm-O.

Encourage children to repeat the saying and substitute the more familiar word, horses, with foals, the key word.

A FARMER'S ALPHABET (71)

By Mary Azarian. Illustrated by the author. New York: Godine, 1981.

Some may think that alphabet picture books are only for the very young child. This is not always true since there are several alphabet books with concepts and illustrations suitable for older children. Azarian's book is one of them. Children enjoy the pleasures of New England with this alphabet of rural life. Bright-red letters complement the black-and-white woodcut illustrations. A viewer sees *Aa* and the key word, apple, along with an accompanying picture of a farmer and his wife harvesting apples. *E* is for eggs and shows the farmer's wife gathering eggs from a hen's nest. Concluding pages have author's notes about the woodcut process.

Extension: A farmer's alphabet chorus

Purpose: To review key words associated with rural New England and to participate in choral reading: unison and solo

Materials: Copy of *A Farmer's Alphabet* (71)

Suggested Grade: 1–2

With the girls and boys, discuss a choral reading activity with solo parts and unison parts. In this activity, all the children say the letter names in unison, then one child says the key word as a solo part. The key words can be accompanied by mime actions. Children should suggest related actions:

Unison: A, Apple
Solo echo: A, apple (Group members mime related actions of
   picking apples from tree and putting them in basket.)

Unison: B, Barn
Solo echo: B, Barn (Group members mime related actions of tenting fingers of both hands to form the shape of a barn's roof.)

Unison: C, Cow
Solo echo: C, Cow (Group members mime related actions of milking the cow as shown by illustration.)

Unison: D, Dog
Solo echo: D, Dog (Group members mime related actions of appearing to sleep as does the dog in the chair.)

Unison: E, Eggs
Solo echo: E, Eggs (Group members mime related actions of gathering eggs and putting them in basket.)

Unison: F, Farm
Solo echo: F, Farm (Group members mime related actions of guiding horse with reins as shown in illustration.)

Unison: G, Garden
Solo echo: G, Garden (Group members mime related actions of raking soil with hand rake seen in illustration.)

Engage children in continuing through selected letters from this rural alphabet about New England for more choral reading and actions related to other letters of the alphabet. As an option, ask the boys and girls to suggest their ideas for key words related to rural life and create their own original alphabet. Ask them to dictate the words and record them on the board. Encourage them to suggest actions to accompany a choral reading in unison and bring their alphabet to "life."

* HISTORY THEME

Alphabet books that relate to historical settings offer an opportunity for children to have an enjoyable experience reviewing the letters and to learn about history in a pleasant manner. The books may tell little-known facts about objects in a certain time period or give accurate pictures of the alphabet rhymes of earlier times. Through the illustrations and text a reader can get a feeling for the general atmosphere of the era. The way people lived, dressed, and their activities are all seen.

A APPLE PIE:
AN OLD FASHIONED ALPHABET BOOK (100)

By Kate Greenaway. Illustrated by the author. New York: Warne, n.d. Originally published in 1886.

Greenaway's old-fashioned ABC book shows youngsters skipping around a giant apple pie. One boy bites it, a girl cuts it, and another deals it. Some boys fight for it and other children jump, kneel and mourn for the pie. Others run, sing, and then take the pie away. For a group of letters, UVWXYZ, all the children have a large slice and go off to bed. The letter *I* is not included because this alphabet goes back to an early use when the letters *I* and *J* were used as one letter. This early use motivated a later use: Charles Schultz, in on "Peanuts" cartoon, has Charlie Brown explain this to his sister, Sally. Charlie Brown approaches Sally who announces that she is writing a report about the thirteenth letter in the alphabet, the letter *M*:

> Charlie replies that *M* would be a twelfth letter if the letter *J* was left out of the alphabet. Questioning, Sally wonders aloud why anyone would leave the letter *J* out of the alphabet. Explaining, Charlie says that *J* was originally a form of the letter *I*, and if Sally did not count *J*, but omitted it from the al-

phabet, then *M* would be the twelfth letter and not the thirteenth. Sally decides to omit her entire report, turns, and impales her paper on the tip of Charlie's nose and stomps out of the room.[1] 1–3.

Extension: Literature of earlier times

Purpose: To promote the display of alphabets in literature from 1800s

Materials: Copy of *A Apple Pie: An Old Fashioned Alphabet Book* (100); collection of display items

Suggested Grade: 2–3

To introduce literature of an earlier time, promote the display of an alphabet book that dates back to the 1800s. In the room, display items that once helped children learn the alphabet. For instance, you might display the Provensen's *A Peaceable Kingdom* (120) or select an attractive wooden puzzle, a replica of an alphabet print originally published in London in 1782.[2] The wooden puzzle shows a youngster making each of the letters with the shape of his body. With his feet resting on the floor, one boy stands on his head and clasps his knees to form the shape of *A*. Underneath, a reader reads words saying the boy has found a way to make a great *A*. Then the boy rearranges his body shape and the words say, ". . . to a *B* he is brought." For *C*, the words tell readers that the boy strains so the *C* is not "mar'd." In that time period, the alphabet had only twenty-four letters and children used the letter *I* for both *I* and *J*. Further, they used the letter *V* for both *V* and *U*.

With a chart showing the words from *A Apple Pie,* engage students in getting acquainted with the vocabulary used by children in the 1880s. Organize a choral reading with solo and unison parts. In this arrangement that follows, lines are brief and can be accompanied by children's actions or children's responses. For instance, children may give suggestions for acting out words from a favorite version. The one that follows is a version with responses by a third-grade class:

Solo: A Apple Pie
Unison: A Apple Pie (act out action of buying a pie)
Responder: I'm tired of apple pie. Why can't we have . . . ?

Solo: B Bought it
Unison: B Bought it (act out action of different ways of buy-
ing a pie)
Responder: I think he paid too much for the pie. It cost . . .

Solo: C cooked for it
Unison: C cooked for it (act out action of cooking)
Responder: I don't like C's cooking. He burned the edges . . . .

Solo: D dropped it
Unison: D dropped it (act out action)
Responder: I think D should have held on tighter.

Solo: E eating it
Unison: E eating it (act out action)
Responder: E is always eating pie. I think he should share.

Solo: F fighting for it
Unison: F fighting for it (act out action of tossing pie in a
game of "Keep Away")
Responder: You might know F would fight for it. F is always
fighting.

Solo: G got it
Unison: G got it (act out action of catching piece of pie and
grinning)
Responder: G got it because G is bigger than the rest of us. G
always gets the pie.

Solo: H held on to it
Unison: H held on to it (act out action)
Responder: I'm tired of H always hanging on to the pie. H
should let some of the rest of us hold the pie.

Solo: J jumped over it
Unison: J jumped over it (act out action of different ways to
jump over pie spilled on floor)
Responder: I'm tired of J always being first to jump over the
pie. Why can't some of the rest of us be first?

Solo: K kicked it
Unison: K kicked it (act out action of kicking it out of the
way)

Responder: K always loses his temper and kicks things.
Instead, I think K should have . . . .

Solo: L lunged for it
Unison: L lunged for it (act out actions of lunging for the pie)
Responder: L tried to keep the pie from landing on the floor.
Three cheers for L!

Solo: M munched at it
Unison: M munched at it (act out action of munching)
Responder: I'm tired of M always munching on something.
He eats pie and everything else . . . .

Invite the girls and boys to continue the choral reading through this old-fashioned alphabet about a large apple pie by suggesting actions and responses for the remaining letters. Take the time to discuss certain words and phrases with them before they suggest actions for these key words: quartered, storm'd for a share like Xantippe, and yeomened.

Option: Alphabet books for thematic reading about literature of the other times

Suggested Grade: 3 up.

A Apple Pie (118) by Tracey Campbell Pearson; *The Adventures of A Apple Pie* (92) by George Burgess; *Peter Piper's Practical Principles of Plain and Perfect Pronunciation* (91) illustrated by Marcia Brown; *Chapbook ABC's: Reprints of Five Rare and Charming Early Juveniles* (122) edited by Peter Stockham.

A APPLE PIE (118)

By Tracy Campbell Pearson. Illustrated by the author. New York: Dial, 1986.

Pearson's alphabet unfolds to show humor and busy children in the illustrations and large text about a hot apple pie. The pie journeys down a long table that stretches across the unfolding pages to 18 feet. When the letter *T* trods on the pie, a child representing the letter stomps his feet in the pie pan; When *U* upsets it, a boy dumps pieces of pie on another's head; when *Y* receives the empty pan, *Y* yearns for pie. The letter *Z* is for zealous who comes from the kitchen with another apple pie. Capitals are introduced by phrases.

Extension: Literature of an earlier time

Purpose: To develop awareness of ways language changes and to compare versions of *A Apple Pie*

Materials: Copy of versions of *A Apple Pie* by Burgess (92) and Greenaway (100)

Suggested Grade: 1

Pearson's text points out that *A Apple Pie* is a traditional verse dating back to around 1671 when it was quoted in writings by John Eachard, theologian. Open the book and unfold the pages to their full length and display as a mural in the room. If interested in finding ways that language has changed over time, the students can compare other versions—such as those by Burgess (92) with the words *curtsied, stormed, yoemaned,* and for the letter *X,* the phrase mounted his zebra which demonstrates the author's difficulty in finding an *X* word; and by Stockham (122) with the words *itch'd, join'd,* and for the letter *X, cross'd*—with *A Apple Pie* by Pearson (118). Students interested further in the topic may locate information about the origins and use of the letters *I, J,* and *O.* A comparison chart might look like this and elicit discussion on ways language changes over time.

===
Language from Two Apple Pies
===

Pearson's Version	Greenaway's Version
A apple pie	A APPLE PIE
B bit	B BIT
C cut	C CUT

D dropped	D DEALT
E enjoyed	E EAT
F fought	F FOUGHT
G got	G GOT
H hoped	H HAD
I inquired	No LETTER I
J jumped over	J JUMPED FOR
K kicked	K KNELT
L longed	L LONGED
M munched	M MOURNED
N nibbled	N NODDED
O opened	No LETTER O
P pined	P PEEPED
Q quarreled	Q QUARTERED
R ran	R RAN
S sat	S SANG
T trod	T TOOK
U upset	UVWXYZ ALL HAD A LARGE SLICE AND WENT OFF TO BED

==

Introduce Pearson's question and answer ending as a choral reading. In the room, side 1 of the class may ask a question such as, *Who made the pie?* Side 2 of the class should answer the question with, *I did.* Side 1 asks the other questions about the pie, i.e., *Who stole it* (ate it, bit it, cut it, and so on)? Side 2 may respond with, *I did.* For an ending, all chant the words: *Who cried for the pie? We did.*

A IS FOR ANNABELLE (125)

By Tasha Tudor. Illustrated by the author. New York: Walck, 1954, 1981. Originally published in 1954.

Like some other authors of alphabet books, Tudor uses the alphabet as a structure for her words. This book tells something about Grandmother's doll with every letter. The words *bright* and *fragrant* help clear up some of the meaning for the letter *N* and key word *nosegay.* Some young children will need to have other words explained further: cloak, shawl, kerchiefs, muff, overskirt, parasol, tippet, and zither. Tudor places letters on one page while other page shows a sentence beneath the illustrations. Black-and-white illustrations alternate with pale watercolors and are encircled with flower garlands.

Extension: High voices, low voices

Purpose: To review the alphabet through choral reading

Materials: Copy of *A Is for Annabelle* (125)

Suggested Grade: K-1

With the girls and boys, introduce different aspects of an antiphonal reading activity for brief time segments on different days.

Add rhythmic beat

Read aloud the book so all the words are heard, and engage children in finger-tapping words as they hear them. Write words from *A* to *Z* suggested by the children on board and invite children to refer to the sequence during a whole group choral reading.

Add high and low voices

Divide the children into two groups, those who have high voices and those who have low voices. Ask children to join in and discuss what parts should be read with high voices and what parts could be read in low voices.

Add character voices

Repeat the high and low groups for another choral reading and add character voices. For instance, when children consider the words about the doll's fan to use at the ball, say those words in "opera voices"—voices that make children sound as if they were speaking in high notes and standing on a stage for an opera. When reading about the muff that keeps the doll's hands warm and cozy, invite children to make their voices sound "warm" during the reading.

With the children's help, prepare the script of Tudor's book for the reading with character voices. Discuss where the voices will be used and mark the children's suggestions on the chart with yellow adhesive notes or on an overhead transparency with an erasable marking pen. For instance, when the children suggest saying two complete lines with the ending rhyming words in an alternating high-low arrangement or want an accumulating effect where every two lines are read by an increasing number of tables or rows or want a finale of all voices blended together saying the words for W, X, Y, and Z, then mark the suggestions on the chart or transparency for the children to see.

Option: In the story?

Purpose: To recall statements from an alphabet book

Materials: Copy of *A Is for Annabelle* (125), collection of statements compiled by students or teacher

Suggested Grade: K-1

With children who can benefit from a sentence recall extension of the book, begin early sentence recall by asking children to respond with a refrain after listening to selected sentences, some from Tudor's book. Related to Tudor's book about grandmother's doll, statements are read in this recall awareness activity. For example, read "C is for clothes," and ask children to echo the phrase. Then read, "Annabelle's clothes box was on the chest in the hall." If children recall that this happened in the book, they respond with, In the story? Yes, yes, yes. If children recall that something did not happen in the book, they respond with, In the story? No, no, no.

Recall statements	*refrain*
A is for Annabelle.	In the story? Yes, yes, yes.
Annabelle is grandmother's doll.	In the story? Yes, yes, yes.

B is for Annabelle's box.	B is for Annabelle's box.
Annabelle's box is in the hall.	In the story? Yes, yes, yes.
C is for Annabelle's cloak.	C is for Annabelle's cloak.
	In the story? Yes, yes, yes.
G is for Annabelle's gloves.	In the story? Yes, yes, yes.
Annabelle's gloves were made of fine cotton.	In the story? No, no, no.

ABC: MUSEUM OF FINE ARTS, BOSTON (111)

By Florence Cassen Mayers. Illustrated by the author. New York: Abrams, 1986.

Some alphabet books are designed to introduce children to objects from art collections and Mayers's book does that. Twenty-six color plates, in turn, introduce various objects from Boston Museum's Fine Arts Collection. A younger child reviews the letters and an older child gets acquainted with some of the items to be found on a tour. One unfamiliar item may be a mummy: A golden mummy case accompanied by informational sentences introduces the letter *M*. An X-ray of the skull and rib cage of the Mummy of the Offerer in Thenes, Egypt, introduces the letter *X*. Oversize letter pairs in color in corners of pages.

Extension: Favorite art works

Purpose: To identify favorite works in an art collection after reviewing the letter sequence

Materials: Copy of *ABC: Museum of Fine Arts, Boston* (111)

Suggested Grade: 2 up

With the students, discuss some of the objects they think they would expect to find in an art collection. As part of the discussion, show Gilbert Stuart's oil painting of *George Washington* (for the letter *W*) and ask if they have seen this picture of Washington and where. Engage them further in a preview of some of the other objects they would see in the Boston Museum Fine Arts Collection beginning with *A* for armchair and going to *Z* for the zigzag designs found in a North Indian court girdle embroidered with silver-gilt thread. If the students live near the Boston Museum, they could check out the book from the school librarian and use it as a guide to search for some favorite objects when they visit. Brief informational notes are found at the foot of each page for the selected objects.

Invite the students to make their own art collections of objects from home and put them in memory boxes (discarded shoes boxes or other containers). Discuss asking an adult in the home for permission to use objects in a memory box for a brief time at school. After displaying the objects and memory boxes in the classroom, invite the children to make an alphabet of some of the items shown in the boxes. As interested students look through books related to objects from other times, include the books by Mayers that feature other art collections:

ABC: The Alef-Bet Book: The Israel Museum, Jerusalem (109) shows the rich diversity of the culture of Israel from arayot (lions) for Alef to takhshitim (jewelry) for Tav;

ABC: Egyptian Art from the Brooklyn Museum (110) introduces images of ancient Egyptian art including a pottery jar more than five thousand years old for *J* (the oldest item in the collection) and an X-ray of a mummified ibis over one thousand years old for the letter *X* (the youngest item in the collection);

ABC: Musical Instruments from The Metropolitan Museum of Art (113) has examples of European and American instruments from *A*, accordion, to *Z*, zither;

ABC, National Air and Space Museum (114) presents images from aviation's early days up through space-age explorations ranging from astronaut for *A* and zeppelin for *Z*; and

ABC, The Wild West Buffalo Bill Historical Center Cody, Wyoming (116) shows objects from the four museums that depict the history of the region and the frontier life from arrowheads and buffalo through decorated soft-leather moccasins to a zigzag pattern found in a corn husk bag of the Nez-Perce tribe.

ABC: THE MUSEUM OF MODERN ART, NEW YORK (112)

By Florence Cassen Mayers. Illustrated by the author. New York: Abrams, 1986.

This alphabet book introduces children to modern art objects arranged in alphabetical sequence. Twenty-six paintings, sculptors, furniture, and other objects are reproduced. Objects familiar to children include a bathrobe, cheeseburgers, and a kitchen. Items unfamiliar to some could be Matisse's *Dance* and Van Gogh's *Starry Night*. *X* is for X-ray, a color lithograph by Robert Rauchenberg (1967).

Extension: Webbing a collection

Purpose: To become aware of objects in the Modern Art collection presented in alphabetical sequence

Materials: Copy of *ABC: The Museum of Modern Art, New York* (112)

Suggested Grade: 2 up

With the girls and boys, discuss their previous trips to museums and what was seen. Ask the students to begin a "webbing of words" about museums on the board. Invite volunteers to take suggestions from the group and write words related to the museum on the board. When a word is suggested that is related to a word on the board, demonstrate how to cluster the two words together in the web.

With the alphabet book, review the sequence of the letters and reread the key words for the painting, sculpture, or design selected for each letter. Ask the students to identify where to put the name of each object on the web, i.e., under the heading of painting, sculpture, or design. Ask them to give reasons for their choices and discuss what information about the time period of its origin the object gives them. The students' identification of items in the book may result in something similar to the categories that follow:

Designed objects

Key words

automobile	car with aluminum body
cheeseburgers	burlap soaked in plaster and painted
elephant	chair and lamp made of steel, iron and cloth
insect	painted metal construction
jewel box	wood box with glass ice cubes and jewelry

Sculpture

Key words

| goat | statue cast in bronze |

Painting

Key words

| bathrobe | lithograph printed in color |
| dance | oil painting, *Dance* by Henri Matisse |

Invite the students to record the web on a sheet of paper or in a notebook about alphabet books. Encourage written reflections (to be read and responded to by you) about what was discussed during the activity.

ABC, NATIONAL MUSEUM OF AMERICAN HISTORY (115)

By Florence Cassen Mayers. Illustrated by the author. New York: Abrams, 1989.

Examples of American history, crafts, and ingenuity begin with the letter *A* introduced by a liberty model automobile (Buick

Runabout). The letter *F* is for flag that inspired Frances Scott Key to write the national anthem, *The Star-Spangled Banner*. The letter *X* stands for xerographic machine invented by Chester Carlson and for an X ray of a woman's foot and shoe taken in 1890 by W. H. McElvain, one of the first X-ray photographs made in the United States. The letter *Z* is for zither, an Arion harp (1891) that is played like a guitar by plucking the strings with the fingers or a pick. Familiar words include automobile, bedcover, clock, and dolls. Of special note are a John Bull railway engine, Uncle Sam as a cast-iron mailbox stand, and a portrait of Washington by John Trumbull, American artist (1795). The letter *Y* is introduced by Yankee stadium and its bright red ticket booth (1923), and *Z* is for a zither made in Washington, Missouri, in 1891.

Extension: Literature of other times

Purpose: To locate literature in alphabet books from different time periods

Materials: Time line, alphabet books showing literature of time periods, pencils

Suggested Grade: 3

With the students, set the stage for an inquiry session:

(To the students:) You are collecting books—especially alphabet books—related to the time periods of objects in the museum's art collection. Look for examples of literature *of* the period to complement Mayers's literature *about* the period when studying the late 1700s and 1800s. Put up mural paper with heading "Books We Found" (or a heading of your choice) and write the titles of any books you find.

===
Books We Found
===

Object in Art Collection	Book
Portrait of George Washington by John Trumbull, American artist (1795)	*A Apple Pie* (18) by Pearson, which dates back to the late 1600s

Nation's first lady:
Martha Washington (1789–1797)

A Apple Pie (100) by
Greenaway, which dates
back to early use.

X-ray of a woman's foot and shoe
taken by W. H. McElvain,
one of the first X-ray photographs
made in the United States (1890).

Edward Lear's ABC (104)

Zither, an Arion harp played
like a guitar by plucking strings
with the fingers or a pick (1891).

The Nonsense Alphabet
(105) by Edward Lear and
illustrated by Art Seiden or
A New Nonsense Alphabet
(106) by Lear and illustrated by Susan Hyman.

===

AN EDWARD LEAR ALPHABET (103)

By Edward Lear. Illustrated by Carol Newsom. New York:
Lothrop, Lee & Shepard, 1983.

Newsom's illustrations and Lear's nonsense verses introduce the letters of the alphabet. Verses have families of word endings—pidy,
widy, tidy, nice insidy. Whether the setting is underwater or in the
air in a hang glider, a small mouse is dressed in appropriate clothing
and found in every scene: it pumps up a bicycle tire (pumpy,
slumpy, flumpy), goes shrimping (shrimpy, nimpy, flimpy), and
mines for zinc (tinky, minky, piece of zinc).

Extension: Be a humorist

Purpose: To review the alphabet through humorous words and
          drawings

Materials: Copy of *An Edward Lear Alphabet* (103)

Suggested Grade: All ages

With students, discuss what makes them laugh. In what ways do playful situations make them laugh? absurd events? wordplay? The students may include Lear's words with unusual spellings, hidden meanings, letter substitutions, and onomatopoetic sounds. Choosing a letter of the alphabet, each student may be encouraged to write humorous words (*vords*) and illustrate them with "piggchurs." If desired, the boys and girls may work with partners and consider some *wurble inwentions* (verbal inventions):

Dd dirtyissimo (This place is vastly dirty. Dirtyissimo.);

Ff frizz (The cold is so great that my nose is frizz so hard that I use it as a paper cutter.);

Nn nokking (Here's somebod a nokking at the dolorous door.);

Tt ted-bime (It is. . . ted-bime.—Goodnight.);

Yy yersell (Noo, just tak cair of yersell . . .); and

Zz zur (Noa zur. [No sir.]).

EDWARD LEAR'S ABC:
ALPHABET RHYMES FOR CHILDREN (104)

By Edward Lear. Illustrated by Carol Pike. Topsfield, Maine: Salem House, 1986.

This rhyming alphabet of Lear's first appeared in *Nonsense Songs, Stories, Botany and Alphabets,* 1871. With sound associations, the rhymes introduce the letters. For example, sound associations for *A,* apple pie, include pidy, widy, tidy, widy. Both upper- and lower-case letters are in bordered inserts in full-color illustrations beginning with apple pie, little bear, little cake, and ending with Xerxes, yew, and zinc.

Extension: An Edward Lear afternoon of lexicon

Purpose: To become aware of Edward Lear's writings of the 1800s and his nonsense verse

Materials: Copy of *Edward Lear's ABC: Alphabet Rhymes for Children* (104)

Suggested Grade: Pre-K; 3-4; 5–6

With young children, Pre-K:

- *Appreciative listening.* Read the book and show illustrations.
- *Oral language.* Discuss with children how they might show Newsom's mouse in the illustrations. Invite some to mime poses of the mouse.
- *Oral/Art Interpretation.* Engage children in creating mouse masks. Depict mouse's actions through finger puppets and puppet production. At one time in his career, Lear wrote an alphabet on light blue linen in dark blue ink. Invite children to choose a favorite Lear verse and write on blue paper with blue markers, crayons.

With middle grade students, 3–4:

- *Oral Language/Art Interpretation.* At one time, Lear was employed by the Zoological Society of London to do animal drawings. With students, plan a bulletin board displaying children's versions of some of Lear's animals from alphabet verses: busy old ants, crafty old cat, dear little duck, stately and wise elephant, lively old fish, good little goat, quaint little quail, and so on.
- *Art/Written Interpretation.* Engage children in designing a poster to entice others to read Lear's verses.
- *Art.* Because of poor health, Lear spent most of his time traveling to the warm countries of Egypt, Greece, Italy, and the Middle East. Invite children to design a travel poster for one of these countries.

With older elementary students, 5–6:

- *Writing.* Lear used the pseudonym of Derry Down Derry to write his first *Book of Nonsense.* Invite children to select their own pseudonyms and write nonsense verses for a class Book of Nonsense. For a final page, they may list their pseudonyms and give written clues to their real identities.
- *Comparing.* Compare *An Edward Lear Alphabet* (103) illustrated by Newsom and *Edward Lear's ABC: Alphabet Rhymes for Children* (104) illustrated by Pike and ask children to discuss/write reasons why they prefer one over the other. Discuss features of preference, i.e., it reminds me of a personal experience, tells me something I did not know, it brings senses from real life (hear, see, smell, taste, touch), it has creative use of words, attractive illustrations, and shows what the author looked like.
- *Recognizing Lear's invented spelling.* Lear delighted in using made-up words. Invite children to dictate/write words for word maps for the following:

  Introducing unusual spellings: F words began with ph: fog becomes phogg; fortunate becomes phortschnit; *Ph* words began with f: physical becomes fizzicle; *H* words began without h: happy becomes appy; words beginning with vowels had an *H* beginning: opposite becomes hopposite; enemies becomes henemies. *A* was added to looking, going, etc: alooking, agoing; Silent g as in gnat was added to other *N* words: gnatural.

  Discovering hidden meanings: the ending "able" was added to words ending in *T:* For example, carrot became carrotable (ask the students to create a definition for this word and others); and

  Locating transposed letters: rejoice becomes erjoice; publisher becomes buplisher; bedtime becomes ted bime.

  Finding onomatopoetic sounds: boshblobberbosh; meloobious, and growlygrumble. Mixed-up letters: Dragon becomes dragging; officers becomes ossifers.

- *Interpreting.* Invite the students to illustrate Lear's phrase, "On the top of the Crumpetty Tree, the Quangle Wangle sat . . . ."

and then compare the interpretation with a published artist's rendition of the Quangle Wangle.

- *Writing.* Invite the girls and boys to finish one of Lear's phrases with original endings: (a) Now, this letter will neither be a nice one not a long one, but, just the *hopposit* for it is to say that I am . . . (b) The knock-shock-sprain which I got in that South Hampton train bothered me a good deal and . . . (c) You see therefore in how noxious a state of knownothingatallabout whatimgoingtodo-ness I am in.

- *Observing reproductions.* Lear promised an alphabet to a child and drew it in deep blue ink on pale blue linen. Show it to the children in *Edward Lear: A New Nonsense Alphabet* (106) by Hyman. Point out the photograph of Lear on the title page, a sample of Lear's letter that accompany the alphabet, the reproductions of the original alphabet pages, and his original sketches.

- *Listening to rhymes.* Lear used cheerful rhymes and sound associations. To promote this use, students may develop flannel board figures for retelling the verses or plan creative drama and act out individual rhymes with movements or movements and words. Some may want to interpret Lear's words in art.

- *Writing limericks.* Lear wrote limericks and some are found in *A New Nonsense Alphabet* (106), a book written for the grandchildren of his patron, the Earl of Derby. One limerick begins with "There was an old man of the west/ who never could get any rest . . . ." This limerick can be a model for students interested in writing original ones.

- *Drama activities.* As rhymes are read, invite students to move to the words, to dramatize the actions silently, to say the verses in refrains, to think of ways to sing the words, and to write Lear-type alphabet rhymes of their own. They can create different shapes of poetry books, make word webs of narrative poems, and sing songs that were popular during Lear's time, i.e., *The Battle Hymn of the Republic* (1861), *John Henry* (1872), and *Sixteen Tons* (1900s).

- *Enjoying.* Create a Lear center in the room and place books written by Lear there. Decorate with students' work about Lear—their posters, puppets, verses, and art compositions.

- *Displaying Lear's Works.* With the help of the school librarian, engage the students in locating other works by Lear—limericks, narrative poems, tongue twisters, and alphabet rhymes—

and discuss the language usage. For example, there is *A Learical Lexicon: A Magnificent Feest of Boshlobberbosh and Phun from the Vorx of Edward Lear* (107) with "vords" selected by Myra Cohn Livingston and "piggchurs" by Joseph Low. The selections focus on Lear's rhymes and letter substitutions in words.

FLANNERY ROW: AN ALPHABET RHYME (89)

By Karen Ackerman. Illustrated by the author. New York: Little, Brown, 1986.

Commander Ahab Flannery says good-bye to his family of twenty-six children before he goes to sea. The commander goes in alphabetical order so no child, from Ahab Junior to Zack, is missed. Unusual names for some children may be Garrick, Justine, Quincy, Upton, Xavier, and Yancy. A reader sees each child's picture above the feature letter of the child's name. Letters are in the same colors as the child's clothing for a matching activity. Rhythmic words. Endpapers show cameos of children in ABC order.

Extension: Saying hello and good-bye

Purpose: To arrange names of class friends in alphabetical order to say hello and good-bye

Materials: Copy of *Flannery Row* (89)

Suggested Grade: 1–2

With the total group, discuss some of the names of the children in their families or in their neighborhood and write the names on the board. Show ways to rearrange the names in ABC order if someone wanted to say good-bye to them in the alphabetical sequence. Read the story about Commander Ahab saying good-bye in alphabetical order to the family members before he goes to sea. Discuss the illustrations showing the children's clothing arranged in alphabetical order under the capital letters in Flannery's kitchen. Point out that the children arranged themselves from A to Z to say farewell to their commander father, and ask children in the class to say their names and then help you alphabetize the names on the board. Invite the girls and boys to arrange themselves from A to Z in the room and role-play Captain Ahab saying good-bye to them. Engage children in making drawings (cameos) of themselves and framing their drawings with a color similar to a color of a clothing article they are wearing. After the children print their names in large print under their drawings, display them in alphabetical order in the room.

Option: Arranging in lines alphabetically

On several subsequent mornings, ask children to arrange themselves alphabetically in a line around the edge of the classroom (for instance, they may line up and stand by their drawings), and invite a classmate to say good morning or hello to them in ABC order.

Each afternoon when getting ready to leave the classroom for home, ask the children to line up in alphabetical order again and invite another classmate to say good-bye in ABC order.

Option: Display alphabet books for themed reading about names

Beginning with Alex, Andrew, and Anne and ending with Zack, Zara, and Zoe, *The Stephen Cartwright ABC* (237) has rhyming couplets with names of children in sequence. The *Arizona Alphabet Book* (230), *The Oregon Alphabet Book,* and *The Washington Alphabet Book* (226) have names of people, places, and activities related to the states in alliterative sentences.

IF THERE WERE DREAMS TO SELL (102)

By Barbara Lalicki, compiler. Illustrated by Margot Tomes. New York: Lothrop, Lee & Shepard, 1984.

For each upper- and lowercase letter, illustrations and verses or poetic phrases are presented along with capitalized key words. Selections include those by Alfred Lord Tennyson, Dickinson, Keats, Donne, and others. As examples, *X* is for "X marks the spot" from American newspapers widely used by the late 1920s; *Y* for yesternight, a word from Donne's "Song"; and *Z* is for Zephyrus, god of the West Wind, from Keats' sonnet, "Oh, How I Love!" Tempera and watercolor illustrations are active ones with scenes of animals, elves, British and American colonial villages.

Extension: Working in inquiring groups (family groups)

Purpose: To become aware of colonial American family groups

Materials: Copy of *If There Were Dreams to Sell* (102), pencils

Suggested Grade: 2–3

With the students, discuss the situation for an inquiry session related to selected key word(s) from *If There Were Dreams to Sell* and to Lalicki's background notes.

> *Inquiring:* Related to key word, *apple,* from *If There Were Dreams to Sell* by Barbara Lalicki, compiler.
>
> What's Going On: Your family is living in the colonies, and to celebrate Twelfth Night in an amusing noisy way, (January 5), everyone plans to gather around the most fruitful apple tree in the orchard. With a fruit drink called Wassail and a toast of "Wassail," your family and friends will dance around the tree and sing a song to the apple tree ("Hail to thee, old apple tree!") in hopes of ensuring plenty of good cider for the coming year. You help prepare the necessary items for this celebration with family and friends on January 5th.
>
> Decide with others in your group (your colonial family), what five things you would need to prepare for this celebration in your orchard:
>
> | | |
> |---|---|
> | mugs | candles |
> | fruit drink | plates and cups |
> | copies of song in print | oil lantern |
> | hats | guns and ammunition |
> | jackets | rope |
> | sacks | printed copies of dance steps |
> | bushels | buckets |
> | caps | other items |

Older students (4–6) may start their own versions of *If There Were Dreams to Sell* in a special notebook and design a front cover, spine, and back cover. When they find words from the literature that represent "a dream" they have, the students may record the quotes in their notebooks. Encourage the students to share the quotes in their discussions, their reports, and in their small group meetings.

IN A PUMPKIN SHELL: A MOTHER GOOSE ABC (90)

By Joan Walsh Anglund. Illustrated by the author. New York: Harcourt Brace Jovanovich, 1960.

Anglund gives readers Mother Goose rhymes in alphabetical order. A letter and key word precede each verse. Some of the verses are familiar ones, i.e., Old Mother Hubbard and the Old Woman Who Lived in a Shoe. Other verses, such as the one describing the fight between the lion and the unicorn, may be less familiar to some girls and boys. Detailed black-and-white drawings alternate with full-color illustrations and show the artist's ability to present the charm of childhood to complement the rhymes.

Anglund's book of rhymes may remind you of other favorites: Walter Crane's *An Alphabet of Old Friends* and *The Absurd ABC,* (94) reprinted in one volume; Craft's Illustrated *Mother Goose ABC* (93), with rhymes inserted over full-color illustrations; and Sonia Delaunay *Alphabet* (95), a series of the artist's original paintings. All three contain nursery rhymes but have contrasting arrangements. Crane, Delaunay, and Craft illustrate only one nursery rhyme for each letter.

Extension: And Mother Goose says . . .

Purpose: To enjoy Mother Goose rhymes

Materials: Copy of favorite alphabet book containing nursery rhymes

Suggested Grade: Pre-K

With the young children, read aloud their favorite nursery rhymes.

For a rereading, engage them in listening again to the rhymes. If desired, begin the rereading with a teacher's verse:

Come, all you children
And listen to me;
Mother Goose
Tells her rhymes
In this A B C.

Reread a rhyme:

There was an old woman
Who lived in a shoe.
She had so many children,
She didn't know what to do.

Remark again:

Come, all you children,
Who listened to me;
Did Mother Goose
Say those rhymes
In her ABC?

Invite the children to call out yes or no and then engage children in repeating the following rhyme:

Come all you children,
And say it with me;
Say the Mother Goose
Rhyme in this ABC.

Encourage the boys and girls to say the rhyme together and then select others to read. For some of the verses read aloud, change some of the words in a well-known nursery rhyme as it is read aloud. For example, the words about the Old Woman Who Lived in a Shoe may be changed:

There was an old cobbler
Allergic to Shoes.

He sneezed so many sneezes
He didn't know what to—Ah Choo!

Continue with:

Come, all you children,
Who listened to me;
Did Mother Goose
Say that rhyme
In her ABC?

When the children answer "No" select another verse to read aloud. Alphabet books by Anglund (90), Craft (93), Delaunay (95), and others have a variety of verses to read aloud. Some clues enabling children to identify and introduce favorite rhymes to be read are: Who jumped over a candlestick? Who fished in other men's ditches? Who had three bags of wool? Who had a great fall? Who lost her sheep? Who could eat no fat? No lean?

Extension: Repeating nursery rhymes with voice and light organ

Purpose: To participate in a listening and repeating rhyme activity; to develop awareness of selected literary elements, to observe sound sensors responding to voices; and to notice effects of voices on a changing light display as rhymes are repeated

Materials: Voice organ and copy of Mother Goose rhymes

Suggested Grade: Pre-K

Turning to the children's favorite selections from an alphabet book of rhymes, read a requested rhyme such as "There was an old woman . . . ," which introduces children to the character in the brief story verse. Invite the children to say the verse in unison. As they repeat the words, show them the effect their voices have on the sound sensors in the voice and light organ. Saying several rhymes in front of the voice organ, children can say aloud different verses with different literary elements and see the effects of their voices on the voice organ in a bright, visual fashion. When a rhyme is repeated aloud near the voice organ, words cause the sensors to react and activate various lights that flash on and off in a colorful quick-changing display.

Indeed, sound sensors in a voice organ respond quickly to children's voices. When the girls and boys repeat a rhyme loud and fast, the light display shows quick changes in the light pattern. If the children say a favorite rhyme slowly and in a low tone, sound sensors reflect this mood with slower-paced changes in color patterns of red, blue, green, and yellow. A high volume of voices causes bright colors, while a low one creates less vivid ones. Invite children to say a rhyme in different ways to see what happens in the color patterns. Ask children to repeat a rhyme fast and loud, fast and soft, slow and forceful, slow and soft, or moderately. The following nursery rhymes from Craft's book (93) illustrate various features of literary awareness that can be introduced:

To develop literary awareness for:	Select a rhyme from *Mother Goose ABC* (93), or another favorite alphabet book of nursery rhymes.
Personification	Some rhymes acquaint children with anthropomorphic animals. In "Pussycat, Pussycat, where have you been?," the cat talks like a wordly traveler.
Movement: Baking, taking	Other rhymes offer verse stories and motion. The words from "Queen of Hearts" are just the ones to say while creating motions for baking the tarts, and for taking them away just as the knave did.
Running, calling, knocking	Motions may be added to the words about "Wee Willie Winkie" running through the town, who knocked at people's windows and called: "Are the children in their beds, For now it's eight o'clock?"
Rhymes Ending Rhymes	Most children find a great deal of pleasure in listening to and in saying ending rhymes. They match "A diller a dollar" with "scholar"

and "soon" with "noon." There are words that rhyme at the end of almost all of the Mother Goose lines.

Internal
Rhymes

Internal rhymes are used in several verses. Boys and girls will listen to "Humpty Dumpty," "Hickety, pickety, My Black Hen," "Hickory, Dickory, Dock," and the verse prank, "Georgie-Porgie."

Tone

There is a festive air in "fiddle-de-dee" when the fly marries the bumblebee, a questioning one in "A diller, a dollar," and an adventurous one in "Three Blind Mice." Some children recognize a comforting tone in Wee Willie's words as he asks, "Are the children in their beds and notice the similarity in "The Man in the Moon."

"The man in the Moon looked out of the moon
    And this is what he said,
Tis time that, now I'm getting up,
    All babies went to bed."

"I had a little nut tree" offers a happy tone for children:

"I had a little nut tree;
    Nothing would it bear
But a silver nutmeg
    And a golden pear.
The King of Spain's daughter
    Came to visit me,
And all was because of
    My little nut tree.
I skipped over water,
    I danced over sea,
And all the birds in the air
    Couldn't catch me."

As options, additional activities may include:

—taking part in an impromptu stage production in the classroom and assigning parts of a rhyme to be repeated aloud.

Reader A: Three little kittens, they lost their mittens, and they
began to cry.

Readers assigned as three little kittens: Oh, Mother dear, we
greatly fear, that we have lost our mittens.

Reader assigned as Mother: What ! Lost your mittens, you
naughty kittens! Then you shall have no pie."

Readers assigned as three little kittens: Mee-ow, mee-ow, mee-
ow, then you shall have no pie.

—developing the idea of dialogue among characters and assigning a reader to read a rhyme and a responder to state who is
talking. For an example, here is Anglund's selected rhyme for
O and the key word owl:

Reader A: Bow-wow says the dog
Responder: said the dog
Reader A: Mew, mew says the cat
Responder: said the cat
Reader A: grunt, grunt goes the hog
Responder: said the hog
Reader A: and squeak says the rat
Responder: said the rat

—assuming the role of an inanimate object in a rhyme and responding to a recited rhyme. For another example from Anglund's book, here is the rhyme for the letter *S* and the key
word, shoe:

rhyme reciter: There was an old woman who lived in a shoe.
Responders as the shoe: I wish somebody else lived here.

rhyme reciter: She had so many children she didn't know what to
do.
Responders as the shoe: I'm being stretched in all directions by
so many children. Why they have made bedrooms in my toe,
they pull on my shoelaces, and use my back as a slippery
slide.

rhyme reciter: She gave them some broth, without any bread,
Responders as the shoe: I hope the broth's not too hot today. The
children spilled some on me yestereday.

rhyme reciter: She whipped them all soundly and sent them to
bed.
Responders as the shoe: I don't know why she waited so long. It's
about time she did something about those kids.

—encouraging older students to use rhymes as the basis for writing creative headlines for a class newspaper about the rhymes,
e.g., Woman and Animal Companion Try to Solve Food
Supply Dilemma may be a headline for "Old Mother
Hubbard."

—encouraging older students to find all the rhymes that relate to
food items and plan a menu for a dinner, e.g., for a snack, students could select the golden pear from "I Had a Little Nut
Tree" or the apple from "If I Were an Apple."

—encouraging older students to find the rhymes related to items
around a house and furnish a room, e.g., for a bedroom, the
students might select the bed from "Little folks, little folks, now
then for bed" and the clock from "Hickory, dickory dock!"

—encouraging older students to study some of the meanings of
words found in the rhymes. Words such as *knave, full sore,
doth, morn,* and *hark* are not in the vocabulary of many of today's children. For a student interested in pursuing this topic
further, the student might compare today's versions of
rhymes with the absurd ones in Crane's *The Absurd ABC* (94)
or study the origins of the rhymes themselves (e.g., some
scholars believe that Mary in the rhyme "Mary, Mary Quite
Contrary" refers to Mary, Queen of Scots) with *The
Annotated Mother Goose* (Bramhill House, 1962) edited by
William S. and Ceil Baring-Gould, and *The Oxford Dictionary of Nursery Rhymes* (Oxford: Clarendon Press, 1951)
edited by Peter and Iona Opie.

ON MARKET STREET (108)

By Arnold Lobel. Illustrated by Anita Lobel. With Afterword by
Richard Meran Barsam. New York: Viking, 1981.

Students can "go shopping," find old-fashioned shops along a cob-
blestone alley, and pretend to buy items from *A* to *Z*. A small boy,
dressed in blue, buys his way through the ABCs, and beside each
capital is a creative image of a person formed from the item itself or
from the item's category. The artist was motivated by seventeenth-
century French trade engravings to develop the images, and for the
letter *A,* the person is made of apples, for *B*, books, and *C,* all clocks.
Students will find lots of details. For example on the page for the letter *M,* a man is arranged from a variety of musical instruments.
With the exception of the face and hands, the image is made up of
a cello for the torso, saxophones for arms, and tubas for legs. Seated
on a bass drum, the man has a banjo in one hand and an oboe in
the other. His hat is decorated with two trumpets, and a violin and
clarinet are placed nearby. Returning from his shopping trip, the
small boy, tired and weary, carries his collection of presents home to
his friend, a large white cat.

Extension: Visiting Market Street

Purpose: To recognize items or an item category for each letter

Materials: Copy of *On Market Street* (108)

Suggested Grade: All ages

With young children, read the book in its big-book format (Scholastic,
1982), and show the filmstrip-cassette version of it.[3] Discuss the
rhyming words heard in the text—doors/stores; eye/buy. Ask children
to recall the items, list words on the board, demonstrate putting the
words in alphabetical order, and ask volunteers to draw an example of
the item by the word. Ask students to identify words that are related
and put them in categories on the board.

　　With older students (grades 4–6), introduce the pattern of the
narrative text and invite them to rewrite a different version and cre-

ate imaginative illustrations. As an example, here is a pattern for words to support the students' illustrations about a wonderful, fascinating school of the future that is located in the world's largest shopping mall:

> At _____ School
>
> The students down
> at _____ school
> were lining up for classes.
> I went along
> to _____ school,
> I stopped at all the windows
> And looked through all the glasses.
> Such wonders there
> at _____ school!
> So much for eyes to spy
> I walked the mall
> at _____ school
> My my, My my, My my . . . .
> And I bought . . .

A PEACEABLE KINGDOM: THE SHAKER ABECEDARIUS (120)

By Alice Provensen & Martin Provensen. Illustrated by the authors. With Afterword by Richard Meran Barsam. New York: Viking, 1978.

Introducing the Shaker alphabet verse suitable for children of today, this verse is literature from the late 1800s and useful during a study of the time period. The Provensens' watercolor and pen-and-ink illustrations go across doublepage spreads to show over one hundred animals and their names that progress through the alphabet. Taken from *The Shaker Manifesto* of 1881, the first line of twenty-six in this rhyming verse begins with an *A* word, the second line a *B* word, and so on. Unfamiliar words for some children include Xanthos, ichneumon, and basilisk. In the Afterword, Richard Meran Barsam relates information about Shaker education, ideals, and behavior with us. Some children may enjoy reviewing the alphabet (as Shaker boys and girls did) with this abecedarius. For a bouncy, rhythmic experience, repeat the lines aloud. For a syllabic romp, sing the words to the well-known ABC song.

Extension: Rhythmic verses

Purpose: To identify syllables in rhyming words and to create a rhythmic verse

Materials: Copy of *A Peaceable Kingdom: The Shaker Abecedarius* (120)

Suggested Grade: 2–3

With children, read *A Peaceable Kingdom* and invite children to read along silently with the words on a chart. Read it again orally and invite children to repeat the words they remember. For another reading, engage children in clicking their fingers and then hitting their hands on their desks to keep the rhythm. Invite students to sing the words to the tune of *The ABC Song*. Children may follow the words written on a chart. Variations of oral interpretation include:

Increase volume by lines. Reread the lines and invite children to be amplifiers of the words. To act as an alphabet word amplifier, children can increase the volume of the words when they echo the lines. Read each line and invite children to say the line back to you as an amplifying echo. When you read:

> Alligator, Beetle, Porcupine, Whale . . .

Students may amplify with:

> Alligator, Beetle, Porcupine, Whale . . .

Add volume by two lines. For another rereading, invite children to amplify two lines after you do the initial reading. These two lines are read aloud:

Alligator, Beetle, Porcupine, Whale . . .
Bobolink, Panther, ...

Continue reading two lines and encouraging children to have their turn at amplifying the lines and increasing the volume.

Introduce other ways to orally interpret the words in the abecedarius. For example, children may divide themselves into side 1 and side 2 in the classroom.

Add increased rate. Increase the rate of the reading and invite children to consider the rate of choral reading for each two lines. For instance, children begin slowly at the start of the first line and go faster near the end of the last line in pairs of lines.

Add voices of characters. The students should be encouraged to look at the illustrations and select figures that suggest certain voices, i.e., the sailing captain on the book's cover may suggest an "Ahoy, me hearties" voice, the child on the page for the letter *J* suggests a "little" voice, the woman sweeping on the *R* page suggests a woman's busy voice, and the man holding an alphabet letter on the *E* page, a "teaching" voice.

Add sound effects. Introduce rhythm in the verses from *The Shaker Manifesto* and chant the beginning words:

Alligator, Beetle, Porcupine, Whale

Rereading the verses again, ask children to accent the rhythm and encourage toe tapping, finger snapping, hand waving, or body-swaying motions.

Add illustrations. Select individual lines to be reread and invite the students to draw sketches of the animals on small squares of paper. If the students are divided into two groups (side 1 and side 2) then side 1 will say the first half of the line and show their sketches. Side 2 responds with its last half of the line and shows its animal sketches. When the lines are slowly chanted aloud, the boys and girls hold up individual sketches of the animals they have drawn.

For example, as they chant the words for Alligator, Beetle, Porcupine, Whale, the ones who have sketches of those animals hold the sketches up for others to see while the words are chanted.

Option: Writing an original abecedarius

Suggested Grade: 3–4

Add observations of syllables. Select some individual lines to reread and ask the students how many syllables they hear in each one of the lines. Write a line on the board and invite the girls and boys to look at its pattern: Engage them in counting the words, tapping out the syllables in the words, and discovering that, in most lines, a three-syllable or four-syllable word is used to begin each line. Invite the students to repeat some of the words—alligator, bobolink, crocodile, dromedary, and elephant—and suggest other three- and four-syllable words related to animals.

Invite the students to look at the second word in each line of verse to see if there is a pattern for the second word in each line. Here, some of the students will see that most of the words have two syllables. Invite them to repeat some of them—beetle, panther, and monkey. Continue looking at the other words in the lines and invite the students to observe the arrangement of the words in some selected lines of verse.

The students should take a look at the lines again to discover the total syllables in the lines. With one exception, every line in the Shaker Abecedarius has ten syllables in it. The observant students will see that words with different numbers of syllables are arranged in different orders but that the most common arrangement begins with a four-syllable word (or a three-syllable word). With the students' suggestions, record an arrangement of the words from selected lines on the board:

four- or three-Syllable Word	two-syllable word	three-syllable word	one-syllable word
_____	_____	_____	_____

With the pattern written on the board, some of the students may be ready to contribute names of animals, insects, or birds to match the pattern. As the students dictate the names, the teacher or student volunteer may record the names under the appropriate heading that indicates the number of syllables in the name(s). For example, the word caterpillar is recorded under the heading "four- or three-syllable word." For a reading in unison, invite the students to repeat the names and roll the syllables over their tongues. After several names are dictated by the students, ask them to find (or dictate) two words from a one-syllable word group that would rhyme. Examples:

one syllable word

Bee

_____

Flea

_____

The students may dictate words for a line of verse and can create lines similar to:

| Caterpillar, | Tortoise, | Ladybug, | Bee |
| Daddy Longlegs, | Spider, | Scorpion, | Flea |

Working in pairs or partners (or independently if desired), the students should be encouraged to write their lines and contribute to an original version of an abecedarius.

*LETTER TRANSFORMATIONS THEME

One of the most popular types of alphabet books is the letter transformation type of presentation. In this type, the letters are changed and transformed into other shapes whose names are related to the letters. The alphabet book that shows a quick change of the letter into an object is the most common. Yet a few books show the changes in steps in panels in the illustrations or show the use of more than one letter to form an object.

ALPHABATICS (132)

By Suse MacDonald. Illustrated by the author. New York: Bradbury, 1986.

Oversize letter pairs in red are introduced by letter transformations that are shown in four steps beginning with the shape of the letter and ending with its transformation as an object whose name begins with the letter. Seeing this approach, a reader finds an original way of looking at the letters, their shapes, and objects that appear from the shapes. Each letter is shrunk, expanded, or manipulated in some way to change the letter into a full-color object that is labeled, e.g., the letter *A* becomes an ark, the letter *M* a mustache, and *Z* a zebra. An astute child may notice that some key words begin with capitals and others with lowercase letters.

Extension: Alphanimals

Purpose: To use shapes of letters to create shapes of animals

Materials: Copy of *Alphabatics* (132)

Suggested Grade: All ages

With young children, discuss some of the shapes of letters that are changed into shapes of animals in *Alphabatics*. For examples, show the illustrations for elephant, fish, giraffe, and other animals and review the steps that show the way a letter is transformed—it is divided or duplicated; it is fattened or given features; it is placed upside down or diagonally on paper. Further, with the illustrations of the elephant, giraffe, and lion, point out the way the artist used the background around the letters as part of each animal's shape.

Sometimes the shapes of the letters are not changed and the outlines of the letters form the shapes of animals. Some observant children will see this in the illustrations of a quail and swan. At other times, certain features are added to the letters, and an example of this is on the page for the letter *F* where the alphabet letter receives an eye and fins to become a fish. On the page for the letter *R,* an eye, beak, and feathers are added to help shape a rooster. At still other times, the letters form only a part of the object, e.g., the letter *W* becomes the shape of a whale's tail, *Y* turns into the horns of a yak, and *Z* transforms into the zigzag stripes of a zebra.

After the children have reviewed the illustrations, invite them to suggest ways they can create unusual alphanimals and select names for the animals. With the children's suggestions, discuss the idea of creating characteristics for the alphanimals. For instance, ask the children to consider an alphanimal's imagined five senses and then suggest characteristics they could create that are related to the senses. Write their ideas on the board as the children discuss some of the following: a) special characteristics of the alphanimal's eyes (perhaps seen at great distances; have stereoscopic sight; have X-ray vision like Superman; have heat sensitive vision); b) characteristics of the animals' hearing (supersensitive; hears from far away); and c) other special characteristics of touch, taste, and smell.

After a discussion, invite the boys and girls to record their thoughts in writing, and if desired, write their ideas on an alphanimal chart similar to the one on the next page:

ANNO'S ALPHABET:
AN ADVENTURE IN IMAGINATION (126)

By Mistumasa Anno. Illustrated by the author. New York: Harper & Row, 1975.

Alpha-Beast Chart	
NAME OF YOUR ALPHA-BEAST:	LENGTH, WIDTH, AND WEIGHT OF YOUR ALPHA-BEAST:
COLOR OF YOUR ALPHA-BEAST:	FEATURES OF THE CLAWS / TOES / FEET:
WHERE CAN YOUR ALPHA-BEAST BE FOUND?	WHAT CLIMATE DOES IT LIKE?
WHAT FOODS DOES IT EAT?	HOW FAST DOES IT TRAVEL?
WHAT ENEMIES DOES IT HAVE?	WHAT FRIENDS DOES IT HAVE?

Anno shows the intricacies of woodblock arrangements to form the alphabet in these illustrations. Examples to point out to children: An *E,* its top and bottom stem pointing to the left, has a center stem projecting toward the viewer; one half of the letter *M* rests against a mirror enabling the viewer to see the entire letter; and the letter *O* is made with two wooden half-circle shapes leaning against one another. Culminating pages are a guide that gives the names of most of the objects. Anno's illustrations ask a viewer, What's missing? as the viewer sees the alphabet letters as if they were carved and assembled from wood. A viewer's careful observation can help find if something is missing from some of the letters. For example, resting against a mirror, the letter M deceives a viewer. The letter *S,* large and solid, slopes upward on an inclined plane and may tempt a viewer to imagine walking up its spiraling, ascending shape. Other objects can be found in the border: snake, spoon, flowers called stock. To find more objects, the viewer may look at the pen-and-ink sketches bordering each page. A glossary is included to help identify some of the objects.

Extension: Object story

Purpose: To predict the objects' names on the pages; to verify names in a guide at the end of the book; and to use objects' names in brief story sentences

Materials: Copy of *Anno's Alphabet* (126)

Suggested Grade: 2-3

With the use of an overhead projector, introduce the fool-the-eye paintings and ask the students to see if they can identify what is "wrong" with each "wooden" letter—some are only half finished and others are twisted or arranged in seemingly unworkable ways. For example, the *M* is only half completed—and the other half shows in a mirror's reflection.

Ask the children to look at the illustration accompanying each letter and to brainstorm a brief story/sentence about the picture; some of the brainstormed narratives can consider the possibilities of a tube of paint growing from an artist's palette and pencil points placed on pen nibs. Some words, such as *anvil, jester, oil paint,* may be unfamiliar to some children. Other words offer material for brief sentences, i.e.:

> the clown in the clock;
> eight Easter eggs;
> an old metal lock heavily embellished; and
> a map of Treasure Island.

Looking at the borders with the projector or a magnifying glass, invite the children to look for the additional flowers, animals, and other creatures to "guess" at the names of the objects, and to use the guide at the back of the book to check their "guesses." Ask the children to use the names of the objects in brief story sentences and then to dictate/write the short sentences. The children draw the objects they select for the sentences and, if interested, create borders for their writing in the manner of the artist.

After reviewing the alphabet in the book again, invite the girls and boys to work as partners and brainstorm names of objects whose names begin with a selected letter and then draw the objects/write the names on chart paper. Ask them to exchange their lists with other partners, who can add more drawings of objects or words to the list.

The completed charts may become an alphabetic resource for future writing activities and the partners may work together to use words from the charts to compose sentences. They should be encouraged to read the sentences to the class and ask other partners to elaborate and add more to each sentence with a choral reading in unison that invites the use of imagination:

> Use imagination.
> Use imagination.
> It's always in your mind.
> Use imagination.
> Use imagination.
> It's in your mind to find.

B chart	*X chart*
bicycle	xylophone
bean	xanthium (burr weed)
bee	

bell
bird
button

Option: Alphabet texture cards

Purpose: To review shapes of letters and provide a tactile experience; to develop visual discrimination skills

Materials: Fabric remnants, sandpaper, cardboard, glue

Suggested Grade: 2-3

To enhance the children's appreciation of textured letters, provide cards for the girls and boys. Focus the attention of children on the texture seen in Anno's wooden letters and on the textures of other materials that can be used to form alphabet letters. Provide children with textures that can be touched and used to make letter shapes in the classroom.

Textured materials can include fabric pieces of corduroy, velveteen denim, and wool. Trimmings can include bright rickrack, leftover braid pieces, and yarns of different colors.

Demonstrate ways to trace upper- and lowercase letter shapes on materials. Once cut, glue manuscript letters to cardboard squares. Prepare cursive letter shapes with trimmings by writing the outline of each letter with fast-drying white glue. Place rickrack, yarn, or braid directly on this glue writing to form the shape of the cursive letter that is needed.

For children who need an extended letter identification activity, show the letter cards to the girls and boys. Invite children to name the letter, touch it, and finger trace. Place cards on display for reference and future use. For instance, if a child has some difficulty forming a certain letter during writing and shows frustration, show the child the letter texture card so the child can touch the shape, trace the shape, and look closely at the letter as the texture touches the child's fingers. Invite the child to keep the letter card while working and writing.

Plan different ways of distributing letter texture cards to the students:

- A teacher distributes letter texture cards from large red, blue, and yellow pockets sewn on a white apron that ties at the waist.
- Another teacher wears an inexpensive letter card vest with odd-shaped pockets to hold different cards.
- A teacher carries an oversized gag wallet purchased at a novelty store and dispenses the textured letter cards like paper money.

CURIOUS GEORGE LEARNS THE ALPHABET (134)

By H. A. Rey. Illustrated by the author. New York: Houghton Mifflin, 1963.

Rey, an author-artist who is fond of monkeys, asks one curious monkey, George, to learn the alphabet. A man in a yellow hat identifies the letters for George from *A,* where the letter becomes the wide, gaping jaws of a green alligator, to the last letter. Capital letter *B* looks like a bird when the letter is changed by adding a tail, bill, and two feet. Lowercase *b* becomes a bee. Capital *C* forms a large crab and lowercase *c* takes the shape of a small one. Children get involved in a prediction puzzle as they try to anticipate what special letter change will take place. What object will *Q* become? The letter *Y* can transform into what object? After George learns the alphabet, he is rewarded with ten dozen doughnuts for his reward. George received this amount because he remembered three letters from the alphabet and added them to the bakery order: *T* and *E* and *N*. Black outlined figures have highlights of red, yellow, blue, and green. On every page, Rey's selected letter is highlighted by a color dot over the letter when found in the text.

Extension: A beginning

Purpose: To participate in observing letters as they form a picture's beginning

Materials: Collection of alphabet books with letter changes and transformations; sketch paper or copies of sketch sheet, A Beginning; crayons, colored pencils or coloring markers

Suggested Grade: 1-2

Transform. If the children have seen Lisl Weil's *Owl and Other Scrambles* (135), Rey's transformations may not surprise them. Like Weil, Rey uses all of the capital letters. Unlike Weil, Rey includes all of the lowercase letters, too. Show the books by Weil, Suse MacDonald, and Jill Downie and distribute them to groups. Invite the children to look at the illustrations and think of ways to begin a unique picture of their own with any uppercase or lowercase letter they want to use.

Create. To provide sketch starters for the students, duplicate a sketch sheet entitled "A Beginning," and distribute these sheets to any students who ask for them.

Extension: Let's draw the letters

Purpose: To create alphabetical transformations

Materials: Copy of *Curious George Learns the Alphabet* (134)

Suggested Grade: 2-3

Draw and say. After each of Rey's letter transformations is shared with the girls and boys, ask the children to help transform more letters. After seeing Rey's capital *A* become an alligator's jaws, a child may be invited to go to the chalkboard to draw or write another capital *A* or sketch another transformation. Observing this take place and joining in by tracing the capital with their fingers in the air, the children may want to say this verse aloud as a total group:

> O, little monkey's alphabet,
> A letter changing alphabet,
> You've never seen A B Cs yet
> Like little monkey's alphabet.

After the verse is said aloud, discuss the writing and drawing that was put on the board and invite the children to repeat together:

> You've never seen
> A B Cs yet
> Like _____ (name of letter) in
> Little Monkey's alphabet.

For those students interested further in letter transformations, duplicate a sketch sheet entitled "A Beginning," and provide a sheet for any student who asks for it.

A Beginning
By

I can make a picture from any letter I like.
Here is my picture.

ED EMBERLEY'S A B C (129)

By Ed Emberley. Color overlays by Barbara Emberley. Color overlays for Bear and Rabbit pages by Michael Emberley. Boston: Little, Brown, 1978.

In this book four panels trace the formation of a selected letter with the actions of animals and insects. For example, two groups of fireflies (a group of five and then four) form the stems of the letter *F* above the heads of two green frogs, one playing a fiddle and the other, a flute. Also, a family of geese watch two grasshoppers gnaw the letter *G* in green grass and then start playing golf. A list of objects to find in the illustrations for each letter concludes the book.

Extension: Creating alphabet books

Purpose: To create original alphabet books to give to someone at school, in the home, or in the community

Materials: Copy of *Ed Emberley's A B C* (129), a selection of other alphabet books, writing paper, color pencils or markers, crayons, watercolors or materials for collage

Suggested Grade: 5-6

With the students, discuss some of the unusual alphabet books you have found. Point out that in some of the books, all of the objects in the illustrations for each letter are related to a topic or theme (alphabet in a topic collection) and show them some of the books that represent the different topics, i.e., history, signs, sounds, and letter transformations. Further, display the alphabet books with puzzles, word games, and stories about life inside and outside the United States. Review with the students the different ways the books are organized. For instance, some books show an alphabetical story that is organized by the sequence of letters and others show how each letter is transformed in some way into an object or animal whose name begins with the letter.

Further, review several books where the objects in the illustrations for each letter are *not* related to a topic or theme (from the alphabet in a milieu collection). In this collection, no apparent theme or topic ties the illustrations or the text together and the alphabet is used as the framework upon which the artist puts his/her collection of objects to illustrate the ABCs.

As you show different books and their features to the students, point out the possibilities that exist for students to consider as they create their own books. For example, the students may cut pages as large as the pages in Marianna Mayer's *The Unicorn Alphabet* (14) or as small as the ones in *Alphabatty Animals and Funny Foods* (48) by Mimi Mazzarella. They can prepare drawings as tiny as the pages hiding behind the hotel door in *Looking for Zebra* (142) by Ron Atlas or as large as the colorful peacock on a double-page spread in

Gyo Fujikawa's A to Z Picture Book (247). They can create a character similar to the searching shepherd who is found on every page of *Alphabet Sheep* (80) by George Mendoza; write dialogue for a talking animal just as Jim Davis did for Garfield in *Garfield A to Z Zoo* (34); or they can highlight the same animal character on every page as Norman Bridwell did with Clifford, the big red dog, in *Clifford's ABC* (29).

Arrangements for alphabet books are organized in different ways and the students can talk about the following features and others:

- the way objects are hidden in *The Most Amazing Hide-and-Seek Alphabet Book* (152) by Robert Crowther and *Demi's Find the Animal ABC* (155);
- the way letters are hidden in *Pigs From A to Z* (162) by Arthur Geisert. In each of the illustrations, Geisert hides five different forms of the featured letter as well as one form of the preceding letter and one form of the following letter.
- the way paper engineering is used; cardboard doors open to show the objects in *The Peek-A-Book ABC* (156) by Demi;
- the way a guessing game adds structure to the alphabet; games are in *Q Is for Duck* (159) by Mary Elting and Michael Folsom and in *Easy as Pie: A Guessing Game of Sayings* (160) by Marcia Folsom and Michael Folsom;
- the way die-cut features add to the illustrations; in *Artemus and the Alphabet* (26) by Scott and Tammy Basset, the students will see that Artemus takes a bite out of every page, thus giving a reader an opportunity to think of other ways to create unusual page formats. Books like these will interest students and motivate them to think of creative ways to organize their own original formats.

HAROLD'S ABC (131)

By Crockett Johnson. Illustrated by the author. New York: Harper & Row, 1981.

Johnson, whose real name is David Johnson Leisk, begins this ABC book with an attic to introduce the letter *A*. A reader can look closely at the picture and see the way the letter is transformed. After

Harold uses his purple crayon to turn the shape of the letter into the attic of a house, he turns the letter *B* into books, *C* into a cake, and continues through the letter sequence. At the letter *W*, Harold escapes from a witch, finds himself in his own yard, and then in his bed sleeping and snoring *z*'s.

Extension: A purple crayon adventure

Purpose: To associate letters with personally selected illustrations

Materials: Copy of *Harold's ABC* (131)

Suggested Grade: 2-3

In this extension, invite children to think of ways to sketch illustrations for the letters. Encourage the girls and boys to think of a favorite object for each letter in their first names and then draw interpretations of the objects. To demonstrate, draw a way to show the letters of your name and the related objects on the board. Suggest that the children find lots of other ways to present their names. Example:

> Patricia is my name.
> P is for _____ (insert picture here).
> A is for _____ (insert picture here).
> T is for _____ (insert picture here).
> R is for _____ (insert picture here).
> I is for _____ (insert picture here).
> C is for _____ (insert picture here).
> I is for _____ (insert picture here).
> A is for _____ (insert picture here).

Invite the children to consider the different ways they can use the illustrations of their names. For example, the children might suggest using the illustrations as book covers, as elaborated signatures on correspondence or letters to friends and relatives. Other suggestions can include:

1. reproducing the name illustration on postcards to friends;
2. writing notes to peers in the classroom and including a name illustration;

3. using the illustrations of names as inserts in holiday cards and letters;
4. decorating lunch boxes and snack sacks with the name illustrations;
5. decorating chairs, desks, binders, and learning centers with the personalized signs;
6. inserting the students' name illustrations as the front pages in their reports; and
7. displaying the illustrations of the names in the classroom.

MOUSE WRITING (127)

By Jim Arnosky. Illustrated by the author. New York: Harcourt Brace Jovanovich, 1983.

Arnosky's book introduces children to letter shapes for cursive writing. To do this, two mice, Cap (a big mouse) and LC (a small mouse), trace each cursive letter shape as they ice-skate on a frozen pond. Invite the children to look closely at the illustrations to the way LC dots the *i*'s and crosses the *t*'s.

Extension: The letter on the page

Purpose: To review the names and sounds of selected consonant letters

Materials: Copy of *Mouse Writing* (127)

Suggested Grade: 1-2

In an integrated music-literature session, invite the boys and girls to tell of past experiences (if any) with ice-skating and discuss some related words such as *twirling, flourish, snowbank,* and *exhausted.* Then with an opaque projector, show the illustrations in *Mouse Writing.* Review the illustrations a second time and stop to point out the shapes of consonant letters and their names. Then, sing or hum the tune of *The Farmer in the Dell* and ask children to sing and hum along. Introduce the idea of singing different words to a familiar tune and invite the children to follow along on a word chart as you point out the words to *The Letter on the Page* and sing them to the music. Ask the children to sing along with you as you turn the pages of the book to show the letter shapes. Encourage them to participate as you introduce the following verses for a selected consonant:

The Letter on the Page
(The Farmer in the Dell)

1. The letter on the page,
   The letter on the page,
   Ay-oh, the letter, oh!
   The letter on the page,

2. The letter has a name,
   The letter has a name,
   Ay-oh, the letter, oh!
   The letter has a name.

3. The letter's name is _____.
   The letter's name is _____.
   Ay-oh, the letter, oh!
   The letter's name is _____.

4. The letter has a sound,
   The letter has a sound,
   Ay-oh, the letter, oh!
   The letter has a sound.

5. The sound is in this word: _____.
   The sound is in this word: _____.
   Ay-oh, the sound, oh!
   The sound is in this word: _____.

(Teacher and children take turns selecting
letters and key words to add to the lines)

Invite the children to notice how Cap, the larger mouse, traces shapes of the capitals and LC, the smaller one, makes the shapes of the lowercase letters. In black-and-white line drawings, the completed letters are shown in bright blue. To add a slight parallel plot feature, a curious bird is in almost every scene. For instance, the bird watches as LC bumps into a bank of snow while tracing the letter *b*. At *E*, both mice exit the pond and land in a large snowbank and leave the imprints of their body shapes. At *F*, the bird lands, beak deep, in snow in a treetop, and at *G*, Cap has to skate fast around several tree stumps to make the shape of the letter. For students interested further in these letter transformations, place large cutout shapes of selected letters on the floor one at a time and invite volunteers to come up and "skate" (or walk) the shape of each letter.

OWL AND OTHER SCRAMBLES (135)

By Lisl Weil. Illustrated by the author. New York: Dutton, 1980.

Owl and Other Scrambles includes that enticing word, scrambles, and Weil uses all of the letters making up a particular word, scrambles them together to make different images, and then draws colorful cartoons from the shapes of the letters. The beginning scrambles include an angel, an ape, and an airplane. Displaying the illustrations, invite a reader to observe the scrambles closely and see if the artist "fooled" the reader in any way, e.g., made it difficult to find some of the letters. A concluding glossary helps a reader unscramble the letters in the words.

Extension: Be a letter scrambler

Purpose: To arrange the letters in a selected word into an illustration

Materials: Uppercase and lowercase letter patterns, art paper, scissors, crayons, markers, opaque projector, copy of *Owl and Other Scrambles* (135)

Suggested Grade: 2-3

With the students, show the scrambled illustrations with the opaque projector and discuss the technique used by Weil to make the illustrations in the book. With the necessary materials (paper, paste, scissors, markers, letter patterns), demonstrate to the boys and girls how you would go about selecting an object, spelling its name with the letter patterns, cutting out the letter shapes, and experimenting with the arrangement of the letters until you formed an illustration to represent a key word. In the illustrations, Weil used capital letters; however, some enterprising students may want to use the lowercase forms. For further extensions, encourage the students to:

1. display their scrambles in a class book to be used as puzzles for others to unscramble;
2. give clues about their words to make a word game;
3. demonstrate to the whole group the way they thought

through the process of scrambling the letters to make the illustration they wanted;

4. unscramble the words they used and write the unscrambled words on labels to place beneath their illustrations when they are displayed in the room;

5. write short stories to place beside their scrambles;

6. arrange the scrambled words and display them in alphabetical order;

7. go through the letters in sequence and talk about the illustrations;

8. ask children to count up to twenty-six and then line up in the room to show each child with a scrambled word and then discover the different scrambled words it takes to add up to the total;

9. say the unscrambled words aloud in alphabetical order while in line;

10. scramble words that represent activities; and mime the activities so others can guess the words.

* PUZZLES AND GAMES THEME

Alphabet books offer puzzles for readers to solve. In some, the alphabetical words tease a reader into seeing the alphabetical sequence of letters, and selected verses have questions and ask a reader for an answer. Some of the illustrations in these books hide letters and objects so a reader can participate in a visual search, and others offer games to be played.

A MY NAME IS ALICE (145)

By Jane Bayer. Illustrated by Steven Kellogg. New York: Dial, 1984.

Bayer's alphabet book does more than introduce the ABCs. The alliterative verses introduce the sequence of the letters, and some wordplay for each, beginning with "A my name is Alice/ and my husband's name is Alex./ We come from Alaska . . ." Bayer's book is another version of the familiar ball-bouncing game. Unfamiliar animals for some children may be echidnas, nutrias, quahogs, zebus, and xigertlings. *X* is for Xena and Xavier from the planet Xigert. With the verses as a model, the children can create their own original sentences and respond to the challenge of selecting words beginning with the same letter.

Extension: Wordplay sentences

Purpose: To create a rhythmical text in alphabetical sequence

Materials: Copy of *A My Name Is Alice* (145) and other alphabet books with rhyming text

Suggested Grade: 3

With the students, read excerpts from the book aloud and take time to discuss any animals that may be unfamiliar ones, such as Emily Emu, Edward Echidna (rodent), Ida Ibis, Ivan Ibex (wild goat), Nancy Nutria (rodent), and Ned Newt. Reread the book again, and point out some of the small signs in the illustrations. Discuss the ideas about selling the objects that are seen in the illustrations. If desired, introduce the pattern of the alphabetical sentences, and show how the pattern forms a beginning letter game of names, animals, places, and objects. Here's Bayer's pattern to display:

==
Wordplay Sentence
==

_____(letter), my name is _____(feminine) and my husband's name is _____ . We come from _____ (location) and we sell _____ (objects).

==

For another review, a grouping of all the animals is shown in Kellogg's last illustration. A list of facts about the less familiar animals and Bayer's note about a way to play the game conclude the book.

Play a game. For interested children, a game can be played by bouncing a ball, one bounce for each word. Each time a word beginning with the featured letter comes up, the player has to put one leg over the ball as it bounces. Similar patterns of text are found in other alphabet books:

> Kuroki's *ABC* (136) has the pattern of A my name is ___ and
> I love _____; and
> *A My Name Is Alice* (169) by Virginia Holt has the pattern of
> ___ (letter) my name is ___ (sister's name) and my brother's name is ___ (brother's name).

Also suitable for older students (5–6), a wordplay pattern from Kuroki's alphabet book may motivate students to write as this sixth-grade student did:

> D my name is Darrell and I love my dog with a D because he
> is delightful. I dislike him with a D because he is dangerous.

His name is Dominic the dog. He comes from Denmark. He lives on doughnuts, dumplings, and Doo-Dads. He is a dopey, devilishly doggie dentist.

The wordplay sentences in any of these books offer an opportunity for students to select their "favorite" letters and then create a rhythmic text to use in a classroom version of the word game. In a classroom display, provide alphabet books, dictionaries, and other library books for additional word sources. Invite the students to read their sentences aloud to partners and then trade them for silent reading and the partner's feedback.

ABC GAMES (175)

By Robert Lopshire. Illustrated by the author. New York: Harper & Row, 1986.

A reader finds a question for each letter pair with several humorous answers to select from for answers. A reader is asked to make a decision and select which object goes with the illustration on a facing page. For example, an acorn introduces *Aa* and the question is "which one will eat the acorn?" A reader chooses from among a fish, snail, squirrel, and turtle. Familiar word choices include bird, clown, yard, and zipper.

Extension: Announce your choice

Purpose: To make decisions to answer questions related to key objects

Materials: Copy of *ABC Games* (175)

Suggested Grade: Pre-1

With the boys and girls, read the page that announces the letter pairs and the key object and clarify the names of the objects on the facing page before the children are invited to listen to the question and answer it. For instance, say the names of the objects and invite the children to chime in on the familiar words. Showing the illustrations, ask them the question on each page and provide time for their responses and thoughts about why they made the choices they made. Invite them to share their reasons for their selections with the whole group. After discussion, encourage them to change their minds about their choices if they wish to do so.

For a rereading, invite the girls and boys to identify the names of the key objects and their related objects by saying a letter-object chant as a total group:

> Children and teacher: Aa, acorns.
> Acorns-O.
> Acorns-O.
> Squirrels eat acorns-O.

The girls and boys will become quite adept at selecting their own words for the chant. For instance, after seeing the bird on the page for the letter *B* and identifying that it lives in a nest and not in a doghouse, aquarium, or a doll cradle, the children may respond with:

> Children and teacher: Bb, birds.
> Birds-O.
> Birds-O.
> Birds live in nests-O.

Seeing a wedge of cheese, a screwdriver, a pencil, and a book on the page for the letter *M*, the children can discuss their responses to "Which one will the mouse eat?" and say:

> Children and teacher: Mm, mice.
> Mice-O.
> Mice-O.
> Mice nibble cheese-O.

On the page for the letter *Z*, the children are asked which object has a zipper, and after choosing an object, they may include the object's name:

> Children and teacher: Zz, zippers.
> Zippers-O.
> Zippers-O.
> Jackets have zippers-O.

ALBERT B. CUB AND ZEBRA:
AN ALPHABET STORYBOOK (187)

By Anne Rockwell. Illustrated by the author. New York: Harper &
Row, 1977.

Rockwell's alphabet book offers more than letters to entertain a
child. It's a mystery that appeals to a child's adventurous spirit. The
storybook has only pictures—there are no words to read except at
the end where Rockwell wisely has included a story glossary. After
his friend, Zebra, is zebranapped, Albert B. Cub begins his long
search for his friend through the alphabetical pages. Cub searches at
the *c*ircus, *d*ays pass, he looks *e*lsewhere, searches in *F*rance, in a *g*arden, in *h*edge country, on an *i*ceberg, and in a *j*ungle. His unevent-
ful travels to *M*aine, *N*iagara Falls, and *T*exas have Cub weeping and
exhausted. Cub finally finds Zebra, who is nibbling a zinnia at the
zoo.

Extension: Bear cub, the character tries . . .

Purpose: To review objects and actions that begin with selected letters of the ABCs through a wordless mystery story

Materials: Copy of *Albert B. Cub and Zebra: An Alphabet Storybook*
(187)

Suggested Grade: 2–3

With the students, show the illustrations in Rockwell's ABC storybook and ask them to talk about what they see in each picture. If
needed as they talk about the illustrations, guide the discussion with
three key phrases to pace the continuity from page to page: a) Bear
Cub, our character tries . . . b) However, Bear Cub . . . and c) And
then, Bear Cub . . ..

Bear cub, the character tries . . .

Each page gives a wealth of information for students to discuss.
Indeed, Albert B. Cub tries something to help his animal friend on
every page. Everything Cub tries is toward the goal of finding his

friend, Zebra. For this wordless story, ask questions such as, What does Cub try? What disappoints him? What discourages Cub?

However, Bear Cub . . .

Encourage the students to always look at the next picture to find out what Bear Cub does next. Discuss what the Cub does when he is disappointed and when he is discouraged.

And then, Bear Cub . . .

With this phrase, the students may be guided toward noticing the episodes in the pictures. Ask them to consider what action Cub tries in each episode and then discuss the "However . . ." part of the picture they can identify. Encourage the students to use the phrases of "Bear Cub tries . . . ," "However . . . ," "And then . . . ," in their discussion of this alphabetical mystery book.

Extension: What can bear and zebra do in our town?

Purpose: To predict a character's action

Materials: Sketch paper, or copy of sketching starter sheet entitled "What Could Bear and Zebra Do in Our Town?," crayons, markers, or colored pencils

Suggested Grade: 2–3

After reviewing Rockwell's illustrations with the students, invite the boys and girls to predict the actions of the characters and then to record and sketch their ideas. Ask the students to think of a picture in their minds about the small bear and his striped friend, Zebra. They can imagine what the two friends would do in the children's town. Possible discussion questions include:

If the bear and zebra could inch out of the illustrations or bounce from the book or project themselves from the pages, what would they do?
What would the animal characters see?
Whom would they visit, and where could they stay?

Where could they eat breakfast, lunch, and dinner, and what
would they eat for meals?

What clothing, if any, would they need to wear?

What other adventure(s) could bear and zebra have?

Working with partners, the students may discuss their ideas,
write their stories, and then sketch the illustrations to go with their
text. Distribute a sketching starter sheet to students who request
one. When finished, each team of partners should meet with another team to read their narratives aloud and show their sketches.

WHAT COULD BEAR AND ZEBRA DO
IN OUR TOWN?
MY IDEA PAPER BY _____.
(Name)

Extension: Find the object

Purpose: To develop oral vocabulary through selected words

Materials: Copy of *Albert B. Cub and Zebra: An Alphabet Storybook*
     (187)

Suggested Grade: 2–3

With children, show illustrations on an opaque projector and ask
them to locate and observe some selected objects. Encourage children to tell information they know about these objects as they find
them in Rockwell's pictures.

- On the *A* page, who sees the *ampersand* on the accountant's
  sign?
- On the page for *B*, who sees the man's *brow* and *bureau?*
- On the *C* page, Who finds the ringmaster's *cravat* and *cum-
  merbund?*
- On the page for *D*, who recognizes a *dinghy?*
- On the *E* page, who finds a young lady wearing *espadrilles?*
- On the page for *F*, who sees the *French flag?*
- On the *G* page, who notices the gardener's *galluses?*
- On the page for *H*, who locates the *huntsmen* and points out
  their riding *habits?*
- On the *I* page, who spots the design of *isosceles* triangles?

Other objects to search for on other pages are jabiru, kiosk,
lozenge, martin, nymphalid butterfly, osprey, obelisk, oculus,
prayerbook, pushcart, pillbox hat, quadrilateral, quiver, quatrefoil,
radiator, Roman numeral, shingle, stilt, serpent, snorkel, toque, ura-
nium hunter, vortex, spiral volutes, whippoorwill, xebec, Yorkshire
terrier, moon at its zenith.

ALL BUTTERFLIES: AN ABC (150)

By Marcia Brown. Illustrated by the author. New York:
Macmillan, 1981.

Brown offers double-page spreads in this alphabet book. Movement in the illustrations is seen as butterflies flutter, cats dance, and mice nibble at cheese and fruit. The turtles swim and climb and sleep; rain falls on a red umbrella, and a zoo is visited. Brown shows two letters on each page with a simple storyline for each woodcut. The linking of the words may nudge a reader into noticing the use of the alphabetical sequence, one that might be somewhat puzzling to some children. A reader sees *E*lephants *F*ly, *G*iraffes *H*igh, and *I*ce-cold *J*umpers, and discovers the use of the sequence in the text. A culminating list helps a reader review all the words.

Extension: Alphabet sequence sentences

Purpose: To identify words in alphabetical order and to arrange words into sentences

Materials: Mural paper to record words in alphabetical order for sentences or copy of pattern sheet, Alphabet Sequence Sentence

Suggested Grade: 3 up

After introducing the use of the alphabetical sequence in the book's text, ask the students to consider words that could be used to write sentences in alphabetical order. Allow plenty of time for the students to discuss their ideas, and as they talk, write their suggestions on the board. Remind them to try and use all of the letters of the alphabet in a sequence in a sentence. Since the letters *X*, *Y*, and *Z* may be difficult for some students, place a collection of alphabet books and dictionaries in the room for references. As an example on the board, write a sentence that uses all the letters in the sequence. Here is one composed by a fourth-grade class:

> A bear caught digging early found great huge insects, jumping kiwis, lassoing monkeys, needling orangutans, pelting quails, rambling somewhat, tugging unnecessarily (and) vainly watched x-ed yellow-jackets zigzagging.

If needed, distribute copies of a duplicated sheet, Alphabet Sequence Structure, to the students for a word arrangement guide.

Alphabet Sequence Sentence by _____.

A word	B word	C word	D word
E word	F word	G word	H word
I word	J word	K word	L word
M word	N word	O word	P word
Q word	R word	S word	T word
U word	V word	W word	X word
	Y word	Z word	

Option: Display Brown's book with Rodney Peppé's *The Alphabet Book* (183). Like the arrangement in *All Butterflies,* Peppé's book also links language alphabetically in its pattern. The guiding letters present the sequence on double-page spreads and the key words are shown in the sentences. An adult may need to point out the linking pattern for the alphabet sequence to some children.

ALL IN THE WOODLAND EARLY: AN ABC BOOK (199)

By Jane Yolen. Illustrated by Jane Breskin Zalben. New York: Putnam, 1983.

Yolen's alphabetic verse questions ask a reader for the answer in this musical story with a surprise. Woodland verses introduce each letter and are sung to music. Verses form the accumulating story as animals in the woods join together. Some names may be unfamiliar ones to some children: Urbanus sees vole and they join woodchuck, Xyleborus, yellow jacket, and zemmi. Dressed in pink and carrying an umbrella, a young girl asks a young man who carries an insect net where he is going. He replies that he is hunting. His response begins the puzzle, i.e., What is the young man looking for?

Extension: Join in!

Purpose: To identify selected animal names, beginning letters, and to write selected letters in manuscript or in cursive

Materials: Copy of *All in the Woodland Early: An ABC Book* (199)

Suggested Grade: Pre-K

Invite the girls and boys to join in and help tell the alphabetic story verses. Engage them in singing about the woodland animals, birds, and insects. Show the illustrations and discuss them. For example, a tiny brown ant runs from a water drop that falls from an umbrella, a black bear watches, and a small chipmunk curls up inside the letter *C.* A proud deer looks outward from the illustration, an eagle flies overhead, and a cinnamon-colored fox paws at the letter *F.* For *G,* a goose stretches her neck through the letter's shape.

For a rereading, write the verses on classroom charts and play music in the back of the book while the children read/sing about the woodland creatures. As an option, distribute letter cards to the children, and as an appropriate verse is sung, ask the child with that letter card to stand up and display the letter:

- A brown hare bounds through the letter *H* and one small green inchworm finds refuge in a leafy tree;
- A screaming jay, a running lynx, and a blinking mouse hurry by;
- A colorful red, blue, and yellow king snake winds around the letters *K, L,* and *M;*
- An opossum hangs by its tail from *O;* and
- A red newt stands beside the letter *N.*

Discuss the situation in the song, e.g., none of the animals seem to know what the child is hunting—and the animals are hunting, too. Invite the children's predictions for the question, What do you think the animals are searching for? Encourage them to give their reasons for their predictions.

ALPHABET PUZZLE (158)

By Jill Downie. Illustrated by the author. New York: Lothrop, Lee & Shepard, 1988.

Downie's purpose is to invite young children to discover the letters of the alphabet and guess the secrets that lie in the scenes seen in the windows on the pages. For examples, after seeing that the letter *A* stands for axe, a reader is asked to predict what the letter *B* stands for in the window on the page. Visual clues show an axe in the bark of a tree. When the page is turned, a reader sees the key word *bark*.

Extension: *A* is for ?

Purpose: To predict key words in an alphabet sequence and use visual clues

Materials: Copy of *Alphabet Puzzle* (158)

Suggested Grade: 1–3

With the students, discuss the questions, e.g., *Bb* is for? and the idea of predicting the key word for the letter. For each letter and question, discuss the visual clues in the scenes that are found in the windows on the pages. Invite the boys and girls to repeat the questions together as a total group. For a rereading, review the illustrations and point out the way pairs of objects are linked (axe, bark/ camel, desert/). Some of the unusual word choices are *garland, jaws, trampoline,* and *reeds.* Allow time for a discussion of the association between the words in the pairs and ask the students to suggest other words that are related to the pairs. Record the students' suggestions on the board:

From the book	*From our heads*

axe, bark
camel, desert
egg, frying pan
garland, hat
icicles, jaws
kite, ladder
moon, nightingale
oven, picnic
quiver, reeds
shoes, trampoline
umbrella, vase
waves, x-ray fish
yak, zigzag

DEMI'S FIND THE ANIMAL ABC: AN ALPHABET GAME BOOK (155)

By Demi. Illustrated by the author. New York: Putnam, 1985.

In Demi's ABC game book, a child is asked to find an illustrated animal whose name begins with the associated letter pairs. For example, an alligator introduces the letter *A,* and in a box on the page, a little alligator waits to be found in the drawing of the large alligator. Many of the animals are familiar ones—whale, yak, zebra—but some may be unfamiliar to certain children—ibis and unicorn. The letter *X* is for x-ray fish. Answers to the challenge are at the end of the book for self-checking. The book ends with one last search, i.e., to find a picture of a small cat somewhere in the book.

Extension: Find the animal alphabet game

Purpose: To find small animals somewhere in the drawings of larger animals

Materials: Opaque projector; 2 copies of *Demi's Find the Animal ABC* (155)

Suggested Grade: Pre-2

Showing the book to the children, discuss how to play the "find the animal alphabet game." For each letter, ask the boys and girls to look closely at the drawing of the small animal in the box on the page when it is projected on an opaque projector. Invite the children to find a little animal somewhere in the drawing of each big animal. Engage the children in playing this game with every page and invite volunteers to look for the answers to the picture puzzles at the end of the book with a second copy. For each letter, ask the children to repeat the question together as a total group, e.g., "Aa, can you find this alligator?"

With the illustrations, discuss the animals, especially the ones that may be unfamiliar to some of the children, e.g., a nine-banded armadillo, ostrich, and vole. Continue with selected letters and talk about the animals, their habitats, and diet. If desired, find the geographical locations of the habitats of some of the animals on a state map or on a world map or a globe.

Option. For an observation extension, distribute additional copies of the book to the boys and girls in groups and ask them to help one another meet the final challenge, i.e., finding the cat somewhere in the book. Discuss this activity and ways to begin to search for the cat. The children could discuss *where* they should begin to look (perhaps, on a page related to the word cat) or *how* they should begin to look (systematically by beginning with page one) and the other ideas they have.

EASY AS PIE: A GUESSING GAME OF SAYINGS (160)

By Marcia Folsom & Michael Folsom. Illustrated by Jack Kent. New York: Ticknor, 1985.

Comparisons such as "easy as pie" and "sly as a fox" may interest children in making up original ones that are new and different. Older students, familiar with the sayings, may predict the endings of the comparisons. Since sequence of the alphabet is guided by colorful capitals that are introduced by clues to words needed to complete the comparisons, the book is best suited for those who already know the alphabet.

Extension: What's the ending?

Purpose: To identify words needed to complete comparisons

Materials: Copy of *Easy as Pie* (160)

Suggested Grade: 1 up

With the book, discuss some of the comparisons the children have heard, e.g., clean as a whistle, shy as a violet, and mad as a wet hen. Read some selected comparisons from the book and ask the girls and boys to predict the words that complete them. To clarify the meanings, discuss each comparison. Reread the book and invite the students to chime in on the familiar phrases. During another reading, review the illustrations and the sequence of the letters as the pages are turned and discussed. Encourage the children to repeat the comparisons aloud, then select a comparison from the book or another comparison they know and illustrate the saying with a related art activity. Some of the sayings that could be chosen are:

> Straight as an _____.
> Snug as a _____ in a _____.
> Cool as a _____.
> Slippery as an _____.
> Sly as a _____.
> Silly as a _____.
> Mad as a _____.
> High as a _____.

When the illustrations are finished, invite the children to hold up their drawings and show one another what they did. Using all of the illustrations, they can select key words and arrange the illustrations in alphabetical order on the chalk rail of the board. If desired, a volunteer can write the letters in order on the board, and the children can line up in that order around the room to show their drawings. Using the drawings as a further resource, invite the children to put their drawings in categories and group them under such headings as "Comparisons with Animals," "Comparisons with Objects," and "Comparisons about Nature." If appropriate, write the headings on the board, and after each child discusses a drawing, take suggestions from the group about the category for the drawing. When a category is decided, invite the child to stand by the board near the appropriate heading. Examples for the board:

Comparisons with Animals	Comparisons with Objects	Comparisons with Nature
Proud as a _____.	Sharp as a _____.	Right as _____.
Crazy as a _____.	Thin as a _____.	White as _____.
Stubborn as a _____.	Tough as _____.	As deep as the _____.

HUMBUG POTION: AN ABC CIPHER (143)

By Lorna Balian. Illustrated by the author. Nashville: Abingdon, 1984.

Numeral symbols are correlated with letters to communicate meaning and a reader is asked to decipher a magic beauty potion for a homely witch. To do this, a reader matches the numeral 1 with the letter *A,* 2 with *B,* and so on. The words in the text that are spelled with numerals are then decoded. Each decoded word is the key word for the object that introduces each letter in the sequence. The code is found on the endpapers.

Extension: Be a code breaker

Purpose: To associate numerals with letters in a code

Materials: Opaque projector; copy of *Humbug Potion* (143)

Suggested Grade: 2–4

Showing the pages of the book on an opaque projector, discuss with the students the idea of cipher, potion, and using numerals to represent letters as a code. Read the story about the homely little witch who longed to be beautiful and was determined to decipher a magic beauty potion she discovered. Reread the numerals for the first ingredient and demonstrate the way to decipher the word. Invite the boys and girls to predict what the ingredients might be from their observations in the illustrations and then cross-check to verify their predictions by deciphering the numerals on the page.

Predict	*Cross-check with the code*
a 1–3–15–18–14	acorn
a 2–9–20 of a witch's 2–18–15–15–13	bit of a witch's broom
a 3–21–16 of 3–15–4 liver oil	a cup of cod liver oil
eight rotten 5–7–7–19	
add five 6–9–19–8	
a bunch of 7–18–5–5–14 7–18–1–16–5–19	

Offer this situation for further discussion: The homely witch was so impatient that she hurried and did not include 19–13–9–12–15. When she finally drank every drop, the potion did not work. How would the 19–13–9–12–15 have helped the recipe?

Extension: Break the code

Purpose: To recognize the relationship of numerals to letters in a code

Materials: Copy of *Humbug Potion* (143), "kettle" made from cardboard container, shape cards, crayons, and markers

Suggested Grade: 2–4

Invite the students to cut shape cards of the kettle and then write on each card the twenty-six ingredients they would include in a beauty potion. The students should use the code to cipher the names of the ingredients into the code on a second kettle-shape card. When finished, all of the cards with the coded ingredients are placed inside a "kettle," and the students may take turns reaching into the container and selecting potions written by their friends. When a student is reaching for a potion, the class says:

Brass kettle, brass kettle,
What do you hide?
What beauty potion
will _____(student's name) find inside?

Each student selects a card and goes to a work area to decipher the coded ingredients. When finished, each student reads aloud the ingredients for the potion. To announce each student before the deciphered potion is read aloud, the whole class may say:

Brass kettle, brass kettle,
What did you hide?
Here's the beauty potion
_____(student's name) found inside.

Everyone who participated in the decoding may receive a kettle-shaped award certificate that states:

Today, _____(name) discovered a numeral-letter relationship to decipher coded words.

_____ name of teacher

THE MOST AMAZING HIDE-AND-SEEK ALPHABET BOOK (152)

By Robert Crowther. Illustrated by the author. New York: Viking, 1978.

Crowther shows readers tabs to pull and flaps to turn on the letters to uncover animals whose names begin with selected letters. A reader uncovers familiar selections—a furry koala bear, a brown monkey, and a feathery, wide-eyed owl. Some hiding animals may surprise a reader when they are found—the unfamiliar umbrella bird, a small newt, a sharp-billed parrot, and a green snake that unwinds in a spiral across the page.

Extension: Imagine

Purpose: To participate in a discussion about an imagined experience

Materials: Copy of *The Most Amazing Hide-and-Seek Alphabet Book* (152)

Suggested Grade: Pre-1

Show Crowther's book to the children, and while reading aloud, hold the book firmly so a child can turn a letter or pull a tab to reveal the animal hiding behind a letter. As each animal is revealed, ask the boys and girls to consider an imaginative experience related to the animal. For example, when the tab for the letter *K* is pulled and the koala slides out from behind a branch of the letter, ask, "What would it feel like if you were to touch this furry koala bear?" "What could have happened to the koala to make it slide out from behind the branch?" "What could happen next?" For other animals, ask such questions as, "What would it feel like if you were to pet the feathers of the parrot? to pet the brown monkey? to touch the small newt? to touch a red lobster?" Discuss the way Crowther portrays a live lobster as red and not as gray green or dark green. If appropriate, talk about the need for safety around animals and suggest cautions about touching any wild animals.

Make lift-up letters and hidden animals. Invite the children to make oversized block letters and draw and color appropriate animals to "hide" beneath the letters. The oversized letters may be hinged at the top to the paper with tape. The children may lift the letters up to see the pictures of the animals they have pasted under the letters. When the hidden animal illustrations are finished, invite each child to show and tell something about the illustration with the whole group.

PIGS FROM A TO Z (162)

By Paul Geisert. Illustrated by the author. New York: Houghton Mifflin, 1986.

Seven little pigs build a tree house, and in the large detailed etchings, Geisert hides at least five different forms of the guiding letter, one form of the preceding letters, and one form of the following letter. Sometimes one of the pigs will try to hide on the page. Oversized capitals are introduced by key words in narrative sentences. For example, on the page for the letter *X*, there are five *X*s, one *W*, one *Y*, and the seven little pigs. The letter *X* is for "extra bracing" for the pigs' house and for "giving Pa some expert help." To self-check while playing this visual game, a student can turn to the last page to find the small illustrations that are a key to the hidden letter shapes on each page.

Extension: Find and discuss

Purpose: To observe letters hidden in the illustrations

Materials: Copy of *Pigs From A to Z* (162)

Suggested Grade: 4 up

With the students, discuss what might happen when seven little pigs (or seven children) try to build a tree house. As the students make their suggestions, write the words/phrases on the board in clusters to show relationships, e.g., words about safety in one cluster, and then words about supplies, words about cooperation, words about tools, and so on, in other clusters. After each page is read, ask, "What might happen next?" and encourage the students to make predictions. After reading the story, lead a discussion about the technique that Geisert used in his illustrations. In his etchings, Geisert has placed at least five different forms of the guiding letter, one form of the preceding letter and one form of the following letter. Point out the value of the self-check key in the back of the book and pass it around to the students.

Extension: Point and tell

Purpose: To observe letters hidden in the illustrations

Materials: Copy of *Pigs From A to Z* (162), opaque projector

Suggested Grade: 1–2

Read the story to the children and review the illustrations on an opaque projector. Invite the children to look for the letters hidden in the illustrations. They may look for:

- five different forms of the selected letter in each illustration,
- one form of the preceding letter and
- one form of the following letter

As a volunteer comes to the screen to point out some of the hidden letters, engage the children in saying a unison chant aloud to introduce the volunteer:

For the page with the letter *B*:

Students:
Where's the A? Where's the B?
Where's the B? Where's the C?
_____ (name) will show us what she (he) sees.

Student taking a turn:
Here's the _____ (A, B, C).
(The student points to one form of the guiding letter *B*,
the preceding letter *A*, and the following letter *C*
and points them out.)

For the page with the letter *C:*

Students:
Where's the B? Where's the C?
Where's the C? Where's the D?
_____ (name) will show us what she (he) sees.

Student taking a turn:
Here's the_____ (B, C, D).

Show the children how to use the key to the illustrations in the back of the book. If some of the boys and girls can benefit from an observation extension activity, ask them to take partners and look for the letters on other pages of the book and use the key for a self-check.

WHAT'S INSIDE: THE ALPHABET BOOK (171)

By Satoshi Kitamura. Illustrated by the author. New York: Farrar, Straus & Giroux, 1985.

Guessing the secret object hidden on every page guides a reader through the sequence of the alphabet. In full-color paintings, a reader sees boxes and other containers that hide different objects. A reader predicts what is hidden and uses the guiding letter as a clue. For example, a reader sees the letters *a* and *b* in the first illustration, makes predictions, and turns the page to discover the names of the objects and to verify the predictions.

Extension: Interact with *What's Inside* (171)

Purpose: To make predictions

Materials: Copy of *What's Inside* (171)

Suggested Grade: K

Sing the Alphabet Song and Make Predictions. Open the book to the end pages and suggest that the children sing the alphabet song to recognize the letters found on the end papers. Ask the boys and girls what they think the book is going to be about with a title that says "What's inside." Write the children's ideas about the title on the board. Show the boxes labeled with the lowercase letters *a* and *b* in the first illustration and ask the title question, "What's inside?" Invite the children to make predictions and talk about the clues they saw that caused them to predict the way they did. Turn the page to show the children what the artist drew inside of the boxes. The prediction may be repeated with the other illustrations, and when the book is finished, point out the children's predictions that were written on the board. Review the predictions and discuss the ones that "came true." Ask the children to discuss some of the clues they used to make the predictions that "came true."

Extension: Create illustrations for predictions

Purpose: To create illustrations for predictions

Materials: Paper and crayons

Suggested Grade: 1

With paper and crayons, engage the boys and girls in working as partners and making a pair of illustrations. The first illustration is to show boxes or other containers labeled with the letter of the object that is hidden inside. The second illustration is to show the boxes or the containers opened to reveal the hidden object. For further extensions, the children may:

1. display the pair of illustrations in a class book to be used as prediction activities for others;
2. give clues about their illustrations to make a word game in front of the whole class;
3. use words that represent animals and mime an animal's behavior so others can guess the hidden animal;
4. demonstrate to the whole group the way they thought through the process of deciding what to hide in the illustration;
5. write the names of the hidden objects on labels to place beneath their illustrations when they are displayed in a classroom book;
6. write short stories to place beside their illustration pairs;
7. arrange the illustration pairs in alphabetical order;
8. go through the letters in sequence and talk about the illustration pairs in that order;
9. count up to twenty-six and line up in the room to see how many pairs of illustrations it takes to make that many in a line; and
10. say the names of the hidden objects aloud in alphabetical order while in line.

* SIGN LANGUAGE THEME

Children can be introduced to American sign language and manual spelling with alphabet books. In some of the books, the illustrations showing manual hand signs for the letters help boys and girls learn the sign for the letter commonly associated with a sound. In other books, the illustrations for hand signs for objects make the signs easy to remember because the signs make pictures of the objects and ideas they represent.

HANDMADE ABC:
A MANUAL ALPHABET (202)

By Linda Bourke. Illustrated by the author. New York: Addison, 1981.

Sign language can be appreciated by everyone because it is expressive, rhythmic, and beautiful to watch, so invite the children to roll up their sleeves, wiggle their fingers, and speak with their hands. Twenty-six hand signs introduce the letters, and once learned, can be used to send messages to others. A manual alphabet guide is included.

Extension: Saying it in sign language

Purpose: To learn the language of signs, i.e., a particular hand shape for a particular meaning

Materials: Copy of *Handmade ABC* (202)

Suggested Grade: 2–3

With the students, show the illustrations and discuss some of the signs that are easy to remember because they make pictures of the ideas they represent:

peel a banana: pretend to act out peeling a banana for the sign
camera: pretend you are looking through the focus window on a
camera
tree: place the elbow of one arm in the palm of the other hand to
show a tree; shake your fingers to show the leaves.
ice cream: pretend to lick an ice cream cone
tickle: pretend to put a finger in your side and tickle yourself
book: put palms of hands together and open them like a book

Discuss the idea that one of the best ways to improve their signing is by practicing with people who use sign language all the time. So the children can grow in their communication skills, plan to invite people to the classroom who use sign language regularly. Ask the children for suggestions about:

- people to invite;
- ways to contact the invited guests;
- what questions the children want to ask;
- what signs they will need to learn to ask their questions;
- what activities they want to provide in sign language for the guest, e.g., "singing" happy birthday and other songs with signs, "reciting" a favorite rhyme or the alphabet, and introducing themselves with finger-spelling signs;
- what signs they will need to say thank you and good-bye to the guest;
- what they want to do to follow up the guest's visit, e.g., writing a thank-you letter.
- who will volunteer for some of the responsibilities during the visit, i.e., meeting the guest at the office, escorting the guest to and from the room, introducing the guest to the total group, and serving as host/hostess for the visit.

I CAN SIGN MY ABCs (205)

By Susan Gibbons Chaplin. Illustrated by Laura McCaul. New York: Gallaudet, 1986.

The alphabet is introduced in sign language with the manual alphabet hand-shapes, pictures, names, and object signs. In color, both oversized capitals and lowercase letters guide the sequence. At the foot of each page is the entire alphabet in lowercase with the appropriate letter identified in color. The word choices are familiar ones with xylophone, yo-yo, and zipper.

Extension: Recognize signs for familiar objects

Purpose: To make signs for familiar objects

Materials: Copy of *I Can Sign My ABCs* (205)

Suggested Grade: All ages

Displaying the book, show the illustrations and discuss the signs for selected objects. Ask the boys and girls to face one another and make some of the signs to their partners. For a review, a child may call out the name of an object and a partner may make the sign. Additional copies of the book should be available as a reference. Then the children trade roles. Other partnership activities may include sending messages, answering riddles, and participaing in a finger-spelling bee.

Send messages, answer riddles, and participate in a finger-spelling bee. Adapt some of the classroom activities to signing and finger spelling. For example, the children can answer roll call each morning by finger spelling their names or signing "here." Select other alphabet books on this topic and display them in the classroom. Titles to consider are:

Finger Spelling Fun (200) by David Adler; a way to spell words with fingers;

The Handmade Alphabet (207) by Laura Rankin; a book with the manual alphabet;

Handtalk: An ABC of Finger Spelling and Sign Language (206) by Remy Charlip and Mary Beth Miller; an introduction to finger spelling and signing;

My First Book of Sign (201) by Pamela J. Baker; a book of words grouped by their initial letters;

Sign Language ABC (203) by Linda Bove; a way to make signs for words that express actions, feelings, and opposites;

A Show of Hands: Say It in Sign Language (208) by Mary Beth Sullivan and Linda Bourke; a book that has been featured on the *Reading Rainbow* television program.

* SPECIFIC PLACES THEME

Alphabet books also have been designed to give information to readers about specific places. In addition to presenting the letters and their relationships to key words, the books offer facts about life north of the fifty-fifth parallel and in Africa and about the animals found in Africa and North America.

JAMBO MEANS HELLO: SWAHILI ALPHABET BOOK (214)

By Muriel Feelings. Illustrated by Tom Feelings. New York: Dial, 1974.

Feelings' alphabet book takes a reader to another country, introduces the people, their customs, and language. Point out the map of Africa that is included and identify some of the countries where Swahili is spoken. You might mention that the language is called Kiswahili while the word Swahili refers to the people who speak the language. Twenty-four (not twenty-six) letters are in this alphabet, and there are no entries for the letters Q and X. With the book, the children acquire information about East African village life, the people, their utensils and musical instruments, words of greeting, and some of the animals that inhabit the region. Brief, informative paragraphs accompany the key words and the illustrations that were painted and covered with wet tissue paper to soften the black ink and white tempera drawings, a process to discuss with interested children.

Extension: Remember this?

Purpose: To recall Kiswahili words featured in alphabetical order

Materials: Copy of *Jambo Means Hello: Swahili Alphabet Book*
(214)

Suggested Grade: K-3

Read some selections from *Jambo Means Hello* and ask the boys and
girls to recall as many of the words as they can. Invite the children
to repeat the Kiswahili words for the key objects, actions, or greet-
ings. If desired, introduce the following "Remember, Remember"
activity:

Words are here for the ABC
Say them aloud in Kiswahili.
Jambo, Jambo,
Boys and girls,
Means . . . clap, clap, . . . clap, clap.
(Teacher claps out number of syllables in the key word, *Hello.*)
Boys and girls.

Children may respond with:

We hear the words in the ABC
We'll say them again in Kiswahili.
Jambo, Jambo,
_____ (name of teacher)
Means Hello, Hello.
_____ (name of teacher).

Option: Display of alphabet books for themed reading about
African life

For a classroom display, titles of alphabet books to consider are:
African Treehouse (234) by Tasker; *Ashanti to Zulu: African Traditions*
(224) by Musgrove; *Afro-Bets Book of Black Heroes from A to Z* (218)
by Wade Hudson and Valerie Wilson Wesley, a book about such heroes as Joseph Cinque (Sierra Leone), Kwame Nkrumah (Ghana),
Phillis Wheatley (Senegal), and Shaka Zulu (South Africa); and *Wild
Animals of Africa* (230) by Hope Ryden.

A NORTHERN ALPHABET (216)

By Ted Harrison. Illustrated by the author. New York: Tundra, 1987.

Harrison's book has alliterative sentences about people, places, animals and objects seen north of the fifty-fifth parallel. Harrison shares facts through words and illustrations about people, their possessions, their environment, and the plants and animals—a valuable source for regional study. Each full-color illustration shows a person, an activity, and additional items related to the featured letter on the page. Point out the names of places in the border of each illustration—a beginning for geographical study. The colorful pictures may motivate interested students to write original stories for selected illustrations.

Extension: Alliterative story starts

Purpose: To elaborate on an alliterative story starter for interpretative reading and original writing

Materials: Copy of *A Northern Alphabet* (216)

Suggested Grade: 3–4

Displaying the book, read the alliterative sentences on the pages from *A* for anorak to *Z* for zero weather. With the total group, discuss ways to orally interpret the sentences during a rereading. For an example, focus on what some of the word meanings could tell a reader about oral interpretation. For instance, write the sentences on the board, "Aa Alex lives in the Arctic. He is wearing the anorak." With the sentences as a pattern, explore some of the oral interpreting possibilities with the students either individually, as partners, as trios or quartets, or by rows or tables. Some of the examples could include:

- "Looking at the page for the letter *A* and saying the word *Arctic,* how could the students say the word to convey the idea of cold weather? For instance, could a reader's voice "shiver" when reading the word? Encourage the students to demonstrate their interpretation of this for the total group.

- Looking at the page for the letter *B* and saying the phrase ". . . being chased by a bear," ask the girls and boys for ways the word *chased* could be interpreted and said aloud to convey its meaning? For instance, would a reader want to interpret the word as "ch--ch--chased" and say it as if out of breath or drum hands on knees to make a "chasing sound?"

- Looking at the page for the letter *C* and reading the phrase, "Above the cabin. . . ," what suggestions do the students have for interpreting the word *above*? For one oral interpretation "experiment," invite them to say *above* in high, "floating" voices.

- Looking at the page for the letter *G* and reading aloud the sentence, "Georgie is greeting his grandmother," how could the word *greeting* be orally interpreted? For a demonstration, invite the students to say the word "greeting" with the same inflection as saying "hello."

- Looking at the page for the letter *L* and reading the phrase, "The lonely loon floats . . .," how could a reader's voice convey a floating tone for the word, *float*? Ask some volunteers to demonstrate their suggestions.

- Looking at the page for the letter *M* and reading the phrase, "a moose munching in the muskeg," how would the students interpret the word *munching*? For another "experiment," encourage each group, row, or table of students to take turns and say *munching* in an accumulating and repetitive manner around the room.

- Looking at the page for the letter *Q* and reading the phrase, "Mother is quietly making a quilt," ask the boys and girls to make suggestions for orally interpreting the word *quietly* and then to demonstrate reading aloud the phrase in a "quiet" way. Encourage the addition of hand motions to mime sewing the quilt.

- Looking at the page for the letter *S* and considering the phrase "soft snow," invite the students' suggestions about ways to make a reader's voice "soft" during a reading.

- Looking at the page for the letter *Y* and reading the phrase "A young Yukoner yells. . . ," ask for suggestions and hand movements to orally interpret the word *yells*. As part of your demonstration, suggest the idea of making an echo.

- Looking at the page for *Z*, ask the students to consider different ways the words *zero weather* could be interpreted. For instance, invite a student to volunteer and be the reader whose voice is "cold" when reading the words.

Option. At the back of the book, Harrison includes a list of things in the pictures that begin with each letter and invites the readers to add still more items to the list. To do this, request that the students suggest a key word for each letter, write their suggestions on the board, and ask them to add more items to the list. The items can be added by writing the object's name or by drawing the object rebus-style. The list might include:

A airplane . . .	N nuggets . . .
B bark . . .	O oil drum . . .
C campfire . . .	P pan . . .
D dandelions . . .	Q quills . . .
E eagle . . .	R ravens . . .
F firewood . . .	S snowshoe . . .
G geese . . .	T toboggan . . .
H hats . . .	U underwear . . .
I ice . . .	V valley . . .
J jackrabbit . . .	W waves . . .
K kettle . . .	X xylophone . . .
L ladle . . .	Y yellow . . .
M mittens . . .	Z zipper . . .

When finished, invite volunteers to talk about what items were added and to show their sketches to others in the group. If appropriate, ask different students to demonstrate in pantomime an activity associated with their object. If desired for a class book collection, gather the students' writing into a class book and place it in the book area for future browsing and for a writing resource.

WILD ANIMALS OF AMERICA ABC (231)

By Hope Ryden. Illustrated by the author. New York: Dutton, 1988.

Wild animals living in North America are seen in full-color photographs. Some, such as the alligator and beaver, will be familiar to children, and others, such as the xanthid crab, urchins, voles, yellow-bellied marmot, and Zone-tailed hawk, will be unfamiliar.

Extension: Animals of North America

Purpose: To introduce wild animals of North America in an alphabetical sequence

Materials: Copy of *Wild Animals of America ABC* (231)

Suggested Grade: 2–3

With the book, read the names of the animals in the book and then return to the illustrations for a discussion about the animals that are seen. For each animal seen, demonstrate the use of the informational notes at the end of the book and read the information related to each animal aloud. If desired, ask the students to mark where they live on a map of their state and see if there is an animal in the book that lives close to them. For a further map activity, ask the students to mark the state where they live on a map of the United States and see if there is an animal shown in the book that lives in states close to the students' state. When the names of the animals are identified, ask the boys and girls to use a grease pencil to write the animal names in the appropriate geographical locations for their habitats on a map of the state or the United States. Here are some animals to consider:

> grizzly bear (Alaska)
> lynx (Alaska)
> kit fox (Arizona, New Mexico, Nevada, California)
> xanthid crab (ocean floor)

The alphabet in a milieu collection consists of ABC books that have the same sharing potential as the books in the alphabet in a topic collection. The print and the pictures in the milieu books, however, contribute mainly to the sequence of the letters and not to related themes or topics in the books. The structure of the alphabet sets the surrounding environment in the books for the illustrations.

ABOUT ALPHABET BOOKS

"Alphabet books introduce letters and show them in use. But many modern alphabet books do more, conveying the flavor of another culture, for example, or teaching some basic facts of science. Teachers can use such books to familiarize students with letters, but many titles also serve as storybooks, or as a source for a colorful variety of pictures. Several alphabet books for older children use the alphabet to develop a theme."

—Joan I. Glazer and Gurney Williams III
Introduction to Children's Literature

"Titles of books may be the center of the writing activity. Children may prepare an eight-course menu of book titles. . . . For dessert they could eat *A Apple Pie* by Kate Greenaway. Children can make up an alphabet of animal names from book titles: *Alligators All Around* by Maurice Sendak . . . ."

—Robert Whitehead
Children's Literature: Strategies of Teaching

"An ABC book may serve as an available language model. An ABC book can be a colorful file of letter, word, or sentence patterns. This file is personal, portable, filled with pictures and examples of language, and protected by hard covers. While interacting with such books, a child asks and answers questions, recalls information, and listens to the words of another reader."

—Patricia L. Roberts
Alphabet Books as a Key to Language Patterns:
An Annotated Action Bibliography

PART TWO
ALPHABET BOOKS IN A MILIEU COLLECTION

Alphabet books also provide outstanding illustrators for a reader to turn to as an art resource and see ways artists have communicated their ideas. Some of the artists share their ideas about sequencing the alphabet with bright paintings, with objects painted in gouache, with tempera drawings, and with cartoon-style illustrations. Additionally, a reader will find the use of color overlays, detailed drafting, and bold poster-style strokes. With alphabet books, a reader inherits a visual legacy from the illustrators and their imaginative ways of presenting the letters and a collection of objects based on the alphabet.

ABC (241)

By Elizabeth Cleaver. Illustrated by the author. New York: Macmillan, 1985.

Best suited for individual use because of its small size, this book introduces each letter with a collage composition. Beginning with alligator, ant, and apple for the letter *A*, each collage contains a number of items whose names begin with the selected letter. In each illustration, both capital and lowercase letters are near the familiar word choices that include X-ray and a sign that reads "Merry Xmas" for the letter *X* and zebra and zipper for the letter *Z*. A young child will enjoy identifying the objects and an older student (grade 4-up) may appreciate the arrangement of the objects in the illustration's page design.

Extension: Tell-and-see

Purpose: To identify objects that introduce the letters

Materials: Copy of *ABC* (241), opaque projector

Suggested Grade: K-1

Displaying the illustrations on an opaque projector, the teacher may discuss some of the objects on the pages and demonstrate different ways to describe the objects. For example, the teacher may show the illustrations for *A, B, C,* and *D,* read the labels for the objects, and then say:

> I see an A and a B
> And a C and a D
> before my eyes.
> What a surprise!
> I see something that is _____.

(The teacher demonstrates a way to describe an object seen on one of the pages and then the teacher and the student trade roles and the student says the rhyme and gives a description of an object.)

The teacher shows the illustrations for the letters *E, F,* and *G,* reads the names of the objects, and then says:

> I see an E
> And an F
> And a G
> before my eyes.
> What a surprise!
> I can name what I see: _____.

(The teacher names an object seen on one of the pages and then the teacher and the student trade roles and the student says the rhyme and names an object.)

The teacher shows other illustrations:

> I see the
> H, I, J, K,
> L, M, N, O, P
> before my eyes.
> What a surprise!
> I can name what I see: _____.

(The teacher and the student trade roles and the student says the rhyme and names an object.)

> I see a Q and an R
> And an S and T
> before my eyes.
> What a surprise!
> I can name what I see: _____.

(The teacher and the student trade roles and the student says the rhyme and names an object.)

Both the teacher and the children may say together:

> I see a V
> and a W,
> and X, Y, Z,
> this ends our
> ABC "tell-and-see."

ABC: AN ALPHABET BOOK (255)

By Thomas Mattiesen. Illustrated by the author. New York: Putnam, 1981.

Mattiesen, a professional photographer, uses uppercase and lower-case letters to accompany each descriptive statement and question to read aloud to children. As an example for the letter *J,* "Jars hold lots of different things—jam and flour, sugar and cereal. Why is there a marble in this one?" Full-color photographs introduce the letters.

Extension: Alphabetical sentences and phrases

Purpose: To match letter cards and phrase cards to make alphabetical sentences

Materials: Teacher and student-prepared cards with set 1 having beginning of sentences, i.e., *A* is for, *B* is for, and so on; set 2 with sentence endings and questions. Copy of *ABC: An Alphabet Book* (255)

Suggested Grade: 1–2

Show the children the models of letter and phrase cards that can be made as a game for others to play. To play the game, invite the girls and boys to match a card from set 1 with a card from set 2 and then make their own sets of cards with photographs cut from discarded magazines. The children may use *ABC: An Alphabet Book* as a data source for examples of sentences and questions to write on the cards. Examples for the two sets can include:

Set 1	Set 2
C is for . . .	Clocks. Clocks help us. How did you learn to tell time?
E is for . . .	Eggs. Eggs change their shape when they are dropped. What does a dropped egg look like?
G is for . . .	Guitars. Guitars make music. How can you make music on this instrument?
J is for . . .	Jars. Jars hold different things. Why is a marble in this one?
P is for . . .	Paints. Paints decorate many things. How do you use paint?
S is for . . .	Shoes. Shoes protect your feet when you run. Why do shoe laces become untied?
T is for . . .	Telephones. Telephones are useful. How can the telephone help you?

A B C, SAY WITH ME (249)

By Karen Gundersheimer. Illustrated by the author. New York: Harper & Row, 1984.

In this book, a small girl demonstrates actions for words that end in "ing." The word choices include actions from asking and balancing through marking (with a color marker) to yawning and zooming. There are no single letters to guide the alphabetical sequence, so there is a need to point out the initial letters in the capitalized words. Best suited for individual use because of the book's small size, a young child can demonstrate the actions.

Extension: Acting out "ing" words

Purpose: To demonstrate actions for "ing" words

Materials: Copy of *ABC, Say with Me* (249), opaque projector

Suggested Grade: K

With an opaque projector, display the illustrations and discuss the actions of the small girl. Invite the boys and girls to mimic the actions and pose to demonstrate what is going on. Clarify any of the words that might be difficult or unfamiliar ones, such as *gnoring*, and elaborate, e.g., that means to pay no attention to something. Reread the key words and ask some volunteers to tell what is going on in each of the illustrations.

Emphasize individual expression. To emphasize some of the physical expressions that children can generate, guide the actions seen in the illustrations with statements such as:

> If A is for asking, find a way to ask something right now while I watch you.
> If B is for balancing, pretend to balance something in your space.
> If C is for cleaning, pretend to clean something once, then twice.
> If D is for dancing, find a way to pretend to dance in the space in front of you.
> If E is for eating, pretend to eat a favorite vegetable right now.
> If F is for floating, imagine that you are floating right now.
> If G is for giggling, show us how you would giggle.
> If H is for hiding, pretend to hide somewhere right in your space.
> If I is for ignoring, pretend to pay no attention to something.

If J is for jumping, let's jump in a make-believe way in our spaces in the room.

If K is for keeping keys, pretend to keep a set of keys in your pocket.

If L is for leaping, let's pretend to leap over something in our spaces.

If M is for marking, pretend to pick up a marker and make a mark on paper.

If N is for nibbling, let's pretend to nibble our favorite food right now.

If O is for observing, let's show we can do this by looking closely at something in the room.

If P is for pretending, let's show one another we can pretend to tie our shoes.

If Q is for questioning, let's ask the person next to us a question right now.

If R is for rocking, let's pretend to rock back and forth in a rocking chair right now.

If S is for sliding, pretend to slide your feet on something in your space.

If T is for tiptoeing, let's stand on tiptoe right now in our spaces.

If U is for undoing, pretend to undo the shoelaces on your shoes right now.

If V is for viewing, let's show others you can look closely at something in the room.

If W is for washing, let's pretend to wash our faces once and then twice.

If X is for x-ing, let's write Xs in the air with our fingers.

If Y is for yawning, let's yawn once, then twice, and then three times this afternoon.

If Z is for zooming, let's make a zooming noise with our voices once, then twice, then three times.

A, B, SEE! (251)

By Tana Hoban. Illustrated by the author. New York: Greenwillow, 1982.

In this book, a reader sees objects in black-and-white photographs taken with a prolonged light source to make photograms. At the foot of each page is the alphabet in a frieze in gray that shows the appropriate letter in oversize black type. Object choices begin with a collection for the letter *A*—apple, abacus, asparagus, acorn—and end with a single object—zipper—for the letter *Z.*

Extension: Recognizing alliteration

Purpose: To review the objects and the beginning letters and sounds in the names of objects

Materials: Copy of *A, B, See!* (251), opaque projector

Suggested Grade: 2

Displaying the illustrations on an opaque projector, identify the objects, their names, and the letters that begin the names. Mention to the children there are different objects whose names all begin with the same letter on each page of the book. On the board, demonstrate a way to write a sentence using as many of the objects' names as possible into an alliterative sentence. When appropriate for the alphabetical sequence, include a student's name in the sentence. As an example for the letter *A*: In the attic, Ann is an actress and adds an apple, abacus, asparagus, and acorn to the act. Take the children's suggestions for additional sentences, and record them on the board. Encourage the children to copy the sentences or to create original ones and then to illustrate what they have written.

Extension: Alliteration accelerators

Purpose: To introduce alliteration through objects shown in alphabetical order

Materials: Copy of *A, B, See!* (251), opaque projector, 3″ × 8″ paper strips with an alliterative sentence on each strip

Suggested Grade: 2

With the use of an opaque projector to display the pages of the book, identify the alliterative names of the objects found on the *A* page, *B* page, and so on. Write the objects' names on the board, chart, or overhead transparency. Introduce the idea of including the names of the objects (and other objects, too) in alliterative sentences with examples such as:

1. Abigail Alligator ate acorns, apples, and asparagus all afternoon, and some army ants attacked Abigail's ankle. After the
attack, Abigail asked an astronaut about the arrow and the abacus at the astrodome. All the animals always asked the astronaut about the arrow and the abacus at the astrodome.

2. Elmer Elephant ate eight extra enormous eggs and eagerly eyed
an eraser and an eggbeater.

3. Finnie Fish floated freely away from a fork, a flower, a 5, and
a frog.

4. In the moonlight, Michael Mouse munched mushrooms.

5. Under silver stars, stout Sylvia Swan and small Sammy
Seahorse swam until they were surprised at seeing a spoon, a
sled, and a pair of scissors.

With the children's suggestions for alliterative words, demonstrate
a way to combine the objects' names into an alliterative sentence and
write the sentence on a paper strip (3″ X 8″ is suggested). Elicit
more suggestions for other sentences and read them aloud together
as a total group. Invite the children to divide into alliteration accelerator groups of four to five students each. A student volunteer in a
group receives an alliteration accelerator sentence and reads it aloud
to the others in the group. With the goal of creating original alliterative sentences, the children receive writing materials. If desired, distribute to the groups additional alphabet books that have examples
of alliterative sentences. Some alphabet books to consider are:

- *The Stephen Cartwright ABC* (237) by Heather Amery and
Stephen Cartwright, a source of alliterative sentences with chil-
dren's names from Alex, Andrew and Anne through Martin,
Maggie, and Mark to Zoe, Zara, and Zack;
- Dick Bruna's *B Is for Bear: An ABC* (238), a collection of sim-
ilar phrases, e.g., *A* is for apple, *B* is for bear, and so on;
- Bobbie Craig's *A Comic and Curious Collection of Animals,
Birds, and Other Creatures* (33), a presentation of curious situ-
ations with comic animals described in alliterative sentences;
- Laurent de Brunhoff's *Babar's ABC* (35), a series of illustrations
with accompanying sentences as alliterative captions;

- Beau Gardner's *Have You Ever Seen . . . ? An ABC Book* (248), a collection of humorous situations with animate and inanimate objects described with alliterative words;
- Susanna Gretz's *Teddy Bears ABC* (41), a presentation of the activities of six teddy bears from arriving at the airport to zipping off to the zoo;
- Carol Mills's *A-Z and Back Again: An ABC Book* (50), an episodic introduction to such personalities as Auntie Ada, Barney Bear, and Zebedee Zebra in alliterative rhythmic text;
- Lilian Obligado's *Faint Frogs Feeling Feverish and Other Terrifically Tantalizing Tongue Twisters* (52), a collection of alliterative phrases that include animal names, their actions, and words of description; and
- *Dr. Seuss's ABC* (259), a group of alliterative answers to the question "What begins with A? with B?" and so on.

DR. SEUSS' ABC (259)

By Dr. Seuss. Illustrated by the author. New York: Random House, 1963, reprinted 1981.

This alphabet book helps girls and boys enjoy the sounds of the letters. On the endpapers, a reader sees a confetti arrangement of large and small letters in bright colors of orange, red, and green, and the text asks, "What begins with A?" and goes on to present the character of Aunt Annie as part of the answer. With guiding reins in her hands, Aunt Annie sits in her sedan chair and goes for a ride on top of a large, smiling alligator. Humorous touches are found in the created words (fiffer-feffer-feff) and in the creature-characters, e.g., a duck-dog, a quacker-oo, and a yellow-eyed pink-and-white checkered creature, a Zizzer-Zazzer-Zuzz.

Extension: Create a creature

Purpose: To enjoy creating an unusual alphabet creature and identify its place in the sequence

Materials: Copy of *Dr. Seuss' ABC* (259), opaque projector, art paper, crayons or markers, scissors, paste, glitter pen or tubes

Suggested Grade: 1–3

After displaying the imaginary creatures in the book—the fiffer-feffer-feff, duck-dog, quacker-oo, and Zizzer-Zazzer-Zuzz—on the opaque projector, invite the boys and girls to cut shapes of circles, triangles, squares, and paste the shapes together in an arrangement to form a head of a Seuss-type creature. After coloring and adding features to the head, each student passes the work along to a second student, who completes the lower body (and tail if there is one) of the creature. When finished, the second student returns the work to the first. The first student may use glitter, sequins, rickrack, and other additions to put the finishing touches to the creature. The two students should name their creature and join with others in the whole class to put the drawings in alphabetical order for a class display.

Extension: Illustrators of alphabets

Purpose: To enjoy the works of artists of alphabet books

Materials: Assorted alphabet books

Suggested Grade: 2

With a collection of alphabet books, discuss some of the ways artists have interpreted key objects that introduce the letters of the alphabet. Some of the artists whose work may be shared with the girls and boys include:

Mary Azarian	Ed Emberley	Mercer Mayer
Leonard Baskin	Marcia Brown	Tom Feelings
Helen Oxenbury	John Burningham	Wanda Gag
Leo and Diane Dillon	Tana Hoban	Lois Ehlert

HAVE YOU EVER SEEN . . . ? AN ABC BOOK (248)

By Beau Gardner. Illustrated by the author. New York: Dodd, 1986.

Gardner's full-color illustrations show images in bright colors and both capitals and lowercase letters guide the sequence. A reader reads alliterative sentences and sees a ladybug riding a lightening bolt, an inchworm on ice skates, and an octopus who eats oatmeal with a spoon in all eight arms. Younger children will enjoy drawing their own versions of alliterative sentences, and older students (grade 3-up) can participate in writing their own original sentences.

Extension: Be a director of alliteration artists

Purpose: To write clear directions

Materials: Copy of *Have You Ever Seen . .?* (248); copy of duplicated sheet, "From the art director of alliteration artists . . . "

Suggested Grade: 3

Display the illustrations to the students with an opaque projector, and discuss the alliteration in the text. Introduce the idea of being an art director for a staff of alliteration artists and talk about the need to give directions clearly to the artists so they will create the appropriate illustrations that are needed to make an alphabet book. Engage the students to role-play the director of alliterative artists, and invite the students to write an alliterative sentence on a duplicated sheet, "From the art director . . . ," and then make comments to help the staff artists prepare the illustration for the sentence.

FROM THE ART DIRECTOR
OF ALLITERATION ARTISTS:

_____
(your name)

Copy of one of your favorite alliterative sentences here.	Write the descriptive comments you would send to your staff of artists here.
_____ _____ _____ _____	_____ _____ _____ _____

HELEN OXENBURY'S ABC OF THINGS (257)

By Helen Oxenbury. Illustrated by the author. New York: Delacorte, 1983.

Oxenbury's alphabet book shows capital and lowercase letters with a list of words labeling the objects in the illustrations. For the letter *B*, a reader finds a baker who holds a baby while a small bear perches on the baker's shoulder. A bird rests on top of the baker's cap and a badger climbs the baker's leg. Other illustrations combine fresh ideas, e.g., an otter riding an ostrich, a hare and a hippopotamus in the hospital, and a vulture playing a violin while a volcano fumes.

Extension: "Freeze" a frame of objects

Purpose: To identify a variety of objects and illustrate them in a single illustration

Materials: Copy of *Helen Oxenbury's ABC of Things* (257), opaque projector

Suggested Grade: K-3

With the book's illustrations displayed on an opaque projector, invite the girls and boys to identify objects and the letters that begin each object's name. Ask the children to each select a letter and think of objects whose names begin with that letter. As the children imagine objects in their thoughts, say, "Freeze that picture in your mind. Can you draw it on our Freeze-a-Frame Idea Sheet?" Invite them to draw, sketch, and then discuss the objects they placed on the Freeze-a-Frame Idea Sheet (see page 161).

JOHN BURNINGHAM'S ABC (239)

By John Burningham. Illustrated by the author. New York: Crown, 1985.

A reader sees a small child join animals, objects, and people on full-color pages. Nouns are in alphabetical order and introduce the capital and lowercase letters. As examples of the actions, the child

Freeze-A-Frame Idea Sheet For _____.

pushes an elephant, is bumped by a goat, and rides on the back of the hippopotamus. For a review, the end pages show all of the lowercase letters in purple.

Extension: Describe it four ways

Purpose: To describe objects in detail

Materials: Copy of *John Burningham's ABC* (239)

Suggested Grade: K-1

First way: Label the object. After reading the book, encourage the boys and girls to review the pages and look for details. Engage the children in using these details when describing the objects. As an example, invite a child to turn to a favorite page and name what is seen. For instance, on the page for the letter *Y*, a child may say, "I see a yacht."

Second way: Describe the object's color. To elaborate—a second way of describing, invite the children to add to the description by using a color word, i.e., "I see a blue yacht."

Third way: Tell something about a feature of the object. To extend still further a third way of describing an object on the page, invite the children to tell something about a feature of the object, i.e., "I see a blue yacht with orange sails."

Fourth Way: Tell something about the setting for the object. To encourage more words when describing an object, invite the children to contribute still more by telling something about the setting, i.e., "I see a blue yacht with orange sails floating on the water" or "In the blue water, I see a blue yacht with orange sails."

To extend the activity further, show other versions of the alphabet by the same author/artist with *John Burningham's ABC* (1964), *John Burningham's ABC* (1967), and *John Burningham's ABC* (1985). In the first book, the letter pairs and names of objects face the illustrations on opposite pages. For example, the word tractor introduces the letter *T* and faces a colorful picture of a tractor driven by a worker. In the second, the upper- and lowercase letters are introduced with bright illustrations. As another example, a green apple, a green iguana, and a large red-yellow orange with a tempting slice of fruit beneath it illustrate the appropriate letters. Additionally, twenty pigs of assorted colors—gray, black, brown, and pink—can be counted, and umbrellas offer a selection of colors—green, black, blue, and fuschia.

Option. As another option, vary this description activity still further and ask the boys and girls to respond in one of the four ways when an illustration is shown and when a certain descriptive direction is given. For instance, when showing the picture of the green apple, you might request, "Please describe it by name and color." Showing the picture for the letter *I* but without identifying the object, you might ask, "Please label it by name," and wait for someone to say *iguana* for a reply. Seeing two jungle cats in a full-page illustration of a jungle, the children could be asked to describe the animals by name, color, feature, and setting. This activity is appropriate for other alphabet books that have a variety of objects to describe.

26 LETTERS AND 99 CENTS (252)

By Tana Hoban. Illustrated by the author. New York: Greenwillow, 1987.

Colorful photographs introduce letters, objects, numerals, and coins. A reader may identify the letters of the alphabet and then turn the book over to find a second text about counting coins from one to ninety-nine cents. Both the uppercase and lowercase letters are introduced by familiar key objects, e.g., egg, fish, jelly beans.

Extension: Seeing a colorful mix

Purpose: To engage in a primary-color experience

Materials: Copy of *26 Letters and 99 Cents* (252); water, glass container, food coloring, shapes of letters cut from sheets of colored plastic acetate, stir stick or spoon, overhead projector, cooking oil.

Suggested Grade: K-1

With the illustrations in the book, show the colorful objects that introduce the letters of the alphabet on the pages and then tell the children you want them to see ways that colors—just like the ones seen in the book—can mix together (they'll be seeing the colors change from a primary state to a secondary one). Fill a glass bowl or clear plastic container with water and place it on the overhead projector stage. Ask the girls and boys to look at three illustrations selected from the book—a red car, a blue airplane, and a yellow (gold) goldfish—and suggest one of the colors to put in the water. In addition, turn on the overhead projector light and invite a volunteer to put three drops of the selected food coloring into the water and stir the mixture. The light of the projector will magnify and illuminate the stirring and the children will see the way the food coloring mixes with the water. Next, invite a volunteer to add three drops of cooking oil and then a colorful letter shape cut from a sheet of acetate plastic. While stirring the mixture, the children will see the way the color mixture swirls around the oil drops and the plastic letter shape refuses to mix completely with the water and food coloring mixture. A bright, colorful effect is achieved when the classroom lights are dimmed. As a variation, invite each child to add a letter shape that stands for the initials of the child's name into the mixture.

To extend the activity further, a second primary color may be selected by the children and added to the mixture. For instance, yellow may be added to blue and when the mixture is stirred, the boys and girls will see the blue color begin to mix with yellow and then change into a shade of green. This activity can be repeated several times so they can see the process magnified by the overhead projector on the screen in the classroom. Before adding other drops of food coloring, the children can predict what color a mixture of blue and red (or red and yellow) might make and then test their prediction. If desired, they can observe the way to make a different *shade* of a color by adding black to the mixture or a way to make a different *tint* of a color by adding white. Further, some of the children may be interested in beginning with a mixture of white and black in the container of water and then adding a color to produce a different color *tone*. Working with partners or in small groups, the children interested further in this activity about color may use fresh water and different color selections to make their own color combinations.

WE READ: A TO Z (244)

By Donald Crews. Illustrated by the author. New York: Harper & Row, 1967.

A reader finds concepts that include positions and shapes to introduce the letters. Both capitals and lowercase letters are found along with the concept words and related phrases. For an example, the letter *E* is introduced by the key word "equal" and a reader sees equal squares on a black-and-yellow checkered page.

Extension: Finding the page

Purpose: To locate the letters on pages

Materials: Several copies of *We Read: A to Z* (244) to distribute

Suggested Grade: 2–3

In Crews's book, each letter (and not the page) is numbered. After reading the book and discussing the concepts with the children, re-

view some selected concept words—horizontal, nothing, colon—
and invite a volunteer to take a copy of the book and turn the pages
to locate the number of a selected letter. The numeral 1 is the locator for the letter *A,* numeral 2 is for *B,* and so on.

Extension: A to Z race

Purpose: To recall letters or key words in alphabetical order

Materials: Chalkboard and chalk

Suggested Grade: 1–6

To prepare for an "A to Z race," the students are in teams in a row
formation or in a line. Each student should write a letter of the alphabet in sequence on the chalkboard facing his or her line (or row).
When the starting instructions are given with "get on your mark,
get set, go—," the first student in each line moves to the chalkboard
and writes the letter *A.* The student walks back and hands the chalk
to the next one in line. The second student goes to the board to
write the letter *B,* the third a *C,* and so on through the alphabet.
The goal is to record the letters in the alphabetical sequence. The
student who writes the letter *Z* is responsible for reading aloud all
of the letters the teammates have written on the board. The team
that finishes first with all of the letters written and read aloud wins
the A to Z Race.

Options: To extend this activity in other ways, certain variations
can be considered. For instance team members may be asked to 1)
write manuscript or cursive letters as capitals; 2) to write manuscript
or cursive letters as lowercase letters; 3) write the name of an object
that begins with the appropriate letter; 4) quickly sketch an outline
of an object whose name begins with the appropriate letter; or 5)
write one (two, three) words that begin with the selected letter.

Part Three contains alphabet books in both the alphabet in a topic collection and the milieu collection. The bibliography, a reference of selected alphabet books, is provided to help a reader select an alphabet book that is related to a child's special interest. A reader may want to choose an ABC book that supports a specific curriculum area or recommend alphabet books to others. The entries represent what can be found in the current world of alphabet books. It is true that a few of the titles are from the mass market area. The titles were included because the books are readily available, inexpensive, and often they are the ones searching relatives may purchase for their favorite girls and boys.

ABOUT ALPHABET BOOKS

"While most alphabet books do help young children learn their ABC's, they also make a contribution to visual literacy, helping the child organize graphic experiences. ABC books are not the only kinds of books that help children in identifying objects, but they do serve as identification books, usually comprising key words that label familiar objects or animals, less often identifying people."
—Zena Sutherland and May Hill Arbuthnot
Children and Books, Seventh Edition

"ABC books can also be used for identification or naming, as they provide the young child with large lovely pictures of animals or single objects to look at and talk about. . . . ABC books do, however, give children practice in the identification of individual letters—necessary when children begin to read and write."
—Charlotte S. Huck, Susan Hepler, and Janet Hickman
Children's Literature in the Elementary School, Fourth Edition

PART THREE

* ANIMALS AS ANIMALS

1. *ABC Colouring Book.* St. Ives, Cornwall, England: British Museum [Natural History]/ Beric Tempest, 1980.

    To foster learning by doing, the British Museum [Natural History] offers a coloring book with animals beginning with an anteater and boa constrictor and ending with zebra. A child finds black-and-white outlines of animals (and a few plants) along with capitals and lowercase letters and the key words in colors on the pages. Size relationships of animals are not emphasized as a fox is almost as large as an African elephant and a snail is as large as a rhino's horn.

2. Argent, Kerry. *Animal Capers.* Illustrated by the author. New York: Dial, 1989.

    A reader sees familiar and unfamiliar animals parade in line in alphabetical order and turns the pages to find out where they are going. Names of animals that may be unfamiliar to some children are kookaburra, numbat, wombat, and umbrella bird. The page arrangement offers capital and lowercase letters with word choices and illustrations.

3. Baskin, Leonard. *Hosie's Alphabet.* Illustrated by the author. New York: Viking, 1972.

    Baskin has full-color pages and colorful illustrations for the words selected by his children. Descriptive words accompany paintings of a blue-eyed baboon, a multicolored jellyfish, a green locust, and others.

4. Broomfield, Robert. *The Baby Animal ABC.* Illustrated by the author. New York: Puffin/The Bodley Head, 1964.

Broomfield shows animals and their young and a reader reviews the use of terms such as zebra foal, goat kid, impala fawn, and others to identify the baby animals. Illustrations show some youthful behavior when an anteater cub rides on its mother's back, an elephant calf grabs its mother's tail, and fox cubs play with a snail.

5. Doubilet, Anne. *Under the Sea from A to Z.* Illustrated by David Doubilet. New York: Crown/Clarkson N. Potter, 1991.

Species of marine life from a red velvety anemone to a beautiful deadly zebra fish illustrate the letters. Illustrations are oversized color photographs, and the text in bold describes the species. Glossary and maps to show locations of photographed animals are included.

6. Farber, Norma. *As I Was Crossing Boston Common.* Illustrated by Arnold Lobel. New York: Dutton, 1973.

Farber introduces a reader to twenty-six animals, and each in turn meets a turtle crossing the common. A culminating page describes the animals from Angwantibo to Zibet.

7. Gág, Wanda. *The ABC Bunny.* Illustrated by the author. New York: Coward, 1933.

The illustrations are in black and white with oversize capitals in red. Couplets describe the bunny's adventures at lunch, in an owl's nook, and meeting other animals. The rhyming text, set to music by Flavia Gág, is a popular read-aloud selection.

8. Jewell, Nancy. *ABC Cat.* Illustrated by Ann Schweninger. New York: Harper & Row, 1983.

Words in alphabetical order begin first line of each rhyming verse about a black-and-white cat who goes through one day and shows a child the selected alphabetical words. In sequence, rhyming lines introduce the letters with an *A* word (awakes), *B* word (blinks), and so on. The cat hurries, jumps, and kneads its claws. A reader finds repetition with words such as "Lick, lick. Click, click. Chomp, chomp," and "Down, cat, down. Go, cat, go!" or "Don't, cat, don't!"

9. Kingdon, Jill. *The ABC Dinosaur Book.* Illustrated by the author. Chicago: Childrens Press, 1982.

Kingdon reviews dinosaurs to introduce the letters. For examples for letters *X*, *Y*, and *Z*, a reader sees xiphactinus (zif AC tin us), a fish that lived during the age of the dinosaurs; the yaleosaurus (yale o SAWR us), a creature only a little taller than a man, and zanclodon (SANK lo don), a meat-gulping dinosaur with strong legs and grasping "hands." Pronunciation guides on pages and alphabetical listing of dinosaurs on the end pages.

10. Kitchen, Bert. *Animal Alphabet.* Illustrated by the author. Fayetteville, New York: Dial, 1984.

Initial letters in animal names are matched with oversized capitals in black. A reader may predict each animal's name— x-ray fish swimming in water held by the sides of a letter, a snail climbing a letter, or a rhinoceros attacking a letter. A concluding page lists the names from armadillo to zebra. Useful as an art resource for older readers.

11. Laird, Jean D. *The Alphabet Zoo.* Illustrated by Barbara Howell Furan. Fayetteville, Ga.: Oddo, 1972.

A reader vicariously goes on a trip to the zoo and sees large, colorful illustrations with some humor. For example, the text reads, "an octopus is not found on farms." Oversize capitals guide the sequence. A review of the letters is on concluding pages, and a teacher's manual is available from the publisher.

12. McConnell, Keith A. *The SeAlphabet Encyclopedia Coloring Book.* Illustrated by the author. Owings Mills, Md.: Stemmer House, 1982.

Descriptive writing about sea animals introduces outlined capitals. Each sea creature from albacore to zebra shark is found in a black-and-white drawing and described in a numbered list. An older student will find facts about the sea animals that have wings to fight their enemies, who camouflage themselves, and who have appendages that look like lures to attract prey. Another alphabet book that is a suitable companion for further reading by older children (grades 5–6) is Tim Arnold's *Natural*

History from A to Z: A Terrestrial Sampler (Macmillan, 1991), a
book that discusses 26 animals and plants in an introduction to
the natural world.

13. MacPhail, David. *David MacPhail's Animals A-Z.* Illustrated by
    the author. New York: Scholastic, 1988.
    In this wordless book, capital letters accompany the illustra-
tions, and the pictures have varying numbers of objects whose
names begin with the letters. A fox with a fish under his arm
holds a frying pan over a fire in the presence of a flute-wielding
frog on a fence in front of some fir trees. Unfamiliar animals are
found e.g., the upside-down catfish from Africa and Xenops, a
small bird. A list of animals appears at the end, a real help to
naming some of the animals. A child may hunt for all the extra
objects in each picture beginning with the selected letter or add
a fox, fish, frog, fife, frying pan, fence, and fire into a story-
telling sequence. An older student (4 up) may examine the illustrations, discuss the artist's style, and talk about the actions.
With white margins, the illustrations are bordered with black
lines broken by capitals.

14. Mayer, Marianna. *The Unicorn Alphabet.* Illustrated by Michael
    Hague. New York: Dial, 1989.
    Mayer's purpose is to draw upon the stories and symbols of
the unicorn in an alphabetical tribute to the one-horned beast
and as a tribute to beliefs of medieval times. Beginning with an
apple (like the unicorn, a symbol of renewed life) and ending
with zephyr, a wind that blows through a unicorn's mane, the
text offers some of the folklore about the animal. In addition,
each capital letter is introduced by a flower that borders the
page. Facts about the border flowers from aster, an altar flower
used in religious ceremonies, to zenry, a flowering mustard plant
used to heal many ills, are at the end of the book.

15. Newberry, Clare Turlay. *The Kittens' ABC.* Illustrated by the au-
    thor. New York: Harper & Row, 1964.
    Oversized yellow capitals begin the verses about kittens, and
the illustrations show alley cats, Persians, and others. Newberry's kindness toward kittens and cats is shared with, " . . . do
not grab, but softly pat."

16. Owens, Mary Beth. *A Caribou Alphabet.* Illustrated by the author. Brunswick, Me: Dog Ear Press, 1988.

    Rhyming couplets review facts about caribou—they have itchy "velvet" on their antlers, insects may cause a stampede, and they are called xalibu by the MicMac, which means pawer of snow. "A Caribou Compendium" is found on concluding pages with informational notes about the word choices.

17. Pallotta, Jerry. *The Bird Alphabet Book.* Illustrated by Edgar Stewart. Boston: Quinlan Press, 1987.

    Beginning with the Atlantic Puffin that introduces *A* and ending with Zebra Finches for *Z,* a reader discovers a variety of birds for key word choices. In text inserted in the full-color illustrations, facts are given, e.g., roadrunners prefer to run, not fly; a kiwi bird cannot fly; and bald eagles are not really bald (but vultures nearly are). A reader interested further in animals may select one of Pallotta's other books (all Charlesbridge Pub., Maine): *The Dinosaur Alphabet Book; The Frog Alphabet Book; The Furry Alphabet Book; The Yucky Reptile Alphabet Book;* and *The Underwater Alphabet Book.*

18. Pelham, David. *A Is for Animals.* Illustrated by the author. New York: Simon & Schuster, 1991.

    Animals in pop-up surprise illustrations introduce the letter pairs. From baboon, crocodile, and dolphin to xenops, yak, and zebra, a child lifts a cardboard door to see the animals hidden behind and read the key words. Unusual word choices for some children may be mandrill, unicorn fish, and wallaby.

19. Robinson, Howard F., ed. dir. *Incredible Animals A to Z.* Art ed. by Judith E. Zatsick. Washington, D.C.: National Wildlife Federation, 1985.

    Unusual animals with names in bold type—cassowary, stag beetle, zebra butterfly—and informative sentences introduce the oversized capitals shown in colors. Full-color illustrations with index included.

20. Small, Terry. *Tails, Claws, Fangs, & Paws: An AlphaBeast Caper.* Illustrated by the author. New York: Bantam, 1991.

    A reader finds the alphabet beginning with an aye-aye intro-

ducing the letter *A,* a boomslang for *B,* and coot for *C.*
Bibliography, full-color illustrations, animal identification
chart, and rhyming text are included. A picture glossary has
black-and-white illustrations with outlines of animals numbered so a reader can identify the unfamiliar animals such as
aye-aye (squirrel-like), agouti (rodent), and others. In addition,
the reader is to look at the front cover to identify some animals
from sayings and then turn to the back cover to find the answers, but this may not be clear to some readers. Some of the
animals in sayings include: a literary lion (a lion writing with
pen and paper), red herring (a herring stained bright red and a
clotheshorse (a horse dressed in suit, white shirt, and tie). To get
the answers, a reader turns the book upside down and peeks at
the answers on the back.

21. Thornhill, Jan. *The Wildlife ABC: A Nature Alphabet Book.*
    Illustrated by the author. New York: Simon & Schuster, 1988.
    Letters are introduced through illustrations of a variety of
    creatures found in North America and with rhyming lines.
    Author's notes about the animals, beginning with auk and
    beaver and ending with yellow jacket and zoo, are included at
    the back of the book. The descriptive notes also include a black-
    and-white key to the full-color zoo illustration. The key has the
    animals numbered, which helps a reader match each animal
    with its name on a list of animal names.

22. Tillett, Leslie. *Plant and Animal Alphabet Coloring Book.*
    Illustrated by the author. New York: Dover, 1980.
    For a child to color, full-page letters have outlines of plants
    and objects whose names begin with appropriate letter. A child
    may see how many items he or she can identify—for example,
    the letter *X* is introduced by the Xenopus (frog), Xiphophorus
    (crab), and Xiphosura (fish). A child may check the names with
    the charts at the end of the book.

23. Whitehead, Pat. *Dinosaur Alphabet Book.* Illustrated by the au-
    thor. Mahwah, N.J.: Troll, 1989.
    Pairs of capital and lowercase letters are introduced with key
    words such as allosaurus, big, and claws. Below the full-colored

illustrations are brief sentences with facts about characteristics of dinosaurs.

24. Wilson, Ron. *100 Dinosaurs A to Z.* Illustrated by Cecilia Fitzsimons. New York: Grosset & Dunlap, 1986.

    Dinosaurs and descriptive paragraphs introduce the alphabetical sequence. Information is given about each dinosaur's weight, length, location, and its time period in history. A chart of dinosaur history that shows Mesozoic and Cenozoic eras is on a final page.

25. Wormell, Christopher. *An Alphabet of Animals.* Illustrated by Cecilia Fitzsimons. New York: Dial, 1990.

    Pairs of letters are introduced by both familiar and unfamiliar creatures in full-color handcut linoleum block prints. Names of creatures are capitalized, in bold type, and oversized. Some unusual word choices include cobra, jackal, umbrella bird, and vulture. Author's notes about some of the less familiar animals conclude the book.

* ANIMALS AS HUMANS

26. Basset, Scott, & Basset, Tammy. *Artemus and the Alphabet*. Illustrated by Scott Basset. Spokane, Wash.: Basset & Burch Pub., 1980.

   A reader discovers Artemus, a fanciful creature with a round head, smiling face, and long slender legs with claws for toes. Artemus gets hungry enough to take a bite out of the pages as he swings, plays with a yo-yo, gets hungry, and adds an extra *x* to box to invent spelling of boxx.

27. Berenstain, Stanley & Janice. *The Berenstain's B Book*. Illustrated by the authors. New York: Random House, 1971.

   Big Brown Bear meets Blue Bull and a beautiful baboon. They blow bubbles, bike backward, bump into a black bug's banana boxes, and other objects whose names begin with the letter *B*.

28. Boynton, Sandra. *A Is for Angry: An Animal and Adjective Alphabet*. Illustrated by the author. New York: Workman, 1983.

   Boynton's alphabet book introduces children to animals acting like humans, their names, and selected adjectives. After a zany zebra hangs upside down from a large *Z*, a second ending shows that *Z* also stands for zoo and the animals sleeping with Zzzzs. A picture review at the end shows all the animals and letters.

29. Bridwell, Norman. *Clifford's ABC*. Illustrated by the author. New York: Scholastic, 1983.

   Each lowercase letter is introduced by initial letters in the noun choices that relate to Clifford, the big red dog, and Emily Elizabeth. Objects such as igloo, elephant, and house are labeled clearly.

30. Charles, Donald. *Letters from Calico Cat.* Illustrated by the author. Chicago: Childrens Press, 1974.

    Pairs of letters are introduced by key word choices related to a personified calico cat. Shown in full-color watercolor illustrations, the word choices are mainly nouns—goldfish, ladder, kite—but other behaviors and attributes of the cat are shown—dance, hungry, quick, slow.

31. Charles, Donald. *Shaggy Dog's Animal Alphabet.* Illustrated by the author. Chicago: Childrens Press, 1979.

    Through a variety of activities, Shaggy Dog introduces the letters with watercolor illustrations and rhymes for each. Activities include making soup, using an insect net, and photographing a zebra at the zoo.

32. Chouinard, Roger, & Chouinard, Mariko. *The Amazing Animal Alphabet Book.* Illustrated by Roger Chouinard. New York: Doubleday, 1988.

    In full-color illustrations, the animal characters introduce letter pairs and alliterative phrases. For examples, *A* is for an anteater waiting for August, *M* is for a mole making a molehill out of a mountain, and *Z* is for a zebra with zippers on his zoot suit. The letter *X* is for an x-ray fish playing on the xylophone at "Xmas." A child may look for the hidden letter in every illustration, e.g., the letter *Y* is hidden in the flag on the yak's yacht.

33. Craig, Bobbie. *A Comic and Curious Collection of Animals, Birds, and Other Creatures.* Illustrated by the author. New York: Modern/Unisystems, 1981.

    Finding alliteration, a reader sees the letter *A* is introduced with an "ant, alligator, ape and adder asleep in the afternoon." In the accompanying full-color, full-page illustration, a smiling alligator sleeps in a hammock, and above in the trees is a sleeping ape and a dozing adder. The rest of the sequence is introduced in a similar manner.

34. Davis, Jim. *Garfield A to Z Zoo.* Illustrated by Mike Fentz & Dave Kuhn. New York: Random House, 1984.

    Imaginary zoo animals with names beginning with selected

letters introduce the alphabetical sequence. Surprised by a grak bird, Garfield hits his head and becomes unconscious. He imagines nonsense zoo animals from Aquawalker, an animal who teaches swamp surfing, to a Zuni bird, who likes talking and giggling on a telephone.

35. de Brunhoff, Laurent. *Babar's ABC.* Illustrated by the author. New York: Random House, 1983.

    In Celesteville, Babar and the other animals introduce the alphabet beginning with Arthur, the little elephant with an accordion, and ending with Zephir, the little monkey. Each object represents a key word shown in bold that is used in an alliterative sentence. The sentences are beneath either the large illustrations or smaller inserts, and both capitals and lowercase letters are presented.

36. DeLage, Ida. *ABC Fire Dogs.* Illustrated by Ellen Sloan. Champaign, Ill.: Garrard, 1977.

    Wearing fire fighters' clothing, personified dalmatians announce they are fire dogs and introduce words related to the topic in alphabetical order from alarm to zone. Examples of word choices include o'clock, very (e.g., Mother Cat is very happy), and quick. The letter *X* is for wax put on the fire engine and bell. Key words are shown in bold in the text. K-1.

37. DeLage, Ida. *ABC Pigs Go to Market.* Illustrated by Kelly Oechsli. Champaign, Ill.: Garrard, 1977.

    A family of Mother Pig and the little pigs go to the market where they find items in alphabetical order from apples to vanilla ice cream. The letter *W* stands for "wait for your change," *X* is for Mrs. Fox; *Y* is for a yard of material; and *Z* is for zero—no money left for Mother pig.

38. Dragonwagon, Crescent. *Alligator Arrived with Apples: A Potluck Alphabet Feast.* Illustrated by Jose Aruego & Ariane Dewey. New York: Macmillan, 1987.

    The rhymes introduce the letters through a Thanksgiving potluck party with the foods and guests in alphabetical order. Two pink pigs wait for the guests at a table set with name tags for animals from alligator to turkey to zebra. The turkey is not

part of the feast, but a guest instead, and brings tomatoes, trifle, and turnips. There is no name tag *X* but the letter stands
for excellent yams. The animals take Thanksgiving naps at the
end of the book, and the endpapers show the labeled foods
from the alligator's apples to the zebra's zucchini. Full-color illustrations.

39. Duke, Kate. *The Guinea Pig ABC.* Illustrated by the author.
New York: Dutton, 1983.
    Duke's full-color illustrations show the actions of guinea
pigs, which introduce large colorful letters and key words in
capitals. The guinea pigs get dirty, get clean, are loud, are
timid, and hang upside down. The letter *X* is for finding an
extra shoe.

40. Eichenberg, Fritz. *Ape in a Cape: An Alphabet of Odd Animals.*
Illustrated by the author. New York: Harcourt Brace Jovanovich, 1952.
    Still other alphabet books, such as Eichenberg's, offer a rich
background for rhyme. Eichenberg creates an unusual assortment of animals in the illustrations along with a short rhyming
caption for each one. For example, the children see a tall lizard
standing beside a wizard who is dressed in a bright red gown.
The wizard waves a wand to sprinkle sparkling stars in a bright
blue sky.

41. Gretz, Susanna. *Teddy Bears ABC.* Illustrated by the author.
Chicago: Follett, 1974.
    Five teddy bears are engaged in lively antics as they move
from letter to letter through the alphabet. They arrive at the airport, find fleas, keep kangaroos in a kitchen, and finally zip off
to the zoo where they watch a big brown bear who in turn stares
back at the teddy bears.

42. Hague, Kathleen. *Alphabears: An ABC Book.* Illustrated by
Michael Hague. New York: Holt, 1984.
    In full-color illustrations, teddy bears with human behaviors
introduce the colorful block letters and the rhymes in large
print. For example, *A* is for Amanda who carries apples in a
wheelbarrow, *Y* is for York, a young bear, who sits in a high chair

at the table, and *Z* is for Zak, who thinks zippers are better than buttons. The letter *X* is for a mark in the sand so an unnamed bear can return to the same spot on the beach.

43. Jefferds, Vincent. *Disney's Elegant ABC Book*. Illustrated by Disney Reproductions. New York: Simon & Schuster, 1983.

    Colorful uppercase letters are introduced by rhyming verses and characters from the Disney movies—Bambi, Cinderella, and Dumbo. Some of Disney's original characters such as Goofy and Donald Duck as well as famous storybook characters such as Eyore and Pinocchio can be recognized. Additional verses in a section in the back give directions for writing selected capitals in manuscript.

44. Kellogg, Steven. *Aster Aardvark's Alphabet Adventures*. Illustrated by the author. New York: Morrow, 1987.

    Having an aversion to the alphabet, Aster Aardvark receives an airplane from her Aunt Agnes, who hopes it will help increase Aster's academic achievement. On her adventures, Aster meets several animal characters beginning with Bertha Bear and her Brooklyn buddies and ending with sleeping zebras. The letter *X* is for Xerxes Ox who became exhausted from exertion after exercise. The catchy alliterative sentences should be chanted aloud and the fingers and feet tapped to keep the beat.

45. Leedy, Loreen. *The Dragon ABC Hunt*. Illustrated by the author. New York: Holiday House, 1986.

    Dragon activities on a scavenger hunt, told in rhymes, introduce colorful capitals and lowercase letters. When ten small blue dragons get bored, Mother suggests they go on a treasure hunt and find objects in alphabetical order, beginning with a red apple and ending with a zebra hiding in the grass. Letters and names of objects are seen in the corners of pages.

46. Lionni, Leo. *Letters To Talk About*. Illustrated by the author. New York: Pantheon, 1985.

    On white backgrounds, gray mice play near, around, and on top of capital block letters in collage illustrations. The actions of the mice have no relationship to the letters of the alphabet on the pages. One mouse juggles on top of the letter *F*, another does a headstand on top of H, and still another balances the letter I on its nose. The sturdy small cardboard pages have no objects or key words. Pre-K.

47. Mack, Stan. *The King's Cat Is Coming.* Illustrated by the author. New York: Pantheon, 1976.

Mack leads a reader to believe the arriving king's cat has human behaviors as he gives descriptive words about it from angry and bashful to zany. A carriage of the Royal Delivery Service delivers a large yellow crate tied with a green ribbon to the king and all wait for a guard to open it so they can see the anticipated cat.

48. Mazzarella, Mimi. *Alphabatty Animals and Funny Foods.* Illustrated by the author. Cockeysville, Md.: Liberty Pub., 1984.

Capitals are introduced by rhymes about twenty-six animals. The personified animals include snappy alligators, a shy bear, and catty cats. No animal introduces the letter X.

49. Merriam, Eve. *Where Is Everybody? An Animal Alphabet.* Illustrated by Diane De Groat. New York: Simon & Schuster, 1989.

In full-color, the animal characters show up in unexpected places and introduce the letters. With humanlike behaviors, the animals range from an alligator in the attic and a bear in the bakery to a yak in the yard and a zebra at the zoo. In most of the illustrations, a little mole is behind a camera and takes pictures of the animals. He is found in such places as a laundry basket, a passing car, and behind a fence. Words that may be unfamiliar to some children are *ibex, narwhal,* and *vicuna.* The letter X is for xenosaurid at the x-ray machine. Some alliteration is in the sentences placed beneath the illustrations.

50. Mills, Carol. *A to Z and Back Again: An ABC Book.* Illustrated by Susanne Ferrier. London, England: Tiger Books, 1962.

Personified animals—Barney Bear, Hilary Hamster, Katy Koala, along with other characters—introduce the letter pairs. A reader finds oversized letters and the character's name as the key word accompanied by a verse and full-color illustration. The letter X is introduced by Xerxes Ox, who lived in a box, and *Z* by Zebedee Zebra, who played the zither with zest and zeal.

51. Milne, A. A. *Pooh's Alphabet Book.* Illustrated by E. H. Shepard. New York: Dutton, 1965.

Milne's character, Pooh, takes a child on an alphabetical tour to meet his animal friends and to see some of their problems. For example, small Piglet tries hard to be brave; taking a bath bothers little Piglet when Kanga gets soap in his mouth; and baby Roo is not bothered at all, but delighted, when Tigger takes Roo's medicine by mistake. Both Pooh and Wise Owl are bothered by some spelling problems, and brave Pooh meets a tree-roosting Jagular, dreams of a big Heffalump in his sleep, and tells how he likes Rabbit's short, one-syllable words.

52. Obligado, Lilian. *Faint Frogs Feeling Feverish and Other Terrifically Tantalizing Tongue Twisters.* Illustrated by the author. New York: Viking, 1983.

A student who takes time to look carefully at this book discovers such humorous pictures as a green frog "feeling feverish" and resting in a wicker chair with an ice pack on his head, a thermometer in his mouth, and a paper fan in his hand; an energetic flamingo who fans the frog "faint with fever," and pandas who patrol for pickpockets (panthers) and are armed with purple pistols. Juggling jackrabbits, zipping zebras, whistling wombats, and adding aardvarks are found in alliterative sentences that offer choices to students for tongue-twister sessions.

53. Potter, Beatrix. *Peter Rabbit's ABC.* Reproductions of original illustrations by author. London, England: Warne, 1987.

The endpapers, designed by Colin Twinn, show several of Potter's characters from the original illustrations—from Appley Dappley and Benjamin Bunny to Yock-Yock, the pig, and Zzz, bzz, the bees. Capital and lowercase letters are in the corners of the pages, in colored inserts, the key object and key phrase are on left-hand pages and the reproductions in full color are on the right-hand pages. Quotes from the stories are beneath the reproductions.

54. Snow, Alan. *The Monster Book of ABC Sounds.* Illustrated by the author. New York: Dial, 1991.

In a house, monsters play a hide-and-seek game with friendly rats, and the story is told in rhyming lines. Capital and lower-case letters are in the illustrations, which are bordered in the objects seen in the full-color scenes. The monsters' sounds from "aaaaah!" to the Zs of their snoring are featured in dialogue balloons and relate to the featured letter on the page. A list of objects that may be unfamiliar to some young children—emu, javelin, x-ray fish—is included at the end of the book.

55. Stock, Catherine. *Alexander's Midnight Snack: A Little Elephant's ABC.* Illustrated by the author. New York: Ticknor, 1988.

This alphabet book introduces children to names of foods in an amusing way. Alexander, the little elephant, wakes up and wants a glass of water but once in the kitchen, he finds that the apple pie looks good. He proceeds to eat (or do) something for every letter beginning with apple pie and buns, and ending with a yawn and sleep (ZZZZZZZZ). The key words are shown with red capitals in black text and the letter *X* is for an X ray of what Alexander's stomach looks like. For a second ending, Mother sees the mess in the kitchen the next morning.

56. Tryon, Leslie. *Albert's Alphabet.* Illustrated by the author. New York: Atheneum, 1991.

Albert, a clever goose who is the school carpenter, is asked to build an alphabet for a path on the playground along with repairing a leaky drinking fountain by three o'clock in the afternoon. To do this, Albert plans and uses the material he has to make unusual letters with innovative building techniques. After Albert uses all his lumber and his only box, he selects other materials to form the letters—rocks, plants, pipes, laundry, sprinklers, and finally, as a surprise, rearranges his house into two stories to make the shape of the letter *Z*. In the final double-page spread, an alert reader will notice that the drinking fountain has been repaired and is in the shape of the letter *U*.

57. Whitehead, Pat. *Arnold Plays Baseball.* Illustrated by G. Brian Karas. Mahwah, N.J.: Troll, 1985.

Letter pairs are introduced by key words in corners of pages.

Key words are from the text about Arnold, who is unhappy and restless when rainy weather keeps him inside and prevents him from playing baseball. When the rain stops and Arnold realizes he can go outside to play, the letter *X* stands for the word, exclaims, *Y* is for yippee, and *Z* is for zipping up his jacket.

58. Whitehead, Pat. *Here Comes Hungry Albert.* Illustrated by G. Brian Karas. Mahwah, N.J.: Troll, 1985.

Hungry Albert, an ape, can always eat more and starts in on a sack of groceries—bananas, carrots, doughnuts. In a search for ice cream, Albert arrives at the zoo's ice cream stand where he orders a strawberry cone.

59. Woolcock, Peter. *Animal ABC.* Illustrated by the author. London, England: Octopus Books, 1980.

Beginning with armadillos acting through monkeys making mischief and ending with zebras zigzagging (while driving a jeep), the letter pairs are introduced by personified animals in full-color scenes. On oversized pages, alliterative phrases that feature "ing" words accompany the colorful letters.

* CITY LIFE

60. Beller, Janet. *A-B-Cing: An Action Alphabet.* Illustrated by the author. New York: Crown, 1984.

Actions are illustrated by children in scenes and 26 words that end in "ing" tell what's going on. In lowercase letters, each word is at the foot of the page below a black-and-white photograph of the action. Girls and boys climb, read, and zip up clothing. There are no single letters to guide the sequence of the alphabet, so a young child will have to recognize the first letter in each action word or know the sequence of letters in the alphabet.

61. Berger, Terry. *Ben's Day.* Illustrated by Alice Kandell. New York: Lothrop, Lee, & Shepard, 1981.

Berger's alphabet book is about doing things in a child's world. Each of Ben's activities begins with a letter of the alphabet from *A,* awakening, to *Z,* quiet snoring with zzzzzzzzz. Clear, full-color photographs provide a photo essay for children. Illustrations for such actions as joking and questioning may be unclear to viewers at first and will need elaboration.

62. DeLage, Ida. *ABC Triplets at the Zoo.* Illustrated by Lori Pierson. Champaign, Ill.: Garrard, 1980.

The ABC triplets go on a walk through the zoo and introduce objects related to the topic in alphabetical order from animals to zebra. Familiar animals are seen—monkey, night owl, tiger. The letter *F* is for feed, *L* is for lunch, and *X* is for train crossing. The key words and letters are in bold on the pages.

63. Hughes, Shirley. *Lucy and Tom's A. B. C.* Illustrated by the author. New York: Viking, 1986.

Lucy and her younger brother, Tom, engage in daily activities that introduce the alphabet letters as they meet people and visit places in their town. The letter *A* is for apples, *Z* is for zoo and *X* is for xylophone. The author includes questions for children to answer, e.g., "Can you see where the children live?" "Can you guess what it is?" and "Which voice do you like best of all?" Full-color illustrations and capital and lowercase letters are in bold type on the full-color pages.

64. Isadora, Rachel. *City Seen from A to Z.* Illustrated by the author. New York: Greenwillow, 1983.

Striking city scenes prepared in textured black-and-white illustrations include a lion design on a T-shirt, an umbrella over a vendor's cart, and a graffiti zoo on a city sidewalk. At first glance, Isadora's illustrations may remind an older viewer of a modern black-and-white pointillistic approach. Block letters in tan are introduced by key words. Subjects are fresh ones, e.g., art for *A,* which shows a large mural of children's faces on a brick building; entrance for *E,* an opening to the subway; and *P* for pigeon, the familiar bird in the city.

65. Johnson, Jean. *Fire Fighters A to Z.* Illustrated by the author. New York: Walker, 1985.

Johnson's alphabet book looks at fire fighters in their working environment, the equipment, and ways they operate as a team. Black-and-white photographs introduce the informational paragraphs, guiding capital letters, and capitalized key words from alarm to zone. The letter *X* is for Xavier, a dalmatian who might have been a fire station mascot some time ago. A concluding section, More about Fire Fighters, provides further discussion material about fire and ways to fight it. Children living in Charlotte, North Carolina, will appreciate the dedication to the fire fighters of their city. Other titles by Johnson in Walker's Community Helpers series are *Police Officers A to Z; Postal Workers A to Z; Teachers A to Z; Librarians A to Z;* and *Sanitation Workers A to Z.*

66. Moak, Allan. *A Big City ABC.* Illustrated by the author. Montreal, Canada: Tundra Books, 1981.

With lowercase letters to guide the sequence, paintings of Toronto introduce traditional sentence beginnings for the alphabet with *A* is for . . . , *B* is for . . ., and so on. Informative paragraphs give facts about the places from Casa Loma, a medieval castle with towers and secret passages, to Toronto's skating rink in front of city hall.

67. Poulin, Stephanie. *Ah! Belle Cite!* Illustrated by the author. Montreal, Canada: Tundra Books, 1985.

    With single word captions in English and French to guide the sequence, paintings of Montreal introduce the letters. Author's notes with additional information at the back of the book.

68. Rosario, Idalia. *Idalia's Proyecto ABC/An Urban Alphabet Book in English and Spanish.* Illustrated by the author. New York: Holt, Rinehart & Winston, 1981.

    In black-and-white illustrations with touches of red, a reader sees life in a city housing project beginning with "asking Papo's mother if he can come out" for the letter *A* and ending with zoo for the letter *Z*. The Spanish alphabet has three more letter/sound relationships (ch, ll, and nn) than the English alphabet and are included.

69. Stevenson, James. *Grandpa's Great City Tour: An Alphabet Book.* Illustrated by the author. New York: Greenwillow, 1983.

    Flying with an alligator pilot on Alligator Airlines, Grandpa takes Louie and Mary Ann on an alphabetical tour of the city through to *X, Y,* and *Z* with a zebra playing a xylophone in the gondola of a balloon decorated with *x*'s and advertising yummy yogurt. Each spread shows a part of the city—the harbor, the park with a carousel, shops, and the museum. The concluding page shows a review with twenty-six colorful balloons each featuring one of the capitals flying above the city.

70. Whitehead, Pat. *Let's Go to the Zoo.* Illustrated by Patti Boyd. Mahwah, N.J.: Troll, 1985.

    Small children visit the city zoo and letter pairs are introduced by key words related to the topic from the letter *A* for the word choice *along,* to *Z* for *zebra.* Unusual word choices that are difficult to show in illustrations include the key word *idea,* for the letter *I, join* for *J, quite* for *Q, unusual* for *U, velvet* for *V, exactly* for *X,* and *can* for *C,* with the accompanying question, "Can you take us to the zoo?"

* COUNTRY LIFE

71. Azarian, Mary. *A Farmer's Alphabet.* Illustrated by the author. New York: Godine, 1981.

    Azarian's book has concepts and illustrations about New England suitable for older children, too. Bright-red letters complement the black-and-white woodcut illustrations. Concluding pages have author's notes about the woodcut process.

72. Burton, Marilee Robin. *Aaron Awoke: An Alphabet Story.* Illustrated by the author. New York: Harper & Row, 1982.

    For each letter, a reader sees Aaron and an alphabetical day of work and play with his friends and finds objects in the illustrations that begin with the letter. Hidden objects are found again on the end pages in a right-to-left ABC sequence that follows the margins. Alliteration.

73. Cameron, Elizabeth. *A Floral ABC.* Illustrated by the author. New York: Morrow, 1983.

    Descriptive writing, folklore, verses, and illustrations of wild flowers introduce the block letters found in inserts. Examples range from anemone, the wind flower, for the letter *A* through ivy, a flower believed to have magical powers when accompanied by holly, and zigzag clover, once called claver, for *Z*.

74. Cameron, Elizabeth. *A Wildflower Alphabet.* Illustrated by the author. New York: Morrow, 1984.

    Beginning with avens, a member of the rose family, hand-lettered descriptions and illustrations of flowers found in Scotland introduce the letters. Lore about the flowers is accompanied by where it's grown and what it is used for.

75. Ehlert, Lois. *Eating the Alphabet: Fruits and Vegetables from A to*

Z. Illustrated by the author. New York: Harcourt Brace Jovanovich, 1989.

Fruits and vegetables such as asparagus, raddichio, and ugli fruit are clearly labeled and shown in bright watercolor collages. A glossary of edibles ends the book.

76. Feldman, Judy. *The Alphabet in Nature.* Illustrated by the author. Chicago: Childrens Press, 1991.

A child may supply the words while learning about the shapes of letters found in the full-color photographs of animals and nature scenes. The photographs are captioned and identify the names of some of the objects, e.g., dewdrops on grass, snake, and the head of a bighorn ram. Unusual scenes from nature are included; for example, the letter *X* is introduced by a spiderweb found in Barbados that is shaped like an *X.*

77. Kinkaid, Eric & Kinkaid, Lucy. *Benji's Book of ABC.* Illustrated by the authors. London: Brimax, 1980.

Rhyming lines and illustrations about Benji, a small boy, introduce key words—apple, bee, zebra—and pairs of capital and lowercase letters. On each page, a second illustration of Benji is inserted, and the sentences are linked across two pages.

78. Lobel, Anita. *Alison's Zinnia.* Illustrated by the author. New York: Greenwillow, 1990.

In the book, flowers are connected to girls' names along with action verbs, and the ending connects back to the beginning. Oversized paintings of flowers introduce the alphabet capitals and are accompanied by alliterative sentences, e.g., "Alison acquired an amaryllis for Beryl," and "Zena zeroed in on a zinnia for Alison." Author's note discusses the interest in painting flowers and concludes the book.

79. Lyon, George Ella. *A B Cedar: An Alphabet of Trees.* Illustrated by Tom Parker. New York: Watts, 1989.

The sequence is with capitals across the tops of pages and the names of leaves of trees from aspen for *A* to zebrawood for *Z* are introduced in order. On white backgrounds, illustrations show hands of children from different ethnic groups holding leaves, catching nuts, and pulling leaves aside to look through branches. A final page mentions a tree's contribution to make the book.

80. Mendoza, George. *Alphabet Sheep*. Illustrated by Kathleen Reidy. New York: Grosset & Dunlap, 1982.

     When a shepherd loses a sheep, he searches in places in alphabetical order beginning in the air for *A* and ending when the sheep is found fast asleep for *Z*. Capitals and the sheep in different poses are found in the corners of pages, and key words—air, barn, coop—are in bold in the text.

81. Miller, Jane. *Farm Alphabet Book*. Illustrated by the author. London: J. M. Dents & Sons, 1981/New York: Prentice, 1984.

     Miller's clear, colorful photographs show farm objects to a reader, and the information in sentences gives facts: A sow is the name of the mother pig, a boar is the father, and a piglet is a young pig. Unfamiliar words for some children may be quill and incubator.

82. Pallotta, Jerry. *The Flower Alphabet Book*. Illustrated by Leslie Evans. Boston: Quinlan Press, 1988.

     Beginning with amaryllis for *A*, a flower named for a shepherdess in classical Greek poetry, and ending with zinnia, named for its discoverer, Professor Zinn, for *Z*, a reader discovers interesting facts—origins of names, uses, and shapes—about the selected flowers. Artist's notes with information about each one conclude the book.

83. Rice, James. *Cajun Alphabet*. Illustrated by the author. Gretna, La.: Pelican Pub., 1976.

     For an older student, Gaston, a personified alligator, gives a Cajun French lesson about Cajun society, language, and culture.

84. Rice, James. *Cowboy Alphabet*. Illustrated by the author. Austin, Tex: Shoal Creek Pub., 1990.

     The book is written with an "eye to the education of adults as well as children" and is a "primer" to initiate the reader into rodeo lore, desert fauna, cowboy dress, and other aspects of cowboy life through illustrations and text. From armadillo for the letter *A* to zillion for *Z*, a reader finds that the illustrated phenomena of the Southwest introduces the letter pairs. Unusual word choices include nighthawk (a guard at night) for *N*, ramrod for *R*, and XIT, one of the biggest ranches in the world, for *X*. For an older student who has an interest in the west, the full-color sequence illustrates word choices that relate to the west, e.g., jerky, kangaroo court, lariat, horned toads, valley, and quarter horse.

85. Watson, Clyde. *Applebet: An ABC.* Illustrated by Wendy Watson. New York: Farrar, Straus & Giroux, 1982.
    A small girl and her mother travel to a country fair to see the entertainment and sample the exhibited foods. In each illustration, a red apple appears and creates a visual game of look-and-point.

86. Whitehead, Pat. *Let's Go to the Farm.* Illustrated by Ethel Gold. Mahwah, N. J.: Troll, 1985.
    A small boy and girl visit a farm, see the animals, and hear the sounds the animals make. For example, the calf's moo introduces the letter *M*, a colt's neigh the *N*, and the piglet's oink for *O*. Block upper- and lowercase letters are found in page corners with word choices found twice—above the illustration and in the text on the page.

87. Wilner, Isabel. *A Garden Alphabet.* Illustrated by Ashley Wolff. New York: Dutton, 1991.
    The letters of the alphabet from *A* for April to *Z* for the zzzing of buzzing bees are introduced by full-color illustrations and rhyming lines. Both print and pictures describe the way a garden can be planted and how vegetables, such as kale, lettuce, onion, and peas grow. The letter *X* is for excitement and the pleasure a garden brings to gardeners who know that "whatever is ready is ready for tasting."

88. Wolf, Janet. *Adelaide to Zeke.* Illustrated by the author. New York: Harper & Row, 1987.
    In a community setting that features a red barn and silo, a central grassy area in the center, a pond, cows, chickens, and goats, twenty-six children interact with one another and intro-

duce the letters in sequence. Colorful capitals are shown one per page, and each features a child, e.g., Adelaide bothers Benny who blows bubbles at Claudia who calls Dr. Dan, and so on. The letter *X* is for Xavier who sails in his boat, the *S. S. Xavier,* *Y* is for Yetta who yawns, and *Z* for Zeke who zigzags home in a hot air balloon. A final illustration shows all of the children for a review.

* HISTORY

89. Ackerman, Karen. *Flannery Row: An Alphabet Rhyme.* Illustrated by the author. New York: Little, Brown, 1986.

   Before sailing at sea, Commander Ahab Flannery says good-bye to his twenty-six children in alphabetical order so no child is missed. Letters are in the same colors as the child's clothing for a matching activity, and each child's picture is above the featured letter in the child's name. End pages show the children in ABC order.

90. Anglund, Joan Walsh. *In a Pumpkin Shell: A Mother Goose ABC.* Illustrated by the author. New York: Harcourt Brace Jovanovich, 1960.

   Detailed black-and-white drawings alternate with full-color illustrations. Mother Goose rhymes are in alphabetical order with a letter and key word for each verse. Some verses, such as the one describing the fight between the lion and the unicorn may be unfamiliar to some girls and boys.

91. Brown, Marcia. *Peter Piper's Practical Principles of Plain and Perfect Pronunciation.* Illustrated by the author. New York: Scribner's, 1974.

   A child may enjoy listening to the alliterative questions about Andrew Airpump, Billy Button, and Captain Crackskull, and others in this version. With the exception of the letters *X, Y,* and *Z,* there is question for every letter in sequence. For example, the tongue twister for *B:* Billy Button bought a buttered biscuit. If Billy button bought a buttered biscuit, where's the buttered biscuit Billy Button bought?"

92. Burgess, George. *The Adventures of A Apple Pie.* Illustrated by the author. New York: 1973.

   Burgess's book is a reprint of an 1835 publication in which

children introduce the beginning traditional phrases about an apple pie. The children demonstrate a curtsy to the pie, dream about it, and fight for it. Some of the words such as illuminated, yeomaned, and Xantippe, may have to be explained to today's young children.

93. Craft, Kinuko. *Mother Goose ABC.* Illustrated by the author. New York: Platt & Munk, 1977.

   Oversized full-color illustrations are bordered and have the Mother Goose rhymes inserted over the pictures. Parts of the paintings blend into the text area. For examples, waves wash down toward the rhyme about a ship a-sailing, a north wind edges into the words about how the wind doth blow, and outlines of fairies fly close to the rhyme about Margery Daw.

94. Crane, Walter. *An Alphabet of Old Friends* and *The Absurd ABC.* Illustrated by the author. New York: Metropolitan Museum of Art/Thames & Hudson, 1981.

   First published in 1874 and now published in one volume, *Old Friends* includes familiar nursery rhymes, and *The Absurd ABC* has rewritten verses of "Hey Diddle Diddle" and other favorites. As an example, the letter *C* stands for a cat who plays the fiddle while the cows jump high . . . "higher than Heigh Diddle, Diddle!" The illustrations are reproduced in full color and gold highlights from the originals in The Metropolitan Museum of Art.

95. Delaunay, Sonia. *Sonia Delaunay Alphabet.* Illustrated by the author. New York: Crowell, 1972.

   Each letter, an original painting by the avant-garde artist, is introduced by English nursery rhymes. For examples, a bright red capital *A* rests over squares of blue, red, green, and black, and the letters *I* and *L* are bordered in bold green and red. Rhymes include such choices as the riddle of "Elizabeth, Lissie, Betsy, and Bess," a tongue twister, "Thomas a'Tattamus," and a chant about jumping.

96. Der Manuelian, Peter. *Hieroglyphs from A to Z.* Illustrated by the author. Boston: Museum of Fine Arts, 1991.

This alphabet book shows the relationship of the English alphabet and Egyptian hieroglyphs. Letters are introduced with hieroglyphs and reproductions of ancient carvings and paintings. At the foot of each page is a smaller hieroglyph that represents the sound of the English letter. History and chart of hieroglyphs and a stencil for writing words and sentences in hieroglyphs are included.

97. *Dolly at Home ABC.* Illustrated by unnamed artist. New York: Merrimack Pub., n. d.
     In a replica of an antique original, a reader of today sees dolls in situations beginning with an artist dolly through a dolly learning ABC lessons to a yawn for a tired dolly. With the exception of a few colored illustrations, black-and-white outlines of activities with dolls illustrate each capital letter. Some of the words in the rhymes may be unfamiliar ones, e.g., Ethelberta fair, frock, jammy tarts, displaced, omnibus, Prudence, tubbing-time, Una, and coverlet.

98. Domanska, Janina. *A Was an Angler.* Illustrated by the author. New York: Greenwillow, 1991.
     Beginning with the letter *A* for an angler and ending with *Z* for zebra, a reader finds a traditional Mother Goose alphabet and illustrations of watercolors, colored pencils, and a black pen. Familiar words are found as most of the choices—custard, egg, fox—but some word usage may not be known by children of today, e.g., pate, betimes, lest, nosegay, bodkin, and Xerxes.

99. Dowdell, Dorothy. *The Secrets of the ABC's.* Illustrated by Marilu Johnson. Fayetteville, Ga.: Oddo, 1958.
     Presents the origin of the English alphabet and traces the history from the time when letters did not exist through times when people drew pictures on walls and carved stories on buildings. Originating from the letter inventions of the Phoenicians, Greeks, and Romans, the letters haven't changed in the last 500 years. As examples, the letter *A* began as the drawing of the head of an ox, the letter *B* began as the plan of a house, and *C* was first drawn to look like the head and neck of a camel.

100. Greenaway, Kate. *A Apple Pie: An Old Fashioned Alphabet Book.* Illustrated by the author. New York: Warne, n.d. original published in 1886.

     Greenaway's old-fashioned ABC book shows youngsters skipping around a giant apple pie. One boy bites it, a girl cuts it, and another deals it. Some boys fight for it, and other children jump, kneel, and mourn for the pie. Others run, sing, and then take the pie away. For a group of letters UVWXYZ, all the children have a large slice and go off to bed. The letter *I* is not included because this alphabet goes back to an early use when the letters *I* and *J* were used as one letter.

101. Jones, Karen H. *From A to Z: A Folk Art Alphabet.* Illustrated by Art Reproductions. Pittstown, N.J.: Main Street Press, 1985.

     Designed like an alphabet primer of the past, works of art of post-Revolutionary America introduce the key words from apple to zebra. Quotations from Noah Webster, Gilbert Stuart, Thomas Bedwick, and others relate to the objects and are followed by informative paragraphs. As examples, a reader sees the paintings of *George Washington on a White Charger* (National Gallery of Art); Joseph Mantel's *Boy with Rooster* (Winterhur); and Jonathan Fisher's *The Male Zebra* (Farnsworth Art Museum).

102. Lalicki, Barbara. *If There Were Dreams to Sell.* Illustrated by Margot Tomes. New York: Lothrop, Lee & Shepard, 1984.

     For each upper- and lowercase letter, illustrations and verses or poetic phrases are presented along with capitalized key words. Tempera and watercolor illustrations have scenes of animals, elves, and British and American colonial villages.

103. Lear, Edward. *An Edward Lear Alphabet.* Illustrated by Carol Newsom. New York: Lothrop, Lee & Shepard, 1983.

     Newsom's illustrations and Lear's nonsense verses introduce the letters of the alphabet. The verses have families of word endings, and adding interest through episodic parallel activities, a small mouse can be found in every scene.

104. Lear, Edward. *Edward Lear's ABC: Alphabet Rhymes for*

Children. Illustrated by Carol Pike. Topsfield, Me: Salem House, 1986.

First appearing in *Nonsense Songs, Stories, Botany and Alphabets,* 1871, the rhymes introduce the letters. Both upper- and lowercase letters are in bordered inserts in full-color illustrations from apple pie to zinc.

105. Lear, Edward. *Lear Alphabet Penned and Illustrated by Edward Lear Himself.* Illustrated by the author. New York: McGraw-Hill, 1965.

Lear's original verses from 1871 are bordered in red and blue beginning with *A* for busy ants trying to build a hillside home. Other versions of Lear's verses are suitable book companions and can be found in *A Nonsense Alphabet* (Doubleday, 1961) illustrated by Richard Scarry, in *The Nonsense Alphabet* (Grosset & Dunlap, 1961) illustrated by Art Seiden, and in *The First ABC* (Watts, 1971) edited by Frank Waters and illustrated by Charles Mozley.

106. Lear, Edward. *A New Nonsense Alphabet.* Edited by Susan Hyman. London, England: Bloomsbury, 1988.

In 1862, Lear promised an alphabet to a new baby, the granddaughter of friends. The alphabet gift was drawn in deep blue ink on pale blue linen and is reproduced in the book along with its accompanying letter to the child, Lear's original sketches, Lear's photograph, and an addendum of his discoveries.

107. Livingston, Myra Cohn. *A Learical Lexicon.* Illustrated by Joseph Low. New York.: Atheneum, 1985.

Livingston selects some of Lear's outlandish words and introduces them in alphabetical order. A reader finds words with unusual spellings, hidden meanings, transposed letters, and onomatopoetic sounds.

108. Lobel, Arnold. *On Market Street.* Illustrated by Anita Lobel. With Afterword by Richard Meran Barsam. New York: Viking, 1981.

A small boy, dressed in blue, buys his way through the ABCs, and beside each capital is a creative image of a person formed from the item itself or from the item's category. The artist was motivated by seventeenth-century French trade engravings to develop the images, and he created a person of apples for the letter *A,* one of books for *B,* and one of clocks for *C.* After shopping, the small boy, tired and weary, brings the presents to a friend, a large white cat.

109. Mayers, Florence Cassen. *ABC: The Alef-Bet Book: The Israel Museum, Jerusalem.* Illustrated by art reproductions selected by author. New York: Abrams, 1989.

A reader turns the book over since a Hebrew book opens from right to left and finds the first letter in this bilingual alphabet book—alef and its key object, the lion, represented by ivory statues of two crouching lions. Other images from the culture of Israel, including the Dead Sea Scrolls, the oldest biblical manuscripts in the world, introduce the letters, and the selected key words are transliterated (spelled in English letters) to show how they may be pronounced.

110. Mayers, Florence Cassen. *ABC: Egyptian Art from The Brooklyn Museum.* Illustrated by art reproductions selected by author. New York: Abrams, 1988.

From a pottery jar more than five thousand years old to a mummy of an ibis that is more than one thousand years old, a reader finds a work of art that is centuries old to introduce each letter pair. At the foot of each page are informative notes about the object. For example, several facts are given about the ibis. The ibis (seen on the page for the letter *I*) was a sacred animal and preserved after death as a mummy (seen on the page for the letter *M*) in a special coffin in the animal's shape. An X ray of an object wrapped in linen showed that a mummified ibis was inside the cloth (seen on the page for the letter *X*).

111. Mayers, Florence Cassen. *ABC: Museum of Fine Arts, Boston.* Illustrated by art reproductions selected by author. New York: Abrams, 1986.

Oversized letter pairs in color and twenty-six color illustrations introduce various objects from the Fine Arts Collection in the Boston Museum. A younger child reviews the letters, and an older child gets acquainted with some of the items to be found on a tour—golden mummy case and an X ray of the skull and rib cage of a mummy.

112. Mayers, Florence Cassen. *ABC: The Museum of Modern Art, New York.* Illustrated by art reproductions selected by author. New York: Abrams, 1986.

    Modern art objects are arranged in alphabetical sequence—a bathrobe, cheeseburgers, and a kitchen. Some paintings that may be unfamiliar to some children are Matisse's *Dance* and Van Gogh's *Starry Night.*

113. Mayers, Florence Cassen. *ABC: Musical Instruments from the Metropolitan Museum of Art.* Illustrated by art reproductions selected by author. New York: Abrams, 1988.

    A reader finds each letter is introduced by one or more instruments from the Metropolitan Museum of Art. Familiar ones are the piano and drum, but most of the selections may be unfamiliar ones to most children in the United States: ipu, jingling Johnnie, nyckelharpa, saron slen tem, udu pots, walking stick instruments, yunluo, and zither.

114. Mayers, Florence Cassen. *ABC, National Air and Space Museum.* Illustrated by art reproductions selected by author. New York: Abrams, 1987.

    Images of objects related to Einstein, Lindbergh, Yeager, and others affiliated with air and space introduce the letter pairs to a reader. A photograph of Einstein, the propeller of Lindbergh's *Spirit of St. Louis,* and the experimental *X-1* flown by Chuck Yeager are seen.

115. Mayers, Florence Cassen. *ABC, National Museum of American History.* Illustrated by art reproductions selected by author. New York: Abrams, 1989.

    Examples of American history, crafts, and ingenuity introduce the letters with *A* for a liberty model automobile (Buick Runabout); *F* for flag that inspired Francis Scott Key to write *The Star-Spangled Banner,* and *X* for xerographic machine invented by Chester Carlson. Unfamiliar choices for some children may be the gowns of nation's first ladies and their names from Martha Washington (1789–97) to Jacqueline Kennedy (1961–1963).

116. Mayers, Florence Cassen. *ABC, The Wild West Buffalo Bill Historical Center, Cody, Wyoming.* Illustrated by art reproductions selected by author. New York: Abrams, 1990.

On tall, slender pages like the other books in the series, each letter is introduced with one or more objects from the Buffalo Bill Historical Center. Familiar objects include dolls, feathers, gloves, jugs, and vests. Of special interest are Buffalo Bill's saddle, a restored stagecoach from his Wild West show, and a Bonheur portrait.

117. Paul, Ann Whitford. *Eight Hands Round: A Patchwork Alphabet.* Illustrated by Jeanette Winter. New York: HarperCollins, 1991.

From the anvil quilt pattern for the letter *A* to the zigzag pattern for *Z,* the letters of the alphabet are introduced with names of early American patchwork quilt patterns and the origins of the designs are explained and related to the activity or occupation they derived from in the past.

118. Pearson, Tracy Campbell. *A Apple Pie.* Illustrated by the author. New York: Dial, 1986.

Capitals are introduced by phrases as this alphabet unfolds to show humor and busy children in the illustrations and large text about a hot apple pie.

119. Postman, Frederica. *The Yiddish Alphabet Book.* Illustrated by Bonnie Stone. New York: Adama, 1979.

Historically, Yiddish is an ancient language that once linked millions of people, and because Yiddish is read from right to left, the book is opened from the right to present the twenty-two basic letters of the Yiddish alphabet and the key words that demonstrate the sound of each letter. The end pages have a guide to transliteration, i.e., Yiddish letters and words in the English alphabet so a reader of English will know how to pronounce them.

120. Provensen, Alice & Provensen, Martin. *A Peaceable Kingdom:*

The Shaker Abecedarius. Illustrated by the authors. With Afterword by Richard Meran Barsam. New York: Viking, 1978.

This Shaker alphabet verse of the late 1800s is useful during a study of the time period. Taken from the *Shaker Manifesto* of 1881, the first line of twenty-six in this rhyming verse begins with an *A* word, the second line a *B* word, and so on.

121. Rubin, Cynthia Elyce, selecter. *ABC Americana from the National Gallery of Art.* Illustrated by art reproductions. New York: Harcourt Brace Jovanovich, 1989.

The National Gallery of Art presents twenty-six examples of American folk art to introduce the alphabet. Beginning with the letter *A* introduced by an angel, a copper weather vane, and ending with a zigzag design in a petit point handbag for *Z*, a child should find interesting things to see. Capitals are introduced and framed at the top of pages. Watercolor paintings are from the Index of American Design. A list of objects identifies artists and concludes the book.

122. Stockham, Peter, ed. *Chapbook ABC's: Reprints of Five Rare and Charming Early Juveniles.* Illustrated by reprints. New York: Dover, 1974.

In the eighteenth and nineteenth centuries, a small chapbook (2″ × 3″) similar to this was offered for about a penny and often sold from door to door as well as in bookstores. Five reprints are offered that represent some of the alphabets for children living in those times: *The Picture Alphabet for the Instruction and Amusement of Boys and Girls* (William Walker, 1830); *The Golden Pippin* (Boyle & Co.); *The Silver Penny for the Amusement and Instruction of Good Children* (J. Kendrew); *The Picture Alphabet* (T. Richardson); and *The Galloping Guide to the ABC* (or *The Child's Agreeable Introduction to a Knowledge of the Gentlemen of the Alphabet*) (J. G. Rusher).

123. Stockham, Peter, ed. *The Mother's Picture Alphabet.* Illustrated by Henry Anelay. New York: Dover, 1975.

Dedicated to her Royal Highness, Princess Beatrice, this is a reprint of a Victorian alphabet book first published in 1862.

For instance, for the letter *Q*, the book pays a tribute to "dear" Queen Victoria and her reign ". . . happy, and useful, and long." For girls and boys of today, a special curiosity may be met as they search and find some of the items that are no longer used on a regular basis in everyday life in the United States. A reader finds such items as a bandbox, inkstand, and slate. Full-page black-and-white drawings face the pages of rhyming verses.

124. Sullivan, Charles, editor. *Alphabet Animals.* Illustrated by art reproductions selected by editor. New York: Rizzoli International, 1991.

The letters are introduced with paintings, photographs of animals, and sculpture from international museum collections. Accompanying each item is a poem that introduces varied moods, rhythms, and sentence structure so that a reader can enjoy different tones of poetry. Of note are the selections from the sixteenth century [Albrecht Durer (1502)] and from the nineteenth century (works of John James Audubon, George Catlin, and Winslow Homer). The author's note mentions that the purpose of the book is to associate each letter with something in the world of animals and with significant works of art, and a list of acknowledgments lists the sources of the included items. Of special interest is the inclusion of *Porcupine,* a 1951 woodcut by Leonard Baskin, author/artist of *Hosie's Alphabet* (3). Further, the author encourages readers to correspond and includes an address: P.O. Box 1775, Annapolis, Md. 21404.

125. Tudor, Tasha. *A Is for Annabelle.* Illustrated by the author. New York: Walck, 1981.

Tudor's alphabet tells something about Grandmother's doll, and the letters are placed on the left-hand page while the right-hand page shows a sentence beneath the illustrations. Black-and-white illustrations alternate with pale watercolors and are bordered with flower garlands. Some young children will need to have certain words, such as overskirt, parasol, and zither, explained. Original printed in 1954.

* LETTER TRANSFORMATIONS

126. Anno, Mistumasa. *Anno's Alphabet: An Adventure in Imagination.* Illustrated by the author. New York: Harper & Row, 1975.

With careful observation, a reader can find if something is missing from the letters. For example, resting against a mirror, only one-half of the letter *M* is shown. Additional objects can be found in the borders of the illustrations. Anno shows the intricacies of woodblock arrangements to form the alphabet in these illustrations. Examples to point out to children: An *E,* its top and bottom stem pointing to the left, has a center stem projecting toward the viewer; one half of the letter *M* rests against a mirror, enabling the viewer to see the entire letter; and the letter *O* is made with two wooden half-circle shapes leaning against one another. Culminating pages are a guide that gives the names of most of the objects.

127. Arnosky, Jim. *Mouse Writing.* Illustrated by the author. New York: Harcourt Brace Jovanovich, 1983.

Arnosky's book introduces children to letter shapes for cursive writing. To do this, two mice, Cap (the big mouse) and LC (the small mouse) trace each cursive letter shape as they ice-skate on a frozen pond. Ask children to look for the way LC dots the *i*'s and crosses the *t*'s.

128. Bonini, Marinella. *I Can Be the Alphabet.* Illustrated by the author. New York: Viking, 1987.

Body postures of children introduce the letters, and full-color illustrations unfold in an accordion format, making the book useful for a display. Directions are given for bending or turning the body to help form the shape of the letters. For example, to shape the letter *C,* a child sits on the floor, curves the torso forward, and curves the right arm up and forward over the head. Children will enjoy posing for the shapes in front of a full-length mirror.

129. Emberley, Ed. *Ed Emberley's A B C.* Color overlays by Barbara Emberley. Color overlays for Bear and Rabbit pages by Michael Emberley. Boston: Little, Brown, 1978.

In this book four panels trace the formation of a selected letter with the actions of animals and insects. A reader follows the scenes from left to right to see four panels of illustrations for each letter and to trace the formation. The visual puzzles of a letter's formation are shown with characters such as an ant aviator who flies a multicolored airplane and lets smoke form the shape of capital *A*; a ladybug who arranges blueberries into the shape of *B*; and a crow who pecks the shape of *C* from corn. For other examples, two groups of fireflies (a group of five and then four) form the stems of the letter *F* above the heads of two green frogs, one playing a fiddle and the other, a flute. Also, a family of geese watch two grasshoppers gnaw the letter *G* in green grass and then start playing golf. A list of objects to find in the illustrations for each letter concludes the book.

130. Fisher, Leonard Everett. *Alphabet Art: Thirteen ABC's from Around the World.* Illustrated by the author. New York: Four Winds, 1978.

For each of thirteen alphabets, a reader finds a brief introduction and the symbols currently in use. English equivalents and pronunciation guides are included along with Arabic characters; angles, circles, and lines of Eskimo symbols; symbols for the Cherokee language; and selected Chinese characters that represent complete ideas, words, or syllable sounds.

131. Johnson, Crockett. *Harold's ABC.* Illustrated by the author. New York: Harper & Row, 1981.

A reader sees the way letters are transformed and become parts of objects. Harold uses his purple crayon to turn the shape of the letter *A* into the attic of a house, *B* into books, *C* into cake, and continues through the letter sequence.

132. MacDonald, Suse. *Alphabatics.* Illustrated by the author. New York: Bradbury, 1986.

A reader sees that each letter expands, shrinks, or is manipulated into the shape of an object the name of which begins with the letter itself. For example, the letter *K* forms the body of a kite that lifts as it changes shape; an ark introduces the letter *A*; and a clown stands for *C*.

133. Neumeier, Marty & Glaser, Byron. *Action Alphabet.* Illustrated by the authors. New York: Greenwillow, 1985.

   Introducing capitals and lowercase letters, drawings of letters portray actions as key word choices. A reader sees the way letters play a part in the key words that introduce them. When appropriate, the letters show action on the pages. For instance, the letter *A* is acrobatic, *K* is flying as a kite, and *Z* is zigzagging.

134. Rey, H. A. *Curious George Learns the Alphabet.* Illustrated by the author. New York: Houghton Mifflin, 1963.

   A man in a yellow hat identifies the letters for George from capital *A,* where the letter becomes the wide gaping jaws of a green alligator and lowercase a where the letter turns into a small apple, to capital and lowercase Z that turn into big and small zebras. Black outlined figures have highlights of red, yellow, blue, and green. On every page, Rey's selected letter is highlighted by a color dot over the letter when it is found in the text.

135. Weil, Lisl. *Owl and Other Scrambles.* Illustrated by the author. New York: Dutton, 1980.

   A reader sees ways the artist uses all of the letters making up a particular word and to draw colorful cartoons from the shapes of the letters. Beginning cartoons formed with scrambles of letters include an angel, an ape, and an airplane. The book includes a glossary for key words.

* PUZZLES AND GAMES

136. *ABC.* Illustrated by Hitomi Kuroki. New York: Little Simon & Zokeisha, Tokyo, 1984.

Kuroki's full-color illustrations are on heavy-stock pages. A child finds it easy to participate by chanting lines about children with "Christopher loves chocolate," "Vanessa loves valentines," and "William loves waterfalls." Point out the pattern to children interested in language patterns they find in books: _____ (letter) my name is _____ (name) and I love____ (object).

137. Alda, Arlene. *Arlene Alda's ABC: A New Way of Seeing.* Illustrated by the author. Millbrae, Calif.: Celestial Arts/Dawne-Leigh Book, 1981.

This "new" way of seeing can be an environmental puzzle when a reader discovers that certain objects resemble shapes of letters. Black or white capital and lowercase letters introduce the objects shown in full-color photographs. The letter *X* is seen in the crossing of two tree trunks, *O* in a car's headlight, and *M* in the lines of the roof of a house.

138. Allington, Richard L. & Krull, Kathleen. *Beginning to Learn About Letters.* Illustrated by Tom Garcia. Milwaukee: Raintree, 1983.

Out-of-sequence letters are introduced with a word guessing game when a reader is asked to look at a full-color illustration and predict names of the animals and objects. To self-check, a reader turns the page to find the key words and upper- and lowercase letters. Culminating pages offer activities for tracing, searching for capitals, and making original alphabet books.

139. *The Alphabet Book.* Illustrated by John Strejan. Paper engi-

neering by I. Penick. New York: Random House/Children's Television Workshop, n.d.

In the book some objects are hidden and appear only when a tab is pulled on a page. For instance, when one tab is pulled on the page for *W,* the mouth of the whale opens. Inside the mouth, a child sees the swallowed objects for *X* and *Y*—xylophone and yak.

140. *The Alphabet Zoo.* Dallas: Texas Instruments, Inc., 1982.

Both upper- and lowercase letters guide the sequence in the text about animals arranged in ABC order at the zoo. A reader puts a Magic Wand™ over zebra bars on the pages to hear the story of acrobatic ants, swimming whales, and other creatures. Culminating pages offer activities for matching, writing, and arranging animal names in alphabetical order.

141. Anno, Mitsumasa & Anno, Masaichiro. *Anno's Magical ABC: An Anamorphic Alphabet.* Illustrated by the authors. New York: Philomel, 1980.

A reader places a silver mylar tube in the center of each page to see the distorted picture become clear in the tube's reflection. The captions serve as clues to the clear images for lowercase letters, e.g., "*a* is for anteater." After the 52 pictures of animals are seen, a reader turns the book upside down to find another alphabet with the capital letters, i.e., *A* Angel. The section "How to Do an Anamorphic Drawing" gives instructions for reversing an image and for transferring that image to a graph.

142. Atlas, Ron. *Looking for Zebra.* Illustrated by Tedd Arnold. New York: Simon & Schuster, 1986.

A young child is asked to search for Zebra and open the windows in the Hotel Zoo to find a full-color picture and its key word. In doing so, the child identifies the letters on the windows, and inside, finds the other animals. The story, told in rhyming lines, is read aloud by a second reader. The young child can join in on the repetitive refrain, e.g., "There's someone in the window, the one marked *A* . . . , *B* . . . ," and so on.

143. Balian, Lorna. *Humbug Potion: An ABC Cipher.* Illustrated by the author. Nashville: Abingdon Press, 1984.

  A reader can discover the secret number code and decipher a magic beauty recipe for a homely witch. On the end pages, *Z* is 26, *Y* is 25, and so on. Replacing each numeral with a letter, a reader uncovers the words and needed ingredients for the chubby witch's potion.

144. Banks, Kate. *Alphabet Soup.* Illustrated by Peter Sis. New York: Knopf, 1988.

  Having lunch, a small boy plays an imaginary game and transforms items around him into an adventure with a teddy bear that comes to life.

145. Bayer, Jane. *A My Name Is Alice.* Illustrated by Steven Kellogg. New York: Dutton/Dial, 1984.

  A child may make a game from the key words that begin with similar sounds in sentence arrangement of: _____ . My name is _____ . My husband's name is _____ . We live in _____ . We sell _____ . Bayer uses language to express a rhythmic pattern. From a playground game, one the author learned in her elementary school, comes this pattern of names and places and things to sell for each letter of the alphabet. From Kellogg's illustrations come a group of zany animals that illustrate the letters. An older child sees some unusual ones, e.g., unau, a two-toed tree mammal, and xigertling, a creature from the planet Xigert. Using this pattern, is any child interested in making his or her own name page?

146. Besche, Tom. *Professor Breads' Alphabet.* Illustrated by the author. Georgetown: Besches' Bread-N-Butter Prod., 1980.

  A child sings along with the alphabet verses in "The Alphabet" heard on the record that accompanies the book. The verses are repetitive ones. Traditional beginnings open the lines. The letter *A* is for the apple, *B* is for a big bee, and *C* is for a carrot. A boy or girl may identify some of the nonfood items that are included: guitar, light bulb, nickel, quarter, umbrella, villain, whistle, x-ray, and yo-yo. This is a book a child may color. Each outlined object in sequence introduces letter pairs. The capitals in sequence are reviewed on a final page and followed by the verses.

147. Bonini, Marinella. *I Can Be the Alphabet.* Illustrated by the author. New York: Viking, 1987.

In this small book, discovering ways to bend or turn the body to form the shapes of the letter can be a puzzle, but the book gives readers directions for doing this. For example, to shape the letter *A*, a reader may bend over at the waist, place arms across the knees, and move the feet apart.

148. Bourke, Linda. *Eye Spy: A Mysterious Alphabet.* Illustrated by the author. San Francisco: Chronicle Books, 1991.

A reader is asked to participate in a guessing game and try to discover the answer (a homonym or homophone) to a picture puzzle for each letter and to predict what is coming on a following page after seeing visual clues. For instance, a reader sees four illustrations in a sequence in a panel across a spread and determines a connection among the illustration. The connection will be that each picture stands for a word that begins with the same letter and is either a homophone (words pronounced alike but spelled differently such as hare and hair), or a homonym (words that are spelled and pronounced alike but have different meanings). As an example for the letter *A,* a reader sees four illustrations—three of different views of an ant—and a fourth of a gray-haired woman dressed in a blue-and-red dress with a matching hat and veil (aunt). Next, a reader can predict the word choice that is coming up next by looking for visual clues. At her neck, the aunt wears a pin showing bowling pins, the key choice that is seen on the next page for the letter *B*. A solution page is included at the end of the book.

149. Brown, Marcia. *All Butterflies: An ABC.* Illustrated by the author. New York: Macmillan, 1981.

Brown shows two letters on each page with a simple storyline for each woodcut. Words are linked by the ABC sequence, an arrangement that might be puzzling to some children. For instance, a child sees *E*lephants *F*ly, *G*iraffes *H*igh, and *I*ce-cold *J*umpers and may discover the alphabetical linkage in the lines. A culminating list helps readers review all the words.

150. Burrows, Roger, Project Director. *My First ABC Book.* Illustrated by Educational Consultants: Verna Burnett, Francie Greanias, and Beverly Dietz. Writers: Rozanne Lanczak Williams, Susan Parker Dietz. Graphic Designers: Lee A. Scott, Judy Walker. Los Angeles: Price Stern Sloan; dist. by Random House, 1985.

Burrows uses activities to show that many words begin with the same symbol and sound. Capital letters are matched with similar letters in rows, columns, and along game tracks. A child matches letters, tracks a path from capital to lowercase letters across pages, and traces the shapes of the colorful letters. One microchip sensor called Questron™ senses right and wrong responses with sounds and lights. Sets of questions or games can be completed. A green light means a child has identified a correct answer while a red light and sound means to try again.

151. Burstein, Chaya. *Hebrew Alphabet Coloring Book.* Illustrated by the author. New York: Dover, 1986.

From Aleph to Tav, Burstein's book presents twenty-two letters of the Hebrew alphabet and an explanation of pronunciation that follows the Sephardic (Spanish) way used in Israel and in the Middle East. A child sees one Hebrew letter per page with Hebrew words beginning with the letter. For Aleph, a child sees such objects as an airplane, goose, and tree. Near each word is a black-and-white drawing of the object. Each word is numbered with an English equivalancy at the foot of the page. Several patterns are mentioned, e.g., sound changes for certain letters when a dot is taken away or moved in the writing, letters that look different when they are at the end of a word, and vowel signs that are often shown in books for beginning readers. A concluding vocabulary section allows a child to look up a word in English and find out what the word is in Hebrew. A final Hebrew alphabet reads from right to left, thus beginning on page 32 and ending on page 30. There are more than twenty pages for coloring if desired.

152. Crowther, Robert. *The Most Amazing Hide-and-Seek Alphabet Book*. Illustrated by the author. New York: Viking, 1978.

   In full-color scenes and a hide-and-seek format, a reader finds familiar selections—a furry koala bear, a brown monkey, a feathery wide-eyed owl, and other animals. Some of the animals that may be unfamiliar ones include an umbrella bird and a small newt.

153. Debnam, Betty. *Alpha Betty's ABC Fun Book*. Illustrated by the author. New York: Collier/ Macmillan, 1982.

   A child is invited to find hidden words that begin with a certain letter, to follow the dots from *A* to *Z* to see the outline of an object, to write words that begin with a selected letter into a simple crossword arrangement, and to write in missing letters in selected nouns.

154. Demi. *The ABC Song*. Illustrated by Leonard Shortall. A Music Box Book. Music Box Concept by Demi. New York: Random House, 1985.

   Opening the pages of this stocky book, a child finds a low-ercase block letter-object-word arrangement: An airplane, bee, and castle in full color on white backgrounds. The names of the objects are in lowercase block letters. A metal handle makes it easy for a child to turn and start the music box and to listen to the music of the familiar ABC song, language expressed in a musical rhythmic pattern. The last page includes all of the words of the song.

155. Demi. *Demi's Find the Animal ABC: An Alphabet Game Book*. Illustrated by the author. New York: Putnam, 1985.

   A reader is asked to find an illustrated animal whose name begins with the associated letter pairs and a picture of a small cat somewhere in the book. For example, an alligator introduces the letter *A,* and in a box on the page, a little alligator waits to be found in the drawing of the large alligator. Answers to the challenge are at the end of the book for self-checking.

156. Demi. *The Peek-A-Book ABC*. Illustrated by the author. New York: Random House, 1982.

A young child finds cardboard doors to open, objects and colorful capital and lowercase letters. For example, opening the sides of the ark reveals animals waiting inside, and a reader finds words that begin with similar sounds and symbols.

157. Doolittle, Eileen. *The Ark in the Attic: An Alphabet Adventure.* Illustrated by Starr Ockenga. Boston: Godine, 1987.

     With oversized full-color photographs, a reader goes on a hunt for small treasures and discovers an open-ended finding game and can point to an object, name it, and invent stories. For the letter *X,* xylophone, Xerox copy of an *X* page, xanthium, and X ray are seen. A key provides the names of items for each letter.

158. Downie, Jill. *Alphabet Puzzle.* Illustrated by the author. New York: Lothrop, Lee & Shepard, 1988.

     Seeing capitals and lowercase letters, a reader recognizes the letters of the alphabet, the key word choices, and looks through the windows on the pages to predict subsequent key words. Letters are linked in pairs through the key words, i.e., *A* and *B* are linked with the key words of axe and bark; *W* and *X* are linked with key words of waves in the ocean and x-ray fish who live in the ocean; and *Y* is for yak, and *Z* for the zigzag in the mountain path along which the yak trudges.

159. Elting, Mary & Folsom, Michael. *Q Is for Duck: An Alphabet Guessing Game.* Illustrated by Jack Kent. Boston: Houghton Mifflin, 1980.

     A reader finds repetitive questions that ask for predictions about associations puzzling to some children, e.g., why does the letter *E* stand for whale (it's enormous), *U* stand for prairie dog (live underground), and *V* stand for chameleon (seems to vanish)? With large colorful capitals to guide the alphabetical sequence, the questions entertain listening children when read aloud.

160. Folsom, Marcia & Folsom, Michael. *Easy as Pie: A Guessing Game of Sayings.* Illustrated by Jack Kent. New York: Ticknor, 1985.

Comparisons such as "easy as pie" and "sly as a fox" may interest children in making up original ones that are new and different. Older students, familiar with the sayings, may predict the endings of the comparisons. Since sequence of the alphabet is guided by colorful capitals that are introduced by clues to words needed to complete the comparisons, the book is best suited for those who already know the alphabet.

161. Forte, Imogene. *From A to Z with Me*. Illustrated by the author. Nashville: Incentive Publications, 1981.

    For each illustrated capital letter, there is a following awareness activity. From *A*, which stands for almost, all, and about, to *Z*, which stands for Zebra, Zipper, and Zachariah, each letter includes an activity that helps a young child become more aware of himself or herself and of the surroundings. For example, at *A*, a child writes a house address. For *B*, a child draws a picture about bumps, bandages, and feeling better after a minor injury. At *C*, there is space for pictures to be drawn on a clock face to show how a child spends his or her time during the day.

162. Geisert, Arthur. *Pigs From A to Z*. Illustrated by the author. Boston: Houghton Mifflin, 1986.

    Seven little pigs build a tree house, and letters are found in the full-page etchings showing its construction. Along with each letter in sequence in each illustration, an observant reader will find five different forms of the letter, one form of the preceding letter, one form of the following letters, and of course, the little pigs. Facing each illustration is the text about the pigs eating apples, chopping down trees, and cutting wood. For a review, a reader turns to the back to find smaller illustrations that point out the hidden letter shapes.

163. Geringer, Laura. *The Cow Is Mooing Anyhow: A Scrambled Alphabet Book to Be Read at Breakfast*. Illustrated by Dirk Zimmer. New York: HarperCollins, 1991.

    Beginning with capital *I* and the arrival of iguanas dressed in pajamas, other rowdy animals represent the capital letter of the alphabet out of sequence and disrupt a child's quiet breakfast. As each creature arrives, its corresponding capital letter is found on the margin of the next page in its proper place to build the sequence. Rhyming lines (crab, cab) tell the story as the goose helps the child drink juice, an albatross spreads toast with applesauce, and a moth chews through the tablecloth. Parallel action is seen in pictures hanging on the wall; the picture of the cow shows a fanciful adventure as the cow enters a grove of birch trees, becomes marked with stripes similar to the bark of birch trees, looks piglike as it eats spotted mushrooms, becomes marked with mushroom spots, plays with a cat, fiddle, dish, and spoon and returns to its original place in time to croon "Moo." With capitals, all the creature names are identified in order on the end pages.

164. Gregorich, Barbara. *Alphabet Avalanche.* Illustrated by Barbara Alexander & others. Grand Haven, Mich.: School Zone Pub., 1986.

A reader is asked to circle letters, color pictures, find hidden letters, connect dots, and play tic-tac-toe. Each page features characters found in other books in this series, Hearty Chicken, a jogging frog, and a bear who puts gum on a drum.

165. Hall, Nancy Christensen. *Macmillan Fairy Tale Alphabet Book.* Illustrated by John O'Brien. New York: Macmillan, 1981.

A reader finds puzzles in a game of titles and is challenged to identify titles from the illustrated scenes of fairy tales. With one letter featured in each illustration, the labels of objects are from unidentified tales. Given a scene for the letter *B,* a reader guesses the title of the fairy tale. A reader sees a boy climbing a large vine up toward a bald giant playing a harp and notes the objects that are labeled *beanstalk, brave boy, butterflies, bluebirds, bald bully,* and *brown boot.* To self-check, a reader turns to the back for the names of the titles.

166. Hargreaves, Roger. *Alphabet Fun.* Illustrated by the author. Los Angeles: Price Stern Sloan, 1983.

When the letters have been identified, a reader is asked to repeat the letter names, trace them, and listen for the sound of the letter in the names of objects from ambulance to zoo. A culmination of activities includes matching, identifying ob-

jects, writing missing letters in the alphabet sequence, and answering riddles.

167. Hawkins, Colin & Hawkins, Jacqui. *I Spy: The Lift-The-flap
     ABC Book.* Illustrated by the authors. Boston: Little, Brown,
     1989.
     A reader finds letter pairs introduced with a variety of per-
     sonified animals in full color illustrations. An alligator pilots a
     plane, a moose drinks milk, x-ray fish dance on the bars of a
     xylophone, and zebras dance to the sounds of a zither.
     Sequence of letter pairs in white on red end papers.

168. Hoguet, Susan Ramsey. *I Unpacked My Grandmother's Trunk:
     A Picture Book Game.* Illustrated by the author. New York:
     Dutton, 1982.
     In this picture book game, a young acrobat unpacks Grand-
     mother's trunk to find a bear, clown, and other objects in an
     accumulating alphabetical pattern. Other characteristics may
     be discussed with interested readers, i.e., the three-quarter page
     that opens like a trunk, the use of white space that intensifies
     the objects, and the parallel pattern of similar postures for the
     acrobat and the animals.

169. Holt, Virginia. *A My Name Is Alice: An Alphabet Book.* Illustra-
     ted by Joe Mathieu. New York: Random House/Children's
     Television Workshop, 1989.
     Alice and the other Muppets introduce the alphabet with
     brief verses about cookies, dinosaurs, ladders, and other ob-
     jects. After a beginning of "*A* my name is Alice and my broth-
     er's name is . . . .," the well-known pattern that includes a girl's
     name, boy's name, a favorite food is ignored for many of the
     letters. The letter *X* is for X ray and *Z* is for zebra.

170. King, Tony. *The Moving Alphabet Book.* Illustrated by the au-
     thor. New York: Putnam, 1982.
     Turning a picture wheel on each page, a reader may be chal-
     lenged with the puzzle of naming the objects shown labeled
     with their names in the windows but not with the repetitive
     sentence on each page i.e., *A* is for _____, *B* is for_____, and so

on. *X* is for X-ray and for a mark on a treasure map. If interested, a reader may make an alphabet picture wheel using the one in the book as a model.

171. Kitamura, Satoshi. *What's Inside: The Alphabet Book.* Illustrated by the author. New York: Farrar, Straus & Giroux, 1985.

Guessing the secret object hidden on every page guides a reader through the sequence of the alphabet. In full-color paintings, a reader sees boxes and other containers that hide different objects. A reader predicts what is hidden and uses the guiding letter as a clue. For example, a reader sees the letters *a* and *b* in the first illustration, makes predictions, and turns the page to discover the names of the objects and to verify the predictions.

172. Lecourt, Nancy. *Abracadabra to Zigzag.* Illustrated by Barbara Lehman. New York: Lothrop, Lee & Shepard, 1991.

A reader discovers ways curious words and phrases have changed over time and ways new ones have been invented—activities for making an original wordplay game. With letter pairs found in page corners, key word choices are illustrated in full color and include bigwig, lickety-split, mishmash, and others. Glossary with information about ways the words and phrases were invented is included.

173. Leman, Martin. *Comic and Curious Cats.* Illustrated by M. Leman. Text by Angela Carter. New York: Harmony, 1979.

After reading Carter's alliterative rhymes, a reader may address the puzzle of using alliterative words and naming a cat, telling where it lives, and what it likes to eat. Moving in the alphabetical sequence, the game continues to the next letter and through *Z*. The game is easily adapted from the topic of cats and applied to a topic of the reader's choice. Letters are introduced by Leman's paintings and Carter's verses about cats. The verses are similar to those in the familiar word game that begins "I love my . . ." Cats are shown chasing insects and birds and sleeping wherever they can.

174. Lionni, Leo. *The Alphabet Tree.* Illustrated by the author. New York: Pantheon, 1968.

An alphabet tree full of leaf-hopping letters survives a blustery gale that leaves the letters huddled in fear. An enterprising red-and-black word bug teaches the letters to join together to form short words, and a purple caterpillar suggests that the words form sentences that "mean something important."

175. Lopshire, Robert. *ABC Games.* Illustrated by the author. New York: Harper & Row, 1986.

When asked a question for each letter, a reader selects an animal, person, or object that is associated with the key word choice. For instance, when asked, "Which one will eat the acorn?" a reader chooses from the possible answers of a fish, snail, squirrel, and turtle. Children interested in this humorous arrangement may be motivated to write their own questions and draw the answers for an original alphabet game book.

176. Lyon, David E. *The ABC Puzzle Book.* Illustrated by Ralph Stobart. New York: Mulberry Books, n.d.

Guided by oversized letters in manuscript style, a reader reads rhyming lines and predicts a rhyming word for an inserted blank line. The clues to the rhyming words are found in the illustrations.

177. McMillan, Bruce. *The Alphabet Symphony: An ABC Book.* Illustrated by the author. New York: Greenwillow, 1977.

As a visual awareness puzzle, black-and-white photographs of musical instruments are accompanied by smaller inserts that show the part of the instrument that looks like the shape of a letter. The culminating pages have a review of the letters and the parts of the instruments.

178. Magel, John. *Dr. Moggle's Alphabet Challenge: A Quest for All Ages.* Illustrated by Claudia Del Col. New York: Rand McNally, 1985.

In a dream, the narrator and Dr. Moggle, an elf, climb the ladder of knowledge to find words that will release them from their dream. In the dream, they visit the circus, a pool, get caught in a dark storm. A reader is asked to find two hidden words located in an illustration and identify as many of the more than one thousand objects as possible. An author's note indicates that the correct two-word solution may be received by sending a self-addressed, stamped envelope to Dr. Moggle Answer Requests, P.O. Box 76600, Chicago, Ill. 60680.

179. Martin, Bill, Jr. & John Archambault. *Chicka Chicka Boom Boom.* Illustrated by Lois Ehlert. New York: Simon & Schuster, 1991.

A coconut tree is full of personified letters when it becomes the site of a race to the top of the tree. A young child should be encouraged to join in on the repetitive refrain of "Chicka chicka . . . BOOM! BOOM!"

180. O'Callaghan, Karen. *Join in with Us! Letters: An Action Alphabet.* Illustrated by Eric Rowe. Cambridge, England: Brimax Books, 1982.

Sound-letter relationships are found in underlined words in sentences. Each full-page and full-color illustration is paired with the upper- and lowercase letters. The caption shows the placement of the letters by highlighting them in red within the black text. Capitalization and punctuation are shown. Each caption encourages a child to respond in different ways, e.g., by pointing, blowing paper, curling up, and with other actions. Words that contain the selected guiding letter are underlined in red.

181. Paré, Roger. *The Annick ABC.* Illustrated by the author. Toronto: Annick Press, 1985.

Each letter pair introduces a humorous situation, e.g., a dinosaur dances, a cat rides in a canoe, and a bathing boa blows bubbles. Accompanying the alliterative text are puzzles and a game that uses letters to spell words from the book.

182. Paris, Pat. *Who's in the Box, Bobby?* Illustrated & paper engineered by Dick Dudley. Los Angeles: Price Stern Sloan, 1987.

A child enjoys puzzles with questions such as "Who's in the airplane, Amy?" and lifts up tabs on pages to find the answers. In the airplane is an artist asking an alligator for an autograph. Both uppercase and lowercase letters are in the corners. For the letter *X,* Xavier, the X-ray technician is X-raying a xylophone.

For *Z*, the question "Who's at the zoo, Zelda?" is answered with, "A zookeeper zipping up a zebra."

183. Peppé, Rodney. *The Alphabet Book*. Illustrated by the author. New York: Four Winds, 1968.

    Using the technique of linking the letters on two facing pages, the author presents familiar words in brief sentences. The complete sequence is reviewed on the last page.

184. Price, Marjorie. *Alphadabbles: A Playful Alphabet*. Illustrated by the author. New York: Pantheon, 1980.

    In these visual puzzles, lines can magnify, minify, or stretch a letter. A reader is encouraged to visualize a letter from different directions—top, bottom, back, and sides.

185. Reasoner, Charles & Hardt, Vicky. *Alphabite! A Funny Feast from A to Z*. Illustrated by the authors. Los Angeles, Calif.: Price Stern Sloan, 1989.

    A reader is asked to predict who is eating the feast of food from *A* to *Z* beginning with "apples, tart and red" and ending with a "zucchini . . . and that was all." The last page reveals the one "who has gone from *A* to *Z* from beginning to end on an eating spree."

186. Rebman, Sybil. *Animal Alphabet*. Illustrated by the author. San Diego, Calif.: Green Tiger Press, n.d.

    With capitals, the letters in an animal's name are used to draw the animal's shape in this visual puzzle. The animal's name may be found in each four-line verse, and its letters then matched to the letters used to make the shape. With each verse is a red animal silhouette.

187. Rockwell, Anne. *Albert B. Cub and Zebra: An Alphabet Storybook*. Illustrated by the author. New York: Harper & Row, 1977.

    After his friend, Zebra, is zebranapped, Albert B. Cub searches for his friend at the *c*ircus, in *F*rance, in a *j*ungle and other places in alphabetical order. His uneventful travels to *M*aine, *N*iagara Falls, and *T*exas have Cub weeping over the loss of his friend and exhausted. Finally, zebra is found nibbling a zinnia at the zoo.

188. Schade, Charlene. *Move with Me from A to Z.* Illustrated by Steve Pileggi. San Diego: The Wright Group, 1982.

Schade's book encourages a child to learn the letters through play in movements. For each letter, there is an animal character and directions for accompanying actions. A young child should enjoy taking turns with someone to show that he or she can make the movements for the action words. The adult describes the movements for the action words. A child jumps and lands gently like Freddy, the frog, runs slowly like Kevin Kiwi, or opens his mouth wide to show his teeth like Henry, the hippopotamus.

189. Shreck, Peter K. *First Letters.* Illustrated by Eleanor Wasmuth. New York: Macmillan, 1982.

At the foot of each page is a key letter and word box. A girl or boy recognizes the letter and the object. For instance, the letter *M* is near a monkey. Other objects on the page are seen: a crescent moon, a rabbit magician, and a red motorcycle. In an accompanying envelope are additional cards to be used in sequence. The cards slide back and forth under a cardboard window frame to show the directions and the correct responses. With these cards, a child is asked to find the pattern of pictures that begin with selected letters, of key words for the pictures, and to name the letter that begins a chosen word. The separate cards for different letters emphasize the twenty-six letters in the English alphabet.

190. Silverman, Maida. *Bunny's ABC Box.* Illustrated by Ellen Blonder. New York: Grosset & Dunlap, 1986.

In this ABC, there are die cuts on every page, shapes of square holes to explore, in this Little Poke and Look Book. A child looks into a bright yellow box along with Bunny. Together, they find objects in alphabetical order from ants and apple to zucchini and zebra. Guiding serif letters, capitals and lowercase ones, are presented in bold type. The brief story lines, both declarative and interrogative, show the use of capitalization and punctuation.

191. Svensson, Borje. *Letters.* Illustrated by the author. New York: Viking, 1981.

Best suited for a child's individual library because of its small size, this book offers letters that are hidden on the pages, and a viewer is challenged to find them. For example, the letter *A* is hidden in the wooden frame of a tall ladder, *D* is hidden in the window of double door, and *E* is seen in the branches of trees. The shapes of *X, Y,* and *Z* are in the frames of kites flying high. A culminating diorama shows children playing with alphabet blocks.

192. Tallarico, Tony. *Alphabet Flip-Book Game.* Illustrated by the author. New York: Grosset & Dunlap, 1981.

A reader matches up component parts of letter shapes to complete the puzzles for making the letters. If a child is puzzled over which pages to flip, colors on pages help in making decisions. There are two letter shapes per page, and beside each are objects whose names begin with that letter, e.g., the American flag and a fish are near the letter *F.*

193. Van Allsburg, Chris. *The Z Was Zapped.* Illustrated by the author. Boston: Houghton Mifflin, 1987.

In black-and-white illustrations, the letters of the alphabet suffer mishaps beginning with *A* getting caught in an avalanche through the melting of *M* and ending with *Z* getting zapped by lightning. Each letter takes its place in the center of a stage when the mishap happens and a reader can predict the key word related to the mishap before turning the page to verify a prediction.

194. *Walt Disney's Flash Ahead with ABC's.* Illustrated. New York: Simon & Schuster, 1983.

Short rhyming verses describe objects used by Disney's characters. There is Goofy's automobile, Dumbo's cupcake, and ice cream for Mickey Mouse. Uppercase letters in black introduce the rhymes. On the back side of these flip pages is a second scene showing the object with both uppercase and lowercase letters. A child is invited to name the letters, identify the objects, and listen to the verse again to say the letter. For another reading, a child may listen to the verse another time to say the object's name when it is omitted by the reader. The objects are reviewed again on the final pages. A child points to an object, names it, flips the page over, and finds the starting letter for the word that names the picture.

195. Weiss, Ellen. *The Alphabet: The Great Alphabet Play.* Art Direction by Robert Pierce. Educational Consultants, Valeria Lovelace & Istar Schwager. Produced in cooperation with Children's Television Workshop. Racine, Wis.: Western, 1986.

Weiss's instructions are on tape and guide a child through this participation book with the Sesame Street characters. There is Bert and Ernie, Big Bird, Oscar the Grouch, Herry Monster, and Cookie Monster. A child lifts the reusable vinyl stickers of objects and places them on the scenes in the book. To the music of "The ABC Song," Prairie Dawn introduces the play. The alphabet is the star of the show. A signal cues a child to turn the pages. The first letter is *A,* and an airplane is brought on stage by Herry Monster. *A* is for airplane. Will a child think of an *A* when the child sees one fly overhead? *D* is for a dusty doorknob contributed by Oscar the Grouch. Big Bird brings an invention, an itch scratcher, for the letter *I.* The vinyl stickers may be returned to a backing sheet and stored inside the book.

196. Wenk, Dina. *Make Zoup! An Alphabet Book.* Illustrated by John Wallner. Project Director, Elaine Chaback. Design, Michaelis/Carpelis Design Associates. Front Cover Illustration, Amy Horowitz. New York: Dell, 1979.

A child is invited to add the ingredients to an ABC soup in alphabetical order. Beginning with one artichoke and three beets and ending with one yam and two zucchini squash, each item may be drawn on the page near the large soup kettle.

197. Wilks, Mike. *The Ultimate Alphabet.* Illustrated by the author. Designed by Bernard Higton. New York: Holt, 1986.

A painting illustrates each of the twenty-six letters, and a reader is encouraged to "read" the paintings, observe the appearance of things, and identify some of the seven thousand, seven hundred, and seventy-seven objects. Objects include artworks by artists, patterns, and even a "mistake" on the page for the letter *M*. In Wilks's companion book, *The Annotated Ultimate Alphabet* (Holt, 1986), the artist includes a key for each of the twenty-six paintings with a full identification of each of the objects painted, ranging from thirty for the letter *X* to more than one thousand for the letter *S*.

198. Wylie, Joanne & Wylie, David. *A Fishy Alphabet Story.* Illustrated by David Graham Wylie. Chicago: Childrens Press, 1983.
A child can make a game of catching the letter fish in order. With the exception of one fish displaying two letters, *VW,* capital letters in groups of three label each fish and are seen again in a list of words in alphabetical order. Each fish shows three letters on its scales. After several fish have been caught, the letters are displayed on one large fish, the alphabet fish. For a final review, there is a fishing game where a child identifies a letter on a fish to catch it. Following the review, a list of words in alphabetical order shows a child which words were introduced in this participation story.

199. Yolen, Jane. *All in the Woodland Early: An ABC Book.* Illustrated by Jane Breskin Zalben. New York: Putnam, 1983.
Woodland verses about animals introduce each letter and are sung to music. Verses form the accumulating story as animals in the woods join together and verse questions ask a reader for the answer that leads to a surprise.

* SIGN LANGUAGE

200. Adler, David A. *Finger Spelling Fun.* Illustrated by Dennis Kendrick. New York: Watts, 1980.

   Black-and-white illustrations with yellow, fuschia, and orange accents show the finger positions for finger spelling the letters and the key words. The author tells readers how to send messages, play "Duck the Duck," answer riddles, and participate in a finger spelling bee.

201. Baker, Pamela J. *My First Book of Sign.* Illustrated by Patricia Bellan Gillen. Washington, D.C.: Gallaudet University Press/Kendall Green, 1986.

   For each pair of letters shown with the finger-spelling, key objects selected from lists of children's early vocabularies are presented with the word signs. Movement for hand signs are designated with directional arrows. Full-color oversized illustrations, chart of manual alphabet, and sign descriptions are included.

202. Bourke, Linda. *Handmade ABC: A Manual Alphabet.* Illustrated by the author. New York: Addison, 1981.

   In this manual alphabet guide, twenty-six hand signs introduce the letters, and once learned, can be used to send messages to others. Each of the letters has a special hand shape and is shown in a black-and-white illustration that accompanies objects whose names begin with the selected letter. On the page for the letter *I,* black inkspots form a line across the top and bottom borders on the page, and facing is a hand shaping the letter *I* dressed in an ink-stained sleeve. The page for the letter *J* is bordered in jewelry, and the hand signing the letter wears a ring and bracelets.

203. Bove, Linda. *Sign Language ABC.* Illustrated by Tom Cooke. In cooperation with National Theater of the Deaf. New York: Random House/Children's Television Workshop, 1985.

 Pairs of capital and lowercase letters appear in bold type on a single page along with hand signs for words, labels in photographs, and a Muppets character. For instance for the letter *A,* Ernie is the pilot of a plane and an alligator who is eating an apple is the copilot. Bove signs the words airplane, alligator, and apple. Arrows inserted in the illustrations show a reader how to move fingers and hands.

204. Bove, Linda. *Sign Language Fun.* Illustrated by Tom Cooke. In cooperation with the National Theater of the Deaf. New York: Random House/Children's Television Workshop, 1980.

 Sign language is introduced along with words and pictures. The manual alphabet from *A* to *Z* is shown on the end pages. Concepts of opposites, actions, and feelings are illustrated by the Muppets. The author suggests asking a child to imitate the hand positions by looking at the arrows on the pictures that show how to move the fingers and hands.

205. Chaplin, Susan Gibbons. *I Can Sign My ABCs.* Illustrated by Laura McCaul. New York: Gallaudet University Press, 1986.

 The alphabet is introduced in sign language with the manual alphabet handshapes, pictures of familiar word choices, names, and object signs. Colorful oversized capital and lowercase letters guide the sequence.

206. Charlip, Remy & Miller, Mary Beth. *Handtalk: An ABC of Finger Spelling and Sign Language.* Illustrated by George Ancona. New York: Four Winds, 1974.

 Capitals are found in corners of double-page spreads along with photographs of features that show a reader the finger spellings and hand signs for the word choices. For example, capital *A* is placed near a black-and-white insert of the signal for *A,* and Miller poses in a full-color illustration for the word choice, *angel.* Additional photographs of the finger spelling for the letters needed to spell the key word are shown at the foot of the page.

207. Rankin, Laura. *The Handmade Alphabet.* Illustrated by Linda Bourke. New York: Harper & Row, 1980.

   The purpose of Rankin's book is to celebrate the expressiveness of signing, and each illustration is related to a letter of the manual alphabet and a word that begins with the featured letter. Full-color illustrations introduce capitals on the pages. For example, the artwork for capital *A* shows the hand shape for the letter in the manual alphabet and a related image, asparagus. Some unusual word choices are ornament, paints and palette, and thimbles and thread. The key words are listed on a final page at the end of the book.

208. Sullivan, Mary Beth & Bourke, Linda. *A Show of Hands: Say It in Sign Language.* Illustrated by Linda Bourke. New York: Harper & Row, 1980.

   A reader discovers how to talk with the hands and hear with the eyes with the included manual alphabet and the suggested signs in categories such as "Love at First Sign," "Flexible Fingers," and "Signs of a Perfect Day." Authors suggest practicing with people who use sign language, signing whenever one can, and watching the vocabulary grow.

* SPECIFIC PLACES

209. Agard, John. *The Calypso Alphabet*. Illustrated by Jennifer Bent. New York: Holt, 1989.

In Agard's verses, a reader discovers words from the Caribbean islands beginning with *Anancy,* a popular folk figure, and ending with *zombie,* one who can break its spell by eating salt. Word list has explanations of *doh-doh, kaison, lickerish,* and other unfamiliar terms.

210. Brown, Ruth. *Alphabet Times Four: An International ABC.* Illustrated by the author. New York: Dutton, 1991.

The purpose of Brown's book is to introduce learning languages in a visual way, and for every letter pair of the alphabet, a key word is offered in four different languages—English, Spanish, French, and German (where all nouns are capitalized). For example, the letter *A* is introduced by a full-color illustration and the word choice, *ark, arca, arche,* and *Arche.* A pronunciation guide is on every page. Unusual word choices include labyrinth, universe, water polo, and yeti. To show that words in different languages may share the same roots, there is a final page listing all of the word choices. Two letters of the Spanish alphabet, ll and n, are not included.

211. Del Rosario, Rubén & De Matos, Isabel Freire. *ABC de Puerto Rico.* Illustrated by Antonio Martorell. Sharon, Conn.: Troutman Press, 1965.

From agua through mango to zapatero, a reader finds key objects and word choices along with accompanying verses in Spanish. Large oversized letters are seen. The letter *X* is for xilfono and *Y* is for yacs (jacks). With special attention given to the letters *LL, W, CH,* and *Z,* instructions for guiding a child are at the back of the book.

212. Douglas, Will. *A Bush Alphabet*. Illustrated by the author. Sydney, Australia: Hale & Iremonger, 1986.

The purpose of the book is to present information about animals from *A* to *Z* that can be found in the bush country of Australia. From anteater to zoology, a reader discovers some of the animals, insects, and birds that live in the undergrowth and vegetation. Facts are given—e.g., Mitchell's Hopping Mice hop like kangaroos, Numbats are found only in Southwestern Australia, and Ospreys live along the coast. The letter *X* is introduced by the unknown bunyip, a legendary water-dwelling creature of the swamps, lakes, and billabongs. Animals shown within the shapes of oversized letters and a game of "Spiders and Vines" concludes the book.

213. Doyle, Emma Lyons. *Aloha Alphabet Coloring Book*. Illustrated by John H. Sugimoto. Cover art by Keani. Honolulu: Tong Pub., 1958.

Doyle's book is a guide to the pronunciation of Hawaiian words from *A* to *Z* as well as an opportunity for a child to learn by doing—to read captions about selected words and, if interested, color the black-and-white outlined drawings. Each large outlined capital is introduced by either an English or a Hawaiian noun used in context in a sentence. For each outlined capital, there is a similar opening, e.g., *A* is for ———— , an English equivalent of a selected Hawaiian word (aloha-hello, cat-popoki, eel-puhi) and a black-and-white line drawing. To say the Hawaiian words, a child pronounces *A* as in father, *E* as ay in play, *I* as ee in sweep, *O* as in old, and *U* as oo in moo.

214. Feelings, Muriel. *Jambo Means Hello: Swahili Alphabet Book*. Illustrated by Tom Feelings. New York: Dial, 1974.

Feelings's purpose is to introduce the reader to Swahili words, properly called Kiswahili words. For each of the twenty-four sounds in Kiswahili, key words are described in the text and illustrated in the double-page spreads in this Caldecott Honor Book. There are no *Q* and *X* sounds in the language. Pronunciation guides are on each page.

215. Feeney, Stephanie. *A Is for Aloha*. Illustrated by Hella Hammid. Honolulu: University of Hawaii Press, 1983.

The book's purpose is to show familiar experiences to which Hawaii's young children can relate and to show glimpses of Hawaiian life to children in other places. The alphabetical arrangement is used to introduce some of the people, places, and experiences that make up everyday life in Hawaii, the only state that once had kings and queens. For example, the letter *A* is introduced by *Aloha*, a Hawaiian word that conveys warm feelings and can be used to say *hello, goodbye*, and *I love you*. Informative notes about the islands, a picture glossary about words that may be unfamiliar to some children—gecko, ipu, zoris—suggestions for sharing the book with children, and notes about the author and photographer conclude the book.

216. Harrison, Ted. *A Northern Alphabet*. Illustrated by the author. Montreal, Canada: Tundra, 1987.
    Colorful pictures of the northern region are accompanied by brief sentences e.g., "Aa Alex lives in the Artic. He is wearing the anorak" and "Zz In zero weather, Zach makes a zigzag path to the zinc mine." Facts about the region are shared through words and illustrations about people, their possessions, animals, and plants found north of the fifty-fifth parallel and make the book a valuable source for regional study. A child may notice additional places named by Harrison in the borders of the illustrations.

217. Jeffares, Jeanne. *An Around-the-World Alphabet*. Illustrated by the author. New York: Peter Bedrick, 1989.
    The purpose is to expose a child to both simple and complex words to make a wide range of vocabulary a part of a child's experience. The book introduces the letters of the alphabet with key words selected from various cultures from around the world. For instance, the letter *X* is introduced by an "xmas tree." There is no map, however, to show where the places might be to locate an ancient Athenian, Babylonian, eskimo, gondola, Indian rope trick, or other items. Size relationships are not considered, and a reader sees a crocodile as long as a carp, frogs as large as a fort, and rabbits taller than a ram. A glossary on the end pages defines Babylonian, Dianthus, Hypericum, and other unusual words.

218. Hudson, Wade & Wesley, Valerie Wilson. *Afro-Bets Book of Black Heroes from A to Z.* Illustrations selected by Cheryl Willis Hudson. Orange, N.J.: Just Us Books, 1988.

The book's purpose is to introduce readers to a few important black men and women who are heroes of their time—the past as well as contemporary times. For examples, the letter *A* is introduced by Ira Aldridge (1805–1867), one of the best-known European actors of his day; Muhammad Ali (1942–), the first fighter to hold the heavyweight boxing crown three times; and Marian Anderson (1902–), a concert singer who received worldwide acclaim. A suggested reading list and photograph credits conclude the book.

219. Knowlton, Jack. *Geography from A to Z: A Picture Glossary.* Illustrated by Harriett Barton. New York: Crowell, 1988.

Knowlton's book introduces the vast world around us to children. Over sixty entries from archipelago and *A* to zone and *Z* are illustrated in full color and describe the features of the earth. A reader is introduced to the world in clear terms. Key word choices include continental shelf, desert, forest, mountain range, swamp, and volcano and are in bold on the pages.

220. McNab, Nan. *A-Z of Australian Wildlife.* Illustrated by Gary Lewis. Victoria, Australia: Lamont Pub., 1987.

The book provides details about the behavior and habits of some of Australia's wildlife. Beginning with anteaters to introduce the letter pairs and ending with a zebra finch, a reader finds full-color photographs. On bright-colored backgrounds, each photo is accompanied by rhyming lines about such wildlife as bandicoots, dingoes, and emus. Most of the key word choices may be unfamiliar ones to children living in the United States. For instance, the letter *X* is introduced by Xenorhynchus asiaicus, a bird that lives near water and searches for fish, crabs and carrion; *L* is for the lyrebird whose tails looks like a lyre and is a good mimic; *N* is for numbat, (English spelling) one colored like a tabby cat that likes termites and bull-ants.

221. Mastin, Colleayn O. *Canadian Birds A-Z.* Illustrated by the

author. Kamloops, British Columbia: Grasshopper Books, 1987.

The book introduces some of Canada's birds to young children. The letter *A* is for albatross, *B* is for bluebird, and *C* for crow, and they are discussed in accompanying rhyming lines, which were "written to be read aloud." Oversized full-color illustrations show the key birds and have captions below. Unusual word choices include Uria for *U*, a seacoast bird called murre,and the almost extinct whooping crane for *X*. No bird is shown for *Z*. Footnotes on each page contain details for the reader.

222. Mastin, Colleayn O. *Canadian Trees A-Z*. Illustrated by Leonard Aguanno. Kamloops, British Columbia: Grasshopper Books, 1989.

The book introduces some of Canada's trees to young children. For each letter pair, rhymes introduce a tree of Canada in alphabetical sequence and give factual information. Captions under the full-color illustrations have information, e.g., an aspen can help someone find a direction by observing the chalky white material that is always thickest on the south side of the tree; a birch is the source of wintergreen; a king nut is a rare sort of hickory tree. Unusual choices are "ex-ceptional tree" for the letter *X* and zillions for *Z*. Additional comments on each page offer details for the reader. Suitable for children (pre-3) is an alphabet companion for this book—Betsy Bowen's *Antler, Bear, Canoe: A Northwoods Alphabet Year* (Little, Brown, 1991).

223. Mastin, Colleayn O. *Canadian Wild Animals A-Z*. Illustrated by J. D. Thompson. Kamloops, British Columbia: Grasshopper Books, 1986.

The book introduces some of Canada's wild mammals to young children. A reader discovers that an antelope introduces the letter *A*, beavers introduce *B*, and coyote, *C*. Rhyming lines are included along with full-color illustrations and their captions. Unusual word choices are quill pig (porcupine) for *Q*, Ursus (bear) for *U*, extinct bison for *X*, and yuma bat for *Y*. A reader interested further in the flora and fauna of Canada may write to the publisher and inquire about Mastin's other alphabets: *Canadian Wildflowers A-Z; Canadian Fish A-Z;* and *Canadian Bugs A-Z.*

224. Musgrove, Margaret. *Ashanti to Zulu.* Illustrated by Leo & Diane Dillon. New York: Dial, 1976.

A reader finds customs of twenty-six different tribes of Africa such as the Dogon who farm, the Wagenia who fish, and the Tendille who live in movable houses. The flora, fauna, and representative members of the tribes are shown in the illustrations.

225. Parker, Nancy Winslow. *The United Nations from A to Z.* Illustrated by the author. New York: Dodd Mead, 1985.

The book is an alphabetical guide to the people, countries, organizations, and activities of the United Nations with a quotation from former Secretary-General, Javier Perez de Cuellar: "Give the United Nations the priority it deserves, and it will yet fulfill its vast potential." A reader is encouraged to flip through the pages and read the parts the reader likes and save some for another time. Full-color illustrations and informational paragraphs introduce the sequence of entries related to the United Nations from the Atlantic Charter for *A* to Zaire for *Z.* Index is included for reference use.

226. Polansky, Leslie & Torrence, Susan. *The Washington Alphabet Book.* Illustrated by Susan Torrence. Eugene, Ore.: T. P. Pub, 1988.

For each pair of letters found in the corners of the page, a reader finds an alliterative sentence that identifies a place in the state, a person, and an activity related to the place, e.g., in Aberdeen, an angler admires an angelfish, and in Zilah, Zazu zooms (shoots with a bow) zillions of zucchini to z zebu. A suitable book companion by the same publisher and authors is *The Oregon Alphabet Book* (1983).

227. Purviance, Susan & O'Shell, Marcia. *Alphabet Annie Announces An All-American Album.* Illustrated by Ruth Brunner-Strosser. Boston: Houghton Mifflin, 1988.

The book introduces an alphabetical list of characters performing various activities in well-known American cities. A reader discovers the capitals are introduced by alliterative sentences that make tongue twisters by including the names of cities in the United States, personified animal characters who live there, and what they do. The alphabetical tour begins in Arizona City with Alice Allosaurus and ends in Zanesville with Zelda Zebra.

228. Rice, James. *Texas Alphabet.* Illustrated by the author. Gretna, La.: Pelican Pub., 1988.

The book's purpose is to teach a reader about the significant Lone Star characters, historical events, and geography. A reader finds Texas Jack, a native jackrabbit, as the narrator who gives humorous comments about each illustrated key word choice. Each oversized illustration is accompanied by informative sentences about Texas history. Facts about Jim Bowie introduce *B,* Davy Crockett for *C,* and Ponce De León for *D.* Unusual word choices include Quivira, Coronado's fabled city of gold for *Q,* and varmint, a small pesky wild critter, for *V.*

229. Roache, Gordon. *A Halifax ABC.* Illustrated by the author. Montreal, Canada: Tundra, 1987.

Paintings of Halifax, Nova Scotia, introduce the letters of the alphabet. Interesting word choices are oil rig, regatta, and explosion. A descriptive list at the end of the book gives facts about each painting, e.g., oil rigs towed by tugs drill for oil from the ocean floor, a regatta for rowers is watched by spectators, and in 1917, the world's greatest man-made explosion before Hiroshima took place in Halifax Harbour when the French ship *Mont Blanc,* loaded with explosives, and the Belgian ship *Imo* collided, causing more than 9,000 injuries and 1,600 deaths.

230. Ryden, Hope. *Wild Animals of Africa ABC.* Illustrated by the author. New York: Dutton, 1989.

The book's purpose is to help a reader learn more about the lives of the animals that live in Africa and in different habitats, e.g., mountains, plains, forests, and deserts. A reader is introduced to the wild animals beginning with aardvark, buffalo, and cheetah, and ending with xoxo, yellow-legged galago, and zebra; each animal is shown in a full-color photograph that accompanies its name and a capital letter. Author's notes at the end of the book give facts about the animals' life, e.g., the name of the xoxo frog is pronounced by clicking your tongue twice against the roof of your mouth, and the galago sleeps in thorn trees during the day and is often tamed for an animal companion.

231. Ryden, Hope. *Wild Animals of America ABC.* Illustrated by the author. New York: Dutton, 1988.

Ryden's purpose is to tell a reader about selected animals' habitats and characteristics and to start a reader looking for the wild animals living nearby. Beautiful wild creatures live in the United States and are introduced in full-color photographs from different regions of the country. Capitals are introduced with key words and photographs of animals that include Alaska's grizzly bear, the desert's kit fox, and the southland's alligator. Author's notes about the animals conclude the book.

232. Schmid-Belk, Donna Dee. *Arizona Alphabet Book.* Illustrated by Michael Ives. Tucson: Donna Dee Books, 1988.

A reader finds alliterative sentences that accompany colorful, and sometimes humorous illustrations. Each sentence names a place in the state, a person, and describes a behavior, e.g., Zack zooming over Montezuma's Castle in a zeppelin. Not all children will be familiar with the names of the places—Baboquivari, Canyon de Chelly below Chinle, and Upper Blue. Map of the state showing the places mentioned is on the back cover.

233. Smith, Robert E. *ABC of Australian Animals.* Illustrated by the author. Sydney, Australia: Angus & Robertson, 1978.

Smith's purpose is to entertain children with humorous illustrations in full color and verses about 26 Australian animals, each introducing a letter of the alphabet. A reader finds animals from anteater through magpie to zaglossus, an anteater's cousin. Unusual word choices include goanna (G), extraordinary bird—the kookaburra (X), and vombatus hirsutus (V), the hairy-nosed wombat.

234. Tasker, James. *African Treehouse.* Illustrated by Kathleen Elgin. New York: Harvey House, 1973.

The book's purpose is to entertain and inform a reader about animals of Africa. Double-page spreads show the vigor of such animals as a bumpity aardvark, running cheetah, and brachiating monkey, and verses offer both sense and nonsense in the words. Internal rhyme and alliteration is found in the verse about the dainty dik-dik and, nonsense is offered in the argument between the baboon and the monkey and whether the world is round or the ground is flat.

235. Wiskur, Darrell. *Silver Dollar City's ABC Words & Rhymes.* Illustrated by the author. Silver Dollar City: Silver Dollar City, Inc., 1977.

The book introduces some of the sights at Silver Dollar City in the illustrations and tells about them in the accompanying rhymes. For examples, the letter *L* is for Lucky Silver Mine and *M* is for miner, and a reader sees an illustration of children riding in an ore barge on an underground river in a mine shaft . The letter *O* is for the "Old-time fun" of visiting the working craftspeople there.

* ALPHABET IN A MILIEU COLLECTION

236. Adams, Pam. *Mr. Lion's I Spy ABC Book.* Illustrated by the author. Restrop Manor, England: Child's Play, 1975.

The book's purpose is to engage a reader to look through die-cut openings on the pages and predict the object to be seen when the page is turned. For instance, a reader looks through the opening for the letter *E* and sees an elephant's ear, eye, and tusk. When the page is turned, an elephant pull toy is seen. Each page has three or more openings showing a variety of objects. A helpful guide of words in alphabetical order is found on the last page.

237. Amery, Heather & Cartwright, Stephen. *The Stephen Cartwright ABC.* Illustrated by Stephen Cartwright. London, England: Usborne House, 1990.

From the letter *A* for Alex, Andrew, and Anne to *Z* for Zoe, Zara, and Zack, children are named in alphabetical order as they are shown in different fanciful situations. They fly in a boat drawn by a huge butterfly, paint an igloo pink and green, and sail in a sandal. The sequence of letter pairs is shown on end pages.

238. Bruna, Dick. *B Is for Bear: An ABC.* Illustrated by the author. London: Methuen, 1971.

In *B Is for Bear: An ABC,* a reader sees familiar objects—duck, fish, and grapes—that are outlined in black and introduce each lowercase serif letter. Some unusual noun choices for children to recognize in this letter-object arrangement are eskimo, jigsaw, and yawn.

239. Burningham, John. *John Burningham's ABC.* Illustrated by the author. New York: Crown, 1985.

In the book, a small child is seen with animals, objects, and people on the full-color pages. For example, the child pushes an elephant, is bumped by a goat, and rides on the back of a hippopotamus. For a review, the endpapers show all of the lowercase letters in purple. In the author's 1964 and 1967 editions, Burningham's collections are guided by capitals and lowercase sans serif letters. Illustrated words are found on the verso pages (1964) along with bright pictures with boldly composed figures on the recto pages. For the letter *T*, the word *tractor* is seen in lowercase letters, which face a colorful picture. One smoking tractor is driven by a seated workman. In *John Burningham's ABC* (Bobbs-Merrill, 1967), pairs of letters are on verso pages and face Burningham's illustrations. As examples, a green apple introduces the letter *A*, a golden orange introduces *O*, and animals at the zoo introduce *Z*.

240. Chwast, Seymour. *The Alphabet Parade*. Illustrated by the author. New York: Harcourt Brace Jovanovich, 1991.

Without words, the book's purpose is to engage a reader in finding the letters of the alphabet that are concealed in different images. A reader finds a procession of images that include a majorette, a clown riding a unicycle, and another clown driving a convertible. The letter *U* is found in the handle of a clown's umbrella, *A* is seen on the front of the car, and *M* is the shape of the baton in the hand of the majorette.

241. Cleaver, Elizabeth. *ABC*. Illustrated by the author. New York: Atheneum, 1985.

Cleaver prepares a collage for each letter. There are uppercase and lowercase letters in black and key objects in each small illustration. Selected objects are placed around each letter. For *X*, one girl models a print of an x-ray and holds a card with the words "Merry Xmas" a possible choice for child-adult discussion in the home. On a background of red, a zebra for *Z* breaks through an opening in the collage near an unzipped zipper.

242. Connelly, Gwen. *El Alfabeto*. Illustrated by the author. Lincolnwood, Ill.: Passport/NTC Pub., 1991.

Spanish sentences present personified objects in humorous

situations, e.g., a pineapple wears a bathing suit, a duck skates on a piano, and a clock laughs at a refrigerator. Notes for parents and teachers and a pronunciation guide are included.

243. Conran, Sebastian. *My First ABC Book.* Illustrated by the author. New York: Macmillan, 1987.

In full-color, a variety of objects introduce each pair of letters found in corners of pages. Most of the choices are large and will be familiar ones—ant, anchor, arrow—but some of them may not be known by all children, e.g., abacus, steamboat, and windmill. An entire alphabet sequence is shown on the end pages.

244. Crews, Donald. *We Read: A to Z.* Illustrated by the author. New York: Harper & Row, 1967.

Crews's book works with vocabulary and reminds a young viewer that all words are made from the twenty-six letters. Concepts that include positions and shapes introduce the words and letters. One pair of upper- and lowercase letters in blue, green, or red announces the concept word and the explanatory phrase. Crews's illustrations of the concepts use double-page spreads and bright colors. *E* is for the equal squares on a black-and-yellow checkered page. *H* is for horizontal blue and green lines from one side of the page to the other side. *N* is for nothing and shows one blank white page. One unusual word choice is Crews's use of the colon, which leads a child to see that in punctuation, it is a signal for more words to come. Each letter, and not the page, is numbered. After reading and discussing the concepts, an adult may read several selected key words and their definitive phrases and ask the child to respond by turning the pages to find the number of the letter for each key word. The numeral one is the locator for *A.* The locator for *B* is the numeral two, and so on.

245. Demi. *The ABC Song.* Illustrated by Leonard Shortall. New York: Random House, 1985.

A reader identifies such objects as airplane, bee, and castle for the lowercase letters and turns a metal handle to start the music for the well-known alphabet song. The words of the song conclude the book.

246. Fredman, Alan. *The Gold Star Alphabet Book*. Illustrated by the author. New York: Modern Pub./Unisystems/Deans, 1981.

Black capital and lowercase letters guide key nouns, which label objects. Double-page spreads are interspersed with single pages. The colorful illustrations show one green alligator who fills the spread, a sleeping giant who needs two pages to stretch out to take a nap, and a colorful rainbow that arches over both pages of hills to one pot of gold. All of the capital letters are reviewed again on a double-page spread. A final alphabet quiz asks a young viewer to match the pictures with the lowercase letters and to fill in the rest of the words in the blanks. A child may self-check with the included answers to the quiz.

247. Fujikawa, Gyo. *Gyo Fujikawa's A to Z Picture Book*. Illustrated by the author. New York: Grosset & Dunlap, 1974.

Fujikawa's collection of labeled alphabetical objects appears on black-and-white pages, which alternate with full-color ones. Capitals and lowercase serif letters are found in the corners of the large pages. Some alliterative phrases are included. For instance, a child hears that the winter wind can whistle, that dreams can be delicious or disgusting, and that the words puddle and polliwog begin with the letter *P*. More of the artist's illustrations are found in a cloth book, *Gyo Fujikawa's A to Z Book* (Grosset & Dunlap, 1981).

248. Gardner, Beau. *Have You Ever Seen . . . ? An ABC Book*. Illustrated by the author. New York: Dodd, 1986.

Full-color illustrations show images in bright colors and both capital and lowercase letters guide the sequence. A reader finds alliterative sentences and sees a ladybug riding a lightning bolt, an inchworm on ice skates, and an octopus who eats oatmeal with spoons in all eight arms. Younger children may enjoy drawing their own versions of alliterative sentences, and older students (grade 3 up) can participate in writing their own original sentences.

249. Gundersheiner, Karen. *ABC Say with Me*. Illustrated by the author. New York: Harper & Row, 1984.

One tiny girl illustrates "ing" words to introduce this imaginative alphabet. Gundersheiner's presentation uses word choices such as asking, balancing, and cleaning to support the illustrations. For the unseen letter *E,* the key words are eating and egg. On top of a red-rimmed drum, the small girl holds a white daisy and dances. In other illustrations, the girl is floating with a feather, giggling in a grape cluster, and hiding under a hat. A young viewer sees the little girl and the objects in an action described by the verb. The illustrations supply the context for the verb used on each page. Printed in capitals, the verbs are emphasized visually. The combined illustrations provide a small language file of *ing* words as the little girl moves through the ABCs. Like Beller's book *A-B-Cing: An Action Alphabet* (60), there are no single letters from the alphabet as a sequence to guide a viewer. The alphabetical order is led by the initial letter in each word choice.

250. Hawkins, Colin & Hawkins, Jacqui. *Busy ABC.* Illustrated by the authors. New York: Viking, 1987.

From acting for the letter *A* to xylophoning for *X* and zipping a jacket for *Z,* a reader finds a collection of activities from A to Z to recognize. Children talking in dialogue balloons are found in full-color scenes. Animals are personified and make comments on the actions.

251. Hoban, Tana. *A, B, See!* Illustrated by the author. New York: Greenwillow, 1982.

A young reader sees objects in black-and-white photographs taken with a prolonged light source to make photograms. At the foot of each page is the alphabet in a frieze in gray that shows the appropriate letter in oversized black type. Object choices begin with a collection for the letter *A*—apple, abacus, asparagus, acorn—and end with a single object—zipper—for the letter *Z.*

252. Hoban, Tana. *26 Letters and 99 Cents.* Illustrated by the author. New York: Greenwillow, 1987.

Colorful photographs introduce letters, objects, numerals, and coins. A reader may say the letters of the alphabet and then turn the book over to find a second text about counting coins from one to ninety-nine cents. Both uppercase and lowercase letters are introduced by familiar key objects, e.g., egg, fish, jelly beans.

253. Johnson, Audean. *A to Z Look and See.* Illustrated by the author. New York: Random House, 1989.
     The book introduces a key object for each letter along with a traditional phrase, e.g., *A* is for Apple, and so on. At the foot of each page, a reader sees the object in different settings. For example, the apple is seen growing on a tree, cut in half to show its seeds, as applesauce in a jar, as juice in a cup, and as a snack eaten by a small boy.

254. King, Tony. *The Moving Alphabet Book.* Illustrated by the author. New York: Putnam, 1982.
     Every large serif capital in black is surrounded by animals and objects whose names begin with that letter. A child turns a wheel and a different object labeled with its name appears in each of the windows. Small color photographs are interspersed with drawings of objects in the windows. *S* shows a snowman, snail, and scarecrow. *X* is for a spot on a treasure map, a xylophone, and an x-ray. A repetitive sentence stem occurs on each page. A child reads the traditional lines: "*A* is for ———— and *B* is for ————." There is a reference list of all of the objects on two culminating pages of the book.

255. Mattiesen, Thomas. *ABC: An Alphabet Book.* Illustrated by the author. New York: Platt & Munk, 1966.
     Mattiesen presents capital and lowercase letters in black manuscript. Beneath the letters are the labels for the photographed objects (guitar, telephone, paint) that are shown on the facing pages. Descriptive sentences follow. In this ABC, a child realizes that in language, he or she communicates by speaking and writing in sentences. With word cards to match the key words on the pages, a child can frame each individual key word as it is found and read. An older child may enjoy writing some additional descriptive sentences for photographs or for magazine pictures brought from home.

256. Nugent, Alys. *My ABC Book.* Illustrated by the author. Racine, Wis.: Western, 1956.
     To listen to the tune of the familiar alphabet song, a child presses a button on the inside of the front cover to start the music. The capitals are introduced by a variety of objects—

acorn, boat, camel—and by traditional sentences, e.g., *A* is for
. . . , *B* is for . . . , and so on.

257. Oxenbury, Helen. *Helen Oxenbury's ABC of Things.* Illustrated
by the author. New York: Delacorte, 1971.
Oversized upper- and lowercase letters are introduced by
scenes of objects whose names begin with the appropriate letters in sequence. For the letter *A*, a child sees an ant on an
apple and reads the word choices, ant and apple. For *T*, a
turkey and two tigers ride a train, and at *Z*, zebras are found in
the zoo.

258. Polak, Johan. *The True-to-Life Alphabet Book Including
Numbers.* Illustrated by the author. New York: Grosset &
Dunlap, 1952.
Polak's endpapers show the musical notes and the sequence
of the letters in the ABC Song. One, and sometimes two objects per page introduce the guiding pairs of letters. The pairs
are seen both as block letters and as cursive ones. With initial
letters in capitals, these word choices are familiar
sights—apple, ball, cat—and are found near each object.
Relative size may be discussed. On facing pages, one large dog
is as large as the elephant. One rabbit is as large as Santa.
Vegetables—one onion, cucumber, and radishes—are as large
as the wagon that could carry the vegetables. Two final pages
offer objects to count from one to ten.

259. Seuss, Dr. *Dr. Seuss' ABC.* Illustrated by the author. New York:
Random House, 1963, 1981.
This alphabet book helps girls and boys enjoy the sounds of
the letters. A reader sees a confetti arrangement of large and
small letters in bright colors of orange, red, and green. The text
asks, "What begins with A?" and goes on to present Aunt
Annie. With guiding reins in her hands, Aunt Annie sits in her
sedan chair and goes for a ride on top of a large, smiling alligator. Humorous touches are found in the created words (fiffer-feffer-feff) and in the creature characters, e.g., a duck-dog,
a quacker-oo, and a yellow-eyed pink-and-white checkered
creature, a Zizzer-zazzer-zuzz.

260. Simpson, Gretchen. *Gretchen's ABC.* Illustrated by the author. New York: HarperCollins, 1991.

The book's purpose is to engage a reader into playing a guessing game about the objects and to introduce the artwork of Simpson, a *New Yorker* artist. In alphabetical order, the illustrations show usual objects—awning, bench, cabbage—from unusual perspectives, e.g., only part of an object is seen in a close-up. For example, the lowercase letter *d* is introduced by dance shoes, the letter *i* by an iris, and *x* by a xylophone, but the tight close-ups may make the shoes, flower, and instrument difficult for some children to recognize.

261. Stillerman, Robbie. *The ABC Book.* Illustrated by the author. Racine, Wis.: Western, 1982.

On small thick cardboard pages with backgrounds in blue, green, yellow. and purple, one object in color introduces each serif capital in white and the accompanying label in black boldface (pie, spoon, umbrella).

262. Szekeres, Cyndy. *ABC.* Illustrated by the author. Racine, Wis.: Western, 1983.

As an introduction, a faint peach background holds all of the capital and lowercase serif letters in the sequence. For *A,* objects gather around on a large red apple. While a mouse in an airplane flies over the apple and one large brown ant crawls across its side, one mouse artist paints a picture of the apple and a second mouse chops off pieces of the apple with a small mouse-sized ax. Pair by pair, the upper- and lowercase letters are located in the upper corners of the pages to be introduced by various objects collected together into each illustration. One-, two-, three-, and four-syllable nouns (ant, bubbles, envelope, caterpillar) in serif lowercase letters in black are near the objects. Two objects include additional explanatory words: do-it-yourself directions and turtleneck sweater. The number of syllables in each word may be tapped out by the adult and counted together with the child.

FOOTNOTES

Animals as Animals Theme

1. As recommended in John T. Gillespie and Christine B. Gilbert in *Best Books for Children: Preschool Through the Middle Grades, Fourth Edition.* New Providence, N.J.: R. R. Bowker, 1991.
2. Paperback reader, cassette, and discussion guide for *As I Was Crossing Boston Common* is available from Listening Library, Inc., One Park Avenue, Old Greenwich, Conn. 06890.

History Theme

1. From "Peanuts" cartoon by Charles Schultz. *The Sacramento Bee.* Sunday, September 20, 1981.
2. From "ABC Puzzle" from The Colonial Williamsburg, Va. Original puzzle is in Colonial Williamsburg Foundation Collection.
3. Filmstrip/cassette of *On Market Street* is available from Random House School Division. Dept. 9036, 400 Hahn Road, Westminster, Md. 21157.

RELATED READINGS

Adkins, Kathryn A. *Masters of the Italic Letter.* Godine, 1986.

Baldwin, Ruth M. *One Hundred Nineteenth Century Rhyming Alphabets in English.* Carbondale, Ill.: Southern Illinois University Press, 1972.

Baring-Gould, William S. and Baring-Gould, Ceil. *The Annotated Mother Goose.* New York: Clarkson N. Potter, 1962.

Coody, Betty. *Using Literature with Young Children,* Third Edition. Dubuque, Iowa: W. C. Brown, 1983.

Cooke, Bridget Litherland. "American Children's Perceptions of the Hebrew Alphabet." Ed. D. dissertation, Yeshiva University, 1979. DA 38:3837A

Cullinan, Bernice E. *Literature and the Child.* In collaboration with Mary E. Karrer and Arlene Pillar. New York: Harcourt Brace Jovanovich, 1981.

Glazer, Joan I. and Williams, Gurney, III. *Introduction to Children's Literature.* New York: McGraw-Hill, 1979.

Gray, Nicolete. *A History of Lettering: Creative Experiment and Letter Identity.* Boston, MA: Godine, 1987.

Hopkins, Lee Bennett and Arenstein, Misha. "From Apple Pie to Zooplankton." *Elementary English* (November 1971): 788–93.

Huck, Charlotte, S., Hepler, Susan and Hickman, Janet. *Children's Literature in the Elementary School,* Fourth Edition. New York: Holt, Rinehart and Winston.

Jones, Marian. "AB (by) C Means Alphabet Books by Children." *The Reading Teacher,* March, 1983. pp. 646–8.

Norton, Donna E. *Through the Eyes of a Child.* Columbus, Ohio: Merrill, 1991.

Ohanian, Susan. "Across the Curriculum from A to Z." *Learning* (April 1987): 34–40.

Opie, Peter and Opie, Iona Archibald. *The Oxford Dictionary of Nursery Rhymes.* Oxford at the Clarendon Press, 1951.

Pellowski, Anne. "AaBbCc." *Top of the News* (January 1974): 144–9.

Roberts, Patricia L. "A to Z: Activities for Alphabet Books in the Classroom." *The Reading Teacher* 44 (October 1991): 182.

Roberts, Patricia L. *Alphabet Books as a Key to Language Patterns.* Hamden, Conn.: Library Professional Publications, 1985.

Schoenfield, Madalynne. "Alphabet and Counting Books." *Day Care and Early Education* 10 (Winter 1982), 44.

Sebesta, Sam Leaton and Iverson, William J. *Literature for Thursday's Child.* Chicago, Ill.: Science Research Associates, 1975.

Smith, Frank. *What's The Use of the Alphabet?* Victoria, British Columbia: Abel Press 1984.

Stewig, John Warren. "Alphabet Books: A Neglected Genre." *Language Arts* 55 (January 1978): 6–11.

Stewig, John Warren. *Children and Literature.* Chicago, IL: Rand McNally, 1980.

Sutherland, Zena and Arbuthnot, May Hill. *Children and Books,* Seventh Edition. Glenview, Ill.: Scott, Foresman, 1986.

Whitehead, Robert. *Children's Literature: Strategies of Teaching.* Englewood Cliffs, N.J.: Prentice-Hall, 1963.

INDEX

247

ABOUT THE AUTHOR

DR. PATRICIA L. ROBERTS received a doctorate from the University of the Pacific and joined the faculty of California State University, Sacramento (1976). She received an award as Distinguished Alumnus of the Year (University of the Pacific) and a meritorious teaching award from California State. Dr. Roberts is the author of *Counting Books are More than Numbers* and *Alphabet Books as a Key to Language Patterns* (Library Professional Publications, 1989 & 1984, respectively) and *A Teacher's Guide to Thematic Units for Literature Based Instruction* (Allyn & Bacon, 1992), as well as articles on literature for children published in *The Reading Teacher, The Dragon's Lode, SIGNAL, Reading Today,* and other publications. Further, Dr. Roberts is coauthor of *A Resource Guide for Elementary School Teaching: Planning for Competence, Second Edition* (Macmillan, 1985) and *Understanding Resiliency Through Children's Literature,* as well as *Modifying Gender Stereotypes: A Guide for Teachers and Librarians, K-8* (both McFarland, 1992).

Dr. Roberts is a national director for the Special Interest Group Network of Adolescent Literature (International Reading Association), a member of the National Council of Research on English, and has served as an educational consultant and a coordinator for a teacher education center for elementary student teachers (multiple subjects credential program, California). She has taught reading and language arts methods, seminars in problems in teaching, and graduate classes in children's literature. Her current research is about multicultural children's literature, wordless books as context for writing, and literature-based instruction. Currently, Dr. Roberts is chair-elect of the Department of Teacher Education at California State University, Sacramento.